Communications
in Computer and Information Science 138

Albert Fleischmann   Werner Schmidt
Robert Singer   Detlef Seese (Eds.)

Subject-Oriented Business Process Management

Second International Conference, S-BPM ONE 2010
Karlsruhe, Germany, October 14, 2010
Selected Papers

 Springer

Volume Editors

Albert Fleischmann
METASONIC AG
Pfaffenhofen, Germany
E-mail: albert.fleischmann@metasonic.de

Werner Schmidt
University of Applied Sciences Ingolstadt
Business Information Systems
Esplanade 10, 85049 Ingolstadt, Germany
E-mail: werner.schmidt@haw-ingolstadt.de

Robert Singer
FH JOANNEUM - University of Applied Sciences
8020 Graz, Austria
E-mail: robert.singer@fh-joanneum.at

Detlef Seese
Institute AIFB
Karlsruhe Institute of Technology (KIT)
76128 Karlsruhe, Germany
E-mail: detlef.seese@kit.edu

ISSN 1865-0929   e-ISSN 1865-0937
ISBN 978-3-642-23134-6   e-ISBN 978-3-642-23135-3
DOI 10.1007/978-3-642-23135-3
Springer Heidelberg Dordrecht London New York

Library of Congress Control Number: 2011934266

CR Subject Classification (1998): H.4, H.5, J.1, D.2

Typesetting: Camera-ready by author, data conversion by Scientific Publishing Services, Chennai, India

Printed on acid-free paper

Springer is part of Springer Science+Business Media (www.springer.com)

Foreword

This volume contains the proceedings of S-BPM ONE 2010 – the Subject-Orientation as Enabler for the Next generation of BPM Tools and Methods. It was the second event in the S-BPM ONE series, which was held in Karlsruhe on October 14, 2010. The success of the first international workshop in 2009 encouraged us to establish a series of conferences which will continue in 2011 in Ingolstadt and in 2012 in Vienna.

The series aims to establish a platform for a multi- and cross-disciplinary interchange of innovative ideas, concepts, methods, tools and results in foundational and applied research as well as studies on the realization of such innovations in real life - all based on the new promising paradigm of subject-oriented business process management (BPM).

The original call for papers attracted a total of 17 submissions, from which the Program Committee selected on the basis of double blind reviews 11 articles for presentation at the conference, giving a rejection rate of 35%. From these 11 articles we present 10 in these proceedings together with the invited keynote talk of A. Komus and three additional papers invited to stimulate discussion in this area. All these papers give evidence of the diversity and enthusiasm of this new area and its promising ideas and first results and achievements.

The contributions in these proceedings are ordered in the same way as they were given at the conference, hence in a quasi-random order determined among other things by train schedules and other more probabilistic reasons. On the other hand this "randomness" reflects perfectly the productive atmosphere of the conference where researchers and practitioners from different areas combined their efforts and their ideas in discussions on how to improve contemporary BPM by paving the way for the new successful paradigm of subject-oriented BPM.

The scientific program of the conference was opened by the invited keynote talk of Ayelt Komus discussing his rich experiences and several studies making evident that good BPM and organizational success go together. Moreover, he investigated the open issue of a holistic integration of various aspects and types of BPM activities, proposing an approach of a "loose coupling" combined with "Wikimanagement success factors" to overcome problems in this area.

Erwin Aitenbichler, Stephan Borgert and Max Mühlhäuser showed in their contribution that S-BPM allows the distributed modeling and execution of processes, without losing the capability to verify the compatibility of processes by describing an engine to execute S-BPM process choreographies.

In the following contribution Oliver Kopp, Lasse Engler, Tammo van Lessen, Frank Leymann and Jörg Nitzsche introduced the language BPEL^{gold} which supports the interaction-based modeling approach and showed that it fulfills all requirements put on a choreography language and how it can be integrated in an enterprise service bus to make it choreography-aware.

The world and markets are highly dynamic. Hence, businesses today also have to adapt their business process models to new conditions. To be able to react instantly to such changes the contribution of Matthias Kurz and Albert Fleischmann suggested a new BPM concept (BPM 2.0) along with a corresponding software system increasing the flexibility of businesses by allowing employees to improve "their" business process. A case study critically examined the feasibility of both the concept as well as the software.

The dynamic connection of business processes between organizations was investigated in the contribution of Nils Meyer, Thomas Feiner, Markus Radmayr, Dominik Blei and Albert Fleischmann. This paper explores the requirements to select flexible and dynamic partners across organizational borders and to react adequately to all arising changes. It evaluates existing approaches regarding cross-organizational process modeling and execution, proposing as a solution the subject-oriented jCPEX! approach.

Konrad Walser and Marc Schaffroth set out in their contribution a paradigmatic BPM framework of public administration developed on the basis of a pioneering organizational concept of public administration and discuss it with the example of the Swiss eGovernment BPM ecosystem.

The research presented in the submission of Alexander Sellner and Erwin Zinser aimed at establishing conceptual and functional links between S-BPM modeling environments and business rule repositories. The contribution presented a prototype for enacting business rules in S-BPM processes.

Complex real-world processes usually require a comprehensive set of control flow constructs and strong semantics. The contribution of Jörg Rodenhagen and Florian Strecker investigated how S-BPM and multi-subjects can handle the process synchronization on different abstraction levels in such situations.

For humans as key players in business processes natural language is the most natural tool with which to communicate. Stephan H. Sneed investigated in his contribution how to enable the generation of natural language documents (as behavior descriptions for human actors, service level agreements, requirement specifications for software systems or test specifications for system testing) out of S-BPM process models by following some modeling guidelines ensuring proper semantics of the S-BPM model as well as the exported natural language.

The contribution of Peter Kesch returned to the dynamics of business processes describing a context-sensitive view on a sequence of process steps. He showed how the problems usually appearing in connection with the use of static data structures in such dynamic contexts can be overcome by a new concept of business objects developed in the Metasonic S-BPM Suite.

Yuliya Stavenko and Alexander Gromoff presented in the last contribution a case study on the subject-oriented approach for automation and process modeling of a service company. They showed how the availability and quality of services and the time of implementing changes can be improved and, moreover, that this approach allows companies to maximize the return on IT investments.

Part II of these proceedings presents three invited contributions. The first contribution by Thomas J. Olbrich is entitled "Why We Need to Re-think Current BPM Research Issues." To understand the character of this paper one has to understand its history. Usually when a long day of interesting and inspiring but nevertheless difficult talks and discussions is over and the conference dinner is approaching even the most intelligent audience becomes tired and more interested in good food than in further discussions of difficult problems and tasks to be solved in the future.

To set a highlight at the end of the conference, to stimulate discussions at dinner and to wake everyone up, we invited Thomas Olbrich to give an especially provocative talk waking up the audience and the community. This he did in an excellent way pointing out what "is wrong" in contemporary BPM research. To reflect his talk in these proceedings we asked him to send us a related contribution to stimulate by this "gunshot" discussions in the community too. This he did, and even if a paper of a few pages simply cannot be as entertaining and funny as an oral presentation of 30 minutes, the submitted paper transports his message "BPM research has – for a number of reasons – failed to make any meaningful contribution over the past several years." In his paper he discusses technical progress vs. deficient process orientation, analyzes where the real issues lie and addresses prospective future research issues. We see this contribution as a "wake-up call" to stimulate discussion at the dinner and of course, with a wink, also in the community.

To reflect the discussions this talk provoked at dinner and to calm down things a bit, we add here two contributions.

The first one is a contribution by Albert Fleischmann focusing on the point of view from industry. He does not agree on all details with Thomas Olbrich but thinks that the research on BPM mainly focuses on technical and technological aspects and does not give enough holistic consideration.

A more fundamental critique to the message of Thomas Olbrich is given in the last contribution of Robert Singer and Erwin Zinser. Both give arguments why his provocative message should be rejected from a more scientific point of view. Moreover, they express and give reason for the huge need for further research, especially for a closer cooperation between academic institutions and industry. They state that we need an intense exchange of knowledge and experience between industry and research and, that moreover, research needs input and funding from industry, while industry needs sound new methodologies and a well-educated workforce to implement BPM to gain sustainable competitive advantage in solving the complex problems of our time and the future.

We are convinced that the results of this conference will not only improve the understanding of the area of BPM and some of its future needs, but it will also prove to be useful in recent and future industrial applications.

As editors of these proceedings we would like to thank all the members of the Program Committee, the keynote speaker Ayelt Komus and the invited speaker of the discussion, Thomas Olbrich, the Chairpersons of all sections, and all authors and speakers for their contributions. We thank Hagen Buchwald, Mathes

Elstermann, Joachim Melcher and Oliver Schöll for their support of the local organization and also for their help in the reviewing. Moreover, we thank Stefan Raß for his support in formatting and building the proceedings, and we also want to thank Alexandra Kulfanova, Katrin Kindermann and Alexandra Gerrard for their support of the local organizers on the day of conference and for correcting the English of the contributions. For his special help as native speaker we thank Richard Wright. Last but not least, we thank Oliver Schöll for his management of the conference website and all his technical work managing the submission process and the generation of the final volume of the proceedings.

The local organizers thank all the participants, and acknowledge the logistic and especially financial support from Metasonic AG with special gratitude. We also thank Alfred Hofmann and Leonie Kunz from Springer for their assistance and support in the production of these proceedings.

June 2011

Albert Fleischmann
Werner Schmidt
Detlef Seese
Robert Singer

Organization

Organizing Committee

Detlef Seese (Chair)	Karlsruhe Institute of Technology (KIT), Germany
Hagen Buchwald	Karlsruhe Institute of Technology (KIT), Germany
Oliver Schöll	Karlsruhe Institute of Technology (KIT), Germany

Program Committee

Detlef Seese (Chair)	Karlsruhe Institute of Technology (KIT), Germany
Freimut Bodendorf	University of Erlangen-Nuremberg, Germany
Alexander Gromov	Higher School of Economics, Russia
Max Mühlhäuser	TU Darmstadt, Germany
Werner Schmidt	University of Applied Sciences Ingolstadt, Germany
Robert Singer	FH JOANNEUM - University of Applied Sciences, Austria
Christian Stary	Johannes Kepler University, Austria

Sponsoring Institutions

METASONIC AG
Münchnerstr. 29
85276 Hettenshausen

www.metasonic.de

Table of Contents

Part I: Invited Key Note

Part II: Contributed Papers

Part III: Discussion

Part I

Invited Key Note

Key Lessons from Wikimanagement and BPM Best Practices: Aspiring for a Truly Holistic Approach in BPM

Ayelt Komus

BPM Laboratory, FH Koblenz,
Fachbereich Betriebswirtschaft Konrad-Zuse-Str. 1, 56075 Koblenz, Germany
komus@fh-koblenz.de

Abstract. Various Studies on BPM show important aspects of good Business Process Management. Also it becomes evident that BPM and organizational success go together. Still an open issue is the holistic integration of various aspects and types of BPM activities. The author suggests an approach of a "loose coupling" combined with "Wikimanagement success factors" to overcome this situation.

Keywords: BPM, success factors, Wikimanagement, technology BPM, business BPM, loose coupling, social media.

1 Studies Conducted by the "BPM Labor" (BPM Laboratory)

The role of business process management as one of the major success factors in today's management has become more and more obvious during the last years. In addition to a better understanding of the relevance of a process-oriented view, advances in the BPMS technology and market offers have given a new boost to BPM.

Nevertheless, many questions on how to manage business processes and how to combine IT's possibilities with the business concepts in a pragmatic and feasible way, as well as many other important questions are still not answered in a satisfactory manner. For this reason various studies have been carried out by the "BPM-Labor" (BPM Laboratory) of the Koblenz University of Applied Sciences to achieve a better understanding on important aspects of good business process management. The studies complement and extend other studies that have been conducted on the topic of BPM [1] [2] [3] [4].

Focus of the BPM-Laboratories' studies have been questions like: "What are the possible business results of good BPM?", "What are the success factors of BPM?", "What are the effects of the combination of BPM with other methods like 6 sigma?", "How does the active involvement of the employees' knowledge base influence BPM?", "How does the integration of social media approaches effect BPM?" etc.

A. Fleischmann et al. (Eds.): S-BPM ONE 2010, CCIS 138, pp. 3–16, 2011.
© Springer-Verlag Berlin Heidelberg 2011

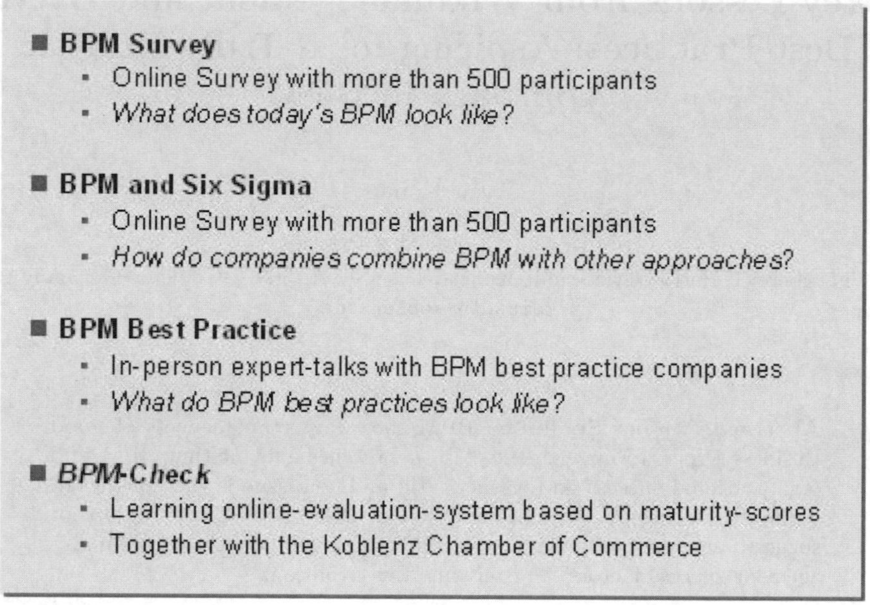

Fig. 1. Recent studies on BPM conducted by the BPM-Labor (BPM Laboratory)

While most studies were conducted as online surveys the BPM best practice study was based on personal in-depth interviews with BPM managers from BPM best practice companies that were identified in the fields of technology BPM and business BPM.

The companies interviewed were Bayer HealthCare AG, Cosmos Direkt, Deutsche Bank AG, DZ Bank AG, E.ON Energie AG, EDEKA Minden-Hannover IT-/logistic service GmbH, EnBW Energie Baden-Württemberg AG, Finanz Informatik Technologie Service GmbH & Co. KG, Generali Deutschland Holding AG, Lufthansa Miles & More, Nordenia Deutschland Gronau GmbH, Paul Hartmann AG, Siemens AG, Siemens Healthcare, VIS Informatik GmbH (Generali Wien), Volkswagen AG and Watt Deutschland GmbH [5].

The "BPM-Check" is based on still another methodological approach. It is designed as an online evaluation for companies to estimate their BPM maturity. By including questions about the company's BPM as well as overall success it was possible to draw conclusions on the relevant set of BPM success factors as well.

2   Empirical Findings

2.1   BPM and Success

It seems that there is a strong correlation between an active management of business processes and the success of a company.

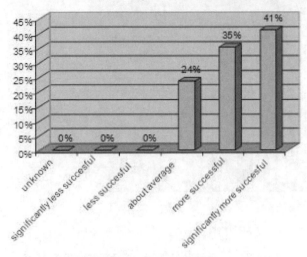

82% ‚know' or ‚believe' their EBIT-margin is above industry average
*How successful was your company compared to
other companies in the industry?**

Source: BPM Best Practice-Study – Prof. Komus – FH Koblenz

Fig. 2. BPM Best Practice Study: Overall Success and BPM

When analyzing the correlations of two of the other studies conducted similar results were achieved as shown in figure 3 and figure 4.

2.2 Strategy Alignment

The study results on the alignment of BPM strategy und corporate strategy showed that 82% of the BPM best practice companies align their BPM to their business unit or company strategy.

Nevertheless, only 18% do their alignment in a "systematic documented process", while 65% stated that it was done in an "implicit process". During the interviews it was shown – at least by the perception of the author – that best practice BPM representatives have a very good understanding of business needs and goals. It was noticeable that the BPM approach in the best practice companies was closely linked to the worries and aims of the management. BPM representatives in those companies were close to the decision makers and streamlined their line of argumentation accordingly.

2.3 Organizational Aspects

The BPM best practice study also revealed interesting organizational facts about the best practice companies studied.

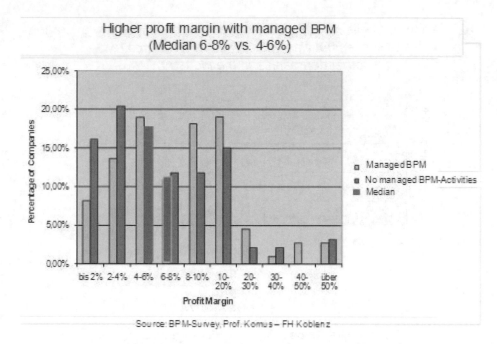

Fig. 3. BPM Survey: Overall Success and BPM

Process owners are widespread. 82% of the companies referred to already had process owners installed. But only in 12% of the companies did the process owners have the authority to issue directives to the employees involved in the respective business process. In many cases a pragmatic approach is chosen where key persons in existing managerial positions take on additional responsibility for processes extending beyond the fields they are already responsible for. This is a strong indicator that in most companies BPM is not successful because it is being forced into the organization in a top-down manner. Top management support may be very important, but in most cases BPM representatives need to be able to convince their audiences by means of good arguments and understanding of the situation rather than by formal power.

Another important success factor that BPM best practice companies have in common is the existence of centers of excellence to support and canalize the BPM efforts in the organization. This again shows that formal authority is not the key to accomplish a widespread realization of practiced process-oriented optimization.

Typical tasks of the BPM centers of excellence included

- definition of standards for BPM
- centralized services
- quality management and quality assurance
- responsibility for the technical BPM infrastructure

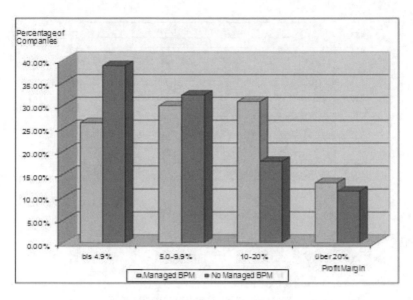

Source BPM + Six Sigma study, FH Koblenz

Fig. 4. BPM + Six Sigma Study: Overall Success and BPM

In many cases the centers of excellence comprised a team of staff members. This was often implemented as a staff division reporting directly to the top management. Still in no case was it found that the manager in charge of the BPM center of excellence was the superior of the employees engaged in the relevant business processes.

2.4 Training and Culture

Another important factor successful BPM companies have in common is the focus on training and culture. As shown in Figure 5 the companies participating in the study paid attention to the know-how and know-why of BPM. Only 12% stated they had almost no training offered. The other companies offered BPM trainings "generally", or "to many employees" showing that those companies found it important to spread the understanding of BPM far beyond the borders of the BPM team. This applied to other skills like project management, too.

The high relevance of training and culture also showed in the perceived attitude towards change (Figure 6). Two third of the companies interviewed stated that "change is an accepted part of corporate culture".

2.5 IT Systems and BPM Models

During the last years the "round-trip" has become one of the important arguments for the potential benefits of BPM. An examination of the links between the IT systems and the process models yielded the following results:

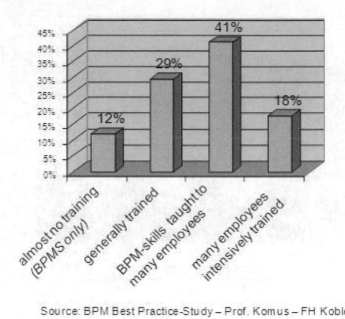

Source: BPM Best Practice-Study – Prof. Komus – FH Koblenz

Fig. 5. BPM + Six Sigma Study: Overall Success and BPM

- only 41% realized links between business models and IT models
- only 25% realized links between IT systems in production and business models

but,

- 71% of development of IT applications was based on process-oriented methods

This leads to the interpretation that the much-discussed round-trip application engineering is the exception rather than the rule. The same seems to apply to the often recommended link between - for example - SAP applications and business process models.

The results of the interviews seem to suggest a practice in which IT application development is based on process-oriented methods, but this doesn't necessarily mean that there is a formal linkage between the business-oriented process models and the IT models; these models are more often being developed independently and without formal links, but based on a common overall understanding of processes, and the resulting application is expected to cover the requirements accordingly. Even if the technical models are being linked to business models this doesn't mean that the models are going to be available and maintained after the application has been put into operations.

This is quite remarkable, considering the fact that the advantages of a close fit between business and technology represent one of the main arguments for BPM.

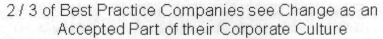
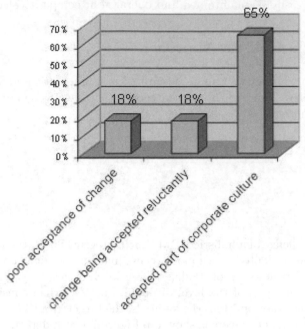

Fig. 6. Change as part of Corporate Culture

Also the missing link between technology and business once the applications are in production will make a continuous alignment impossible and therefore set back the efforts to continuously improve applications at low cost.

This fits well together with another observation of this and other studies. Most BPM activities can easily be classified as business BPM or technology BPM [6]. This separation also shows in the differentiation between BPMS (Business Process Management Suites or Systems) and BPMA or BPA (Business Process Modeling and Analysis).

In BPM companies this means, depending on the kind of BPM, the responsibilities are mostly being assigned to different departments. Technology BPM often is focused on business processes, but this focus is narrower and determined by the application to be developed. The discussion and the management attention are very much influenced by the IT. Business BPM on the other hand very often comes from a top-down perspective displayed in a process landscape ranging over the whole company. No focus is placed on the possibilities and restrictions of IT tools for supporting the processes.

The reasons for this divide between technology and business may lie in the different backgrounds and traditions of general management and IT management. Perhaps the different academic traditions of computer science and management studies are also contributing to the divergent understanding of BPM. In any case the gap observed between technology and business BPM is not beneficial to aspirations for optimized processes supported by flexible yet powerful IT applications which can easily be maintained and operated at competitive cost.

3   Aspiring for a Holistic Approach

Ideas on how the two perspectives can be integrated in a pragmatic and feasible way shall be given below. There are 3 main categories that seem to be important when aspiring for a holistic BPM approach.

- Methods
- Structure
- Human Side

3.1   Methods

To understand the challenge of a holistic BPM which integrates both the technological and the business-oriented aspects of process management it is necessary to realize that the different types of models in use in BPM are very different. This is true not only in terms of the level of detail, but also when considering the aspects being depicted or omitted, the symbols, the target groups and so on.

An overview of the different layers is shown in Figure 7 which depicts 3 levels of business BPM models and 3 levels of technology BPM models [7], overlapping in the Computation Independent Models.

Each of the layers shown has a special purpose. Even though the models of the lower layers do show more detailed information, they cannot be understood as a simple drill-down, but rather have to be interpreted as models for different purposes. For example, in the 2 lowest levels of modeling, necessary technical details (platform specific or platform independent) could be given while the business process landscape could be addressing the perspective of the top management, including strategic decisions like outsourcing business processes, strategic understanding of core competencies and other aspects.

In the daily BPM business this means there are not only 5 levels of models with different target groups and methodologies to consider, but going top-down there is a growing number of models, objects, links and more and more technical details being depicted in a large number of models which are closely interrelated and in many ways interdependent. As a result every change in any of the models – no matter if being driven by technological or business needs – has to be taken into account not only in one model, but in most cases in many models with many different types of relations to the main model in which the specific change occurs.

The question moving into focus is therefore how to realize a modeling and linking structure that is not only realistic in day-to-day business life when initially modeling processes, but even more so how to maintain those models considering the large number of inevitable changes.

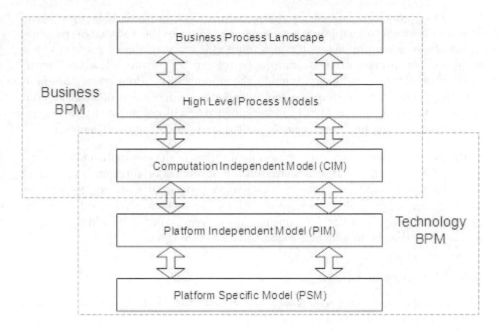

Fig. 7. Layers of Models in BPM (Technology BPM and Business BPM)

One approach to deal with this challenge is to implement flexible structures within the architecture of the models. Following an approach of a loose coupling it is necessary to avoid rigid structures that cause follow up changes in a too large number of models when changing just one element of the models.

Some important aspects of achieving a more flexible structure that is realistic, efficient and still meaningful enough to keep the different perspectives of the business processes and their models synchronized are the following:

Flexible Pointers. Formal pointers like process interfaces, hierarchical decompositions, etc., increase the maintenance efforts necessary. Other forms of coupling might allow a higher degree of freedom and a more fuzzy way of linkage without losing the relationship altogether, so that not every change necessarily has to be followed by maintenance work.

The use of less formal description methods – in an intelligent combination with traditionally more formal methods – allows the mapping of different models and the documentation of important information about the processes and their relationship to other processes and models. A very simple but effective type of software tool may be a wiki, which allows easy and collective maintenance of process information. Also, a wiki can offer a very simple access to process documentation and meta-knowledge in the BPM field.

Social Links. Following the insight that it is impossible to document all knowledge about processes in the organization, an important recommendation from the field of knowledge management can help to find an acceptable alternative. "Include pointers to people" [8] shows the way to make the knowledge resources inside the organization accessible in a more efficient way. Social networks that emphasize on process-oriented knowledge related to persons allow the identification of experts within and outside the organization. Pointers of this kind will allow obtaining necessary process information in a context of situation and personal knowledge. This kind of meta-knowledge will not substitute for documented knowledge, but it can complement it in a feasible and efficient way.

Culture. Another cornerstone of loose coupling is developing a culture supportive for the aims of BPM. A shared vision of process orientation, a culture of open discussion, fault tolerance in the creative process of searching for process improvements, openness to change and the willingness to share and exchange process knowledge are the prerequisites for a living and value-adding process architecture that is holistic and feasible at the same time.

3.2   Structure of BPM

Another important factor to achieve a holistic BPM is the design of the processes and the organizational structure of BPM.

The processes of process management should assure that the different – especially business- and IT-oriented – perspectives are being taken into consideration in the course of process design, implementation and improvement. This has to be reflected in all different aspects of BPM processes, for example in the procedures documented, communicated, trained and controlled, as well as in the incentive systems and the IT systems supporting BPM and the execution of the processes later on.

Concerning the organizational structure of BPM, it is very questionable whether a holistic BPM is possible in the common structure of separate organizational units for business BPM and technology BPM. An alternative organizational design calls for an integrated organizational BPM unit that serves as a link between the needs of the business unit and the IT fulfillment (Fig. 8). There are several important aspects that should be considered when changing the organizational structure in this way – for example the balance of power in the new organizational unit [5]. But considering the different arguments for and against this structure, the setup as an integrated organizational BPM unit promises to be a suitable step on the way towards a more holistic BPM.

3.3   Human Side

As stated above, the human side of BPM is the most important lever to implement a working BPM that will have a major impact on organizational performance.

The BPM software industry has understood the potentials of offering functionalities that will improve the collaboration and motivation of the organization's members. Today, the ideas and functionalities of web 2.0 or social media offerings

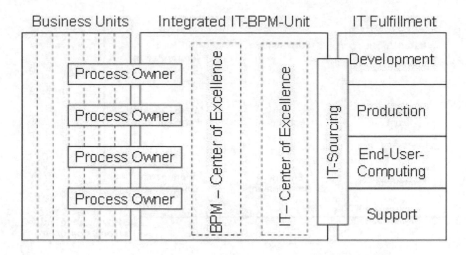

Fig. 8. Organizational Structure of an integrated BPM Unit

are being integrated in the BPM tools available. These range from the integration of weblogs over social networks and mash-ups to wiki export features. The subject-oriented BPM method [9] can also be considered as an approach to more readily benefit from employees' capabilities.

Based on the idea of benefiting from the success factors of social media, the Wikimanagement success factors [10] derived from organizational patterns of social media communities can give valuable ideas on how to manage a company to benefit from the employees potential to optimize business process management. (Fig. 9)

The potential benefits can be structured in three groups:

Motivation. A common shared vision of the relevance and potential benefits of BPM in a process-oriented organization is one cornerstone for a bottom-up BPM. This, in combination with the possibility to work on topics of importance for the employees themselves, lays the foundation for self-fulfillment as an important motivator.

Another opportunity to further strengthen those motivational factors is a personal image given to BPM activities. Examples for ways to achieve this might consist of personal blogs and other social media which are displayed in the BPM representation. These can be important aids in supporting an emotional approval of BPM.

Creative Freedom. Social media systems like Wikipedia allow participation based on a culture of trust. Different forms of rules are being combined with a very flexible rule interpretation. Simplicity of the tools used ensures that nobody is being excluded as a result of know-how deficits or lack of interest in matters of tool handling or tool technology.

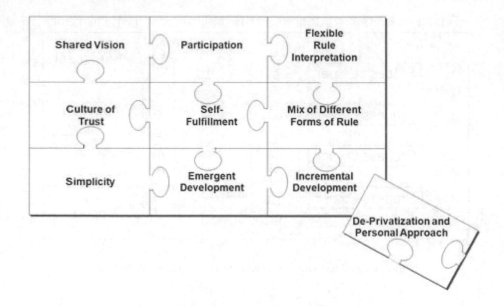

Fig. 9. Wikimanagement Success Factors

Emergent und Incremental Development. Social media systems as well as successful open source software projects have shown that advantages can be achieved by taking into consideration the fact that a path develops dynamically along the way and is the result of a series of small steps taken in a sensible and meaningful way as they approach. In sharp contrast to the philosophy of analyzing, predicting, planning and controlling on a large scale, some aspects of social media very often seem to be more flexible, faster and more efficient. At the same time this approach is very well aligned with the aims of creative freedom and motivation and therefore represents an interesting new way of managing the company's business processes.

Obviously the Wikimanagement success factors can only give some general guidance for developing the management of the organization. The implementation of a new leadership approach supporting a holistic BPM will depend on a holistic implementation of the management approach itself. Credibility and authenticity of the top management combined with efforts in change management, training, culture development and incentive systems represent just of few of the influencing factors.

4   Challenges on the Way to a Holistic BPM

A holistic BPM depends on many different aspects. Methods, structure, and the human side are just some of the important factors to be considered on the way towards a holistic BPM. Empirical evidence shows the relevance of soft and fuzzy factors.

Challenges like

- how to motivate and involve employees and partners,
- how to find an architecture of model layers that are linked together, but not so rigidly interdependent that they not maintainable without disproportional cost or
- how to implement a BPM organization that will still be able to guarantee a business-driven process view and at the same time ensures IT-reliability in the future at affordable costs

are still far from being mastered conclusively.

Future research, accompanied by continuous improvement of BPM practices in day-to-day management, will have to search in many different directions to find better solutions. Also organizations will have to make sure they find the way best-suited to their specific challenges, resources and backgrounds.

Altogether it will be critical for success to find a holistic approach for the change process itself on the way towards a more holistic BPM.

References

[1] Pritchard, J.-P., Armistead, C.: Business process management – lessons from European business. Business Process Management 5, 10–32 (1999)
[2] Palmer, N.: 2009 BPM – State of the Market Report,
    http://www.bpm.com/2009-bpm-stateof-the-market-report.html
    (download May 2010)
[3] IDS Scheer AG, Pierre Audoin Consultants (PAC) GmbH (eds.): Business process report 2007 – Geschäftsprozessmanagement in Deutschland, Österreich und der Schweiz. München und Saarbrücken (2007)
[4] Knuppertz, T., Schnägelberger, S., Clauberg, K.: Umfrage Status Quo Prozessmanagement 2009/2010 (February 2010),
    http://www.bpm-expo.com/bpmexpo/opencms/fachinfo/Trend_und_studien/
    BPMO_Status_Quo_Prozessmanagement_2009-2010.pdf
    (download February 2011)
[5] Komus, A.: BPM Best Practice: Erfolgsfaktoren der Prozessorientierung. In: Komus, A. (ed.) BPM Best Practice: Wie führende Unternehmen ihre Geschäftsprozesse Managen, pp. 3–57. Springer, Heidelberg (2011)
[6] Kruppke, H., Jost, W., Kindermann, H.: ARIS-Software, Method and Instrument. In: Scheer, A.-W., et al. (eds.) Agility by ARIS: Business Process Management: Yearbook Business Process Excellence 2006-2007, pp. 3–10. Springer, Heidelberg (2006)
[7] Allweyer, T.: BPM-Round-Trip: Wunsch oder Wirklichkeit. In: Komus, A. (ed.) BPM Best Practice: Wie führende Unternehmen ihre Geschäftsprozesse managen, pp. 219–234. Springer, Heidelberg (2011)
[8] Davenport, T., Prusak, L.: Information Ecology – Mastering the Information and Knowledge Environment. In: Why Technology is not enough for Success in the information age, Oxford University Press, Oxford (1997)

[9] Fleischmann, A.: What Is S-BPM? In: Buchwald, H., Fleischmann, A., Seese, D.,
     Stary, C. (eds.) S-BOM One – Setting the Stage for Subject-Oriented Business Pro-
     cess Management – First International Workshop, Karlsruhe, Germany, October 22,
     pp. 85–106. Springer, Berlin (2010)
[10] Komus, A., Wauch, F.: Wikimanagement: Was Unternehmen von Social Software
     und Web 2.0 lernen können. Verlag Oldenbourg (2008)

Part II

Contributed Papers

Distributed Execution of S-BPM Business Processes

Erwin Aitenbichler, Stephan Borgert, and Max Mühlhäuser

Technische Universität Darmstadt,
Hochschulstrasse 10, 64289 Darmstadt, Germany
{erwin,borgert,max}@tk.informatik.tu-darmstadt.de

Abstract. Subject-oriented business process management (S-BPM) introduces a new technique for process modeling that emphasizes the importance of the actors in business processes (subjects) and gives a balanced consideration to subjects, their actions, and goals. Because of the formal foundation and the clear declaration of subjects, S-BPM allows the distributed modeling and execution of processes, without losing the capability to verify the compatibility of processes.

Executing cooperating processes in a distributed system also poses new requirements to the communication middleware, which is responsible for routing messages from one process instance to a remote peer process instance. In this paper, we describe an engine to execute S-BPM process choreographies. It is based on subject-oriented process modeling and a publish/subscribe middleware as communication basis. Our process engine also runs on mobile devices.

Keywords: Business Process, Business Process Management, Process Execution, Distributed Execution, CCS, PASS, S-BPM, MundoCore.

1 Introduction

Internet-based marketplaces for mobile phone end-user applications ("apps") have been very successful recently. As a second trend, we observe the increased adoption of service-oriented architectures in enterprises. Such architectures make systems modular and components become interchangeable. The combination of both – marketplaces and services – promises to enable an *Internet of Services*, which offers marketplaces where services become tradable goods. The basis for such an Internet of Services is currently developed in the large-scale Theseus Programme [3].

The Internet of Services gives businesses the opportunity to outsource certain business functions to external contractors by using external services, instead of implementing them in-house. From the business process perspective, the consequence of outsourcing is that a subprocess of the overall internal business process is moved to an external contractor. This subprocess is then implemented by the external service used. However, in an open service market, where anybody is allowed to offer services, it seems natural that there will be multiple offers for services providing the same functionality.

Hence, the services offered on the market will be different in many details, such as their quality and how their internal processes are realized. In many cases, the process implemented by an offered service will not exactly match the subprocess a customer asks for. As long as the remaining internal process and the outsourced subprocess fulfill *interaction soundness* [20], they can be composed. Consequently, it is vitally important that the parties interacting in a B2B scenario ensure that their processes are compatible

A. Fleischmann et al. (Eds.): S-BPM ONE 2010, CCIS 138, pp. 19–35, 2011.

with each other. It is desirable that this compatibility check is performed on the models during design or composition time, thereby detecting any incompatibilities before some process instance actually fails at runtime.

As a direct consequence of the Internet of Services, the distributed execution of business processes also increases in importance. By distributed execution of a business process we mean that every process participant may use her own process execution engine. The overall process is then executed by interconnecting multiple engines. These engines may be used by different enterprises, but there may also be multiple engines within the same enterprise. The engine may also run on the mobile device of an employee, giving her the opportunity to work on processes during times without a network connection. This paper addresses the following two aspects of distributed process execution:

- the composition-time compatibility check of services and
- the execution-time message routing between process engines.

1.1 Requirements

For the distributed execution of a process, two important prerequisites are needed: A *suitable process modeling* technique and a *flexible communication platform*. We expect that the process modeling technique can fulfill the following requirements:

- It should be possible to split a process up into subprocesses describing the work of each process participant separately.
- If a process is modeled in a distributed manner, it should be possible to perform the same model checks regarding the communication between interacting partners, as if it would be modeled as a whole.

In order to execute the process in a distributed manner, it must first be clear which activities are performed by which actor. Subject-oriented process modeling introduces an approach that gives balanced consideration to the actors in business processes (persons and systems as subjects), their actions (predicates), and their goals or the subject matter of their actions (objects) [21, 8]. Every one of them receives and delivers information by exchanging messages. Humans, e.g., exchanges emails, office documents, or voice messages.

Because subjects are modeled separately, it is easy to split up a process into its subprocesses for all its subjects. It is also possible that subjects are modeled by different enterprises at different places. Because the formal framework offers the functionality to hide all internal communication and communication with other third parties for a particular interaction, companies only have to expose minimum knowledge about their internal processes.

1.2 Contributions

In this work we make the following contributions:

- We show that subject-orientation and the process modeling language Parallel Activities Specification Scheme (PASS) [7] provide a good basis for the distributed modeling and execution of business processes. Parties do not have to disclose their internal processes and can still ensure the compatibility of their processes.

– We describe the *process embedding* concept and its implementation in a distributed system. It allows to reduce the number of process variants that would otherwise have to be modeled and maintained explicitly.
– We show how the publish/subscribe abstraction can be used for the flexible message routing needed in distributed process execution.

The rest of the paper is organized as follows. In section 2 we discuss related work. Subject-oriented BPM and the modeling language PASS are introduced in section 3. Next, section 4 describes how PASS can be mapped to its formal foundation CCS. The execution of PASS processes and the separate modeling of the embedding information is presented in section 5. In section 6 we show how publish/subscribe can be applied to message routing in distributed process execution. The implementation is described in section 7. Finally, the paper is concluded in section 8.

2   Related Work

2.1   Process Description Languages

The mainstream process description languages used today lack a formal foundation and well-defined semantics (e.g., EPC, BPMN). This impedes to perform verifications on the models or to directly execute the models. Execution-oriented languages (e.g., BPEL, XPDL) are also not suitable for verification, because they hardly allow the description of choreographies. Consequently, in practice business experts often start with a business-oriented model (BPMN), which is then one-shot transformed into an execution-oriented model (BPEL) by engineers. In contrast to using multiple languages, PASS can be used throughout the whole process lifecycle. It has a formal basis suitable to perform verifications and is executable at the same time.

Several approaches are working on the execution level and extend the functionality of the BPEL standard by using proxy services or additional annotations or descriptions. A representative work is described in [12], where the authors introduce the VxBPEL language, which is an extension of BPEL by incorporating variability. It enables re-binding of services during runtime, substitution of service for optimizing purposes or in case of in sudden unavailable services. In contrast to our approach, choreographies are not supported. In addition, services provided by humans are not considered and there is a shortage of formal verification techniques.

2.2   Formal Methods for Verifying Interaction Soundness

Process algebras like the π-calculus provide strong means for modeling concurrent systems like service compositions and are based on formal terms. Choreography modeling, refining, and clustering are inherently supported. In addition, a rich theory to analyze processes for equivalence is provided and also the capability to perform reasoning on system properties and to verify process behavior. For this reason, current research efforts in this area focus mainly on approaches for formal verification of services and business process. Work on compliance and compatibility checks investigate the issue of when a service can be replaced by another one [22, 4]. This is necessary when a service of a process fails during runtime or for finding redundant services. COWS [13] and SOCK [9] are designed for the purpose of automatic service composition. Furthermore, process algebras are often combined with other formalisms in order to be able to specify more aspects of a service in a formal manner. E.g., some extensions exist, that combine the π-calculus with ontologies and formal logics [1, 14] to describe non-functional properties and access control policies. While these formal approaches are also capable of formal verification and matchmaking, they usually do not consider other aspects, such as the execution of the models, or the seamless integration of human services. In this work we use CCS, which can be considered as a subset of the π-calculus. The additional concepts of the π-calculus, like mobility of channels, were not required here.

A Petri Net is a formal language for modeling concurrent systems and has been widely accepted as formal foundation for business process modeling. Furthermore, it provides a graphical and easily understandable notation. Petri Nets are object of research for many years and current efforts are focusing on suitable constructs for choreography descriptions. For example, Huangfu et. al. [10] present an approach that addresses the issue of dynamic service composition by modeling service behavior by Object Petri Nets. A service consists of a set of operations and mapping rules from services to Object Petri Nets are introduced. One main drawback of using Petri Nets is that the entire process has to modeled in a single net. In contrast to this, many process algebras directly support parallelism. That allows to model each service separately and then compose them simply by using the parallel operator. Furthermore, Petri Nets do not support all of the workflow patterns[1]. Several extension overcome this issue partly but lead often to a lower expressiveness [19]. Consequently, a higher modeling effort is necessary in order to describe processes.

2.3 Distributed Execution of Business Processes

Process execution engines are usually centralized systems that execute an entire business process and manage all its instances. A comprehensive survey of methods for the distributed execution of business processes can be found in [23].

To achieve scalability, a simplistic approach is to replicate the centralized engine and distribute the process instances among the replicas. However, this approach is not sufficient for an Internet of Services scenario. In the following, we only consider methods that allow a distributed execution even of individual process instances.

The distributed process execution engine described in [17] decomposes a single BPEL process into its individual activities and deploys these activities to any set of execution engines. These activities then communicate over the PADRES publish/subscribe platform. An important aim is to deploy activities close to the data they operate on, thereby minimizing network communication costs. The work reported in [23] is based on a similar approach, which allows the distributed execution of an unmodified BPEL process. Algorithms for the automatic partitioning of processes among the partners participating in their execution are provided. In contrast to that, we do not assume that we already have a complete and consistent process model in the beginning - which would

---

[1] http://www.workflowpatterns.com

be very unlikely in multi-party Internet of Services scenarios. Instead, we allow for distributed modeling and ensure interaction soundness of the process parts by formal verification methods.

3 Subject-Oriented Business Process Management (S-BPM)

Subject-orientation gives special consideration to the actors (subjects) in business processes, beside their actions (predicates), and their results (objects) [21, 8]. It is based on the fact that humans, machines, and software services can be modeled in the same manner. Every one of them receives and delivers information by exchanging messages. Humans, e.g., exchanges emails, office documents, or voice messages.

The company Metasonic [15] provides modeling, validation and execution tools that cover the entire business process lifecycle. Subject-oriented business process management (S-BPM) places the focus on the flow of communication among employees instead of defining a rigid central control flow as in traditional BPM. Subject-oriented BPM (S-BPM) acknowledges that employees themselves drive processes. The advantages of subject-oriented BPM (S-BPM) include greater motivation, savings in time and costs, increased flexibility, improved employee integration and simpler compliance.

The following explanation gives a general overview of the subject-oriented approach. The term subject is used for processes executed by one organization, role, IT-organization etc. These are the acting entities in a business process. They synchronize their activities in order to execute a business process triggered by a corresponding event. In a process description from a subject-oriented view, the focus lies on the involved subjects, which have got a role in the process. That can be people or systems performing the process steps (subjects of a process). The subject-oriented view on a process describes which activities the involved subjects (persons, actors, applications) need to perform at what time. Furthermore, which interactions (sending and receiving of messages) are necessary for the coordination of the respective activities. Each subject defines its own control flow, which coordinates and synchronizes itself with the control flows of other subjects via messages. A subject encloses the interactions and activities executed by a certain involved organizational unit, or person within a considered process. During the execution of a process, a subject sends messages to other subjects, receives messages from other subjects or performs internal activities.

To execute business processes, the Metasonic Business Suite [15] contains the tools jLIVE! and jFLOW!. jLIVE! allows to test processes directly without any coding effort. This tool directly acts on the subjects and does not consider *process embedding* (see Section 5.1). Using an Internet browser, all of the process participants can then immediately test the process together on the basis of roles (subject-related).

jFLOW! allows the actual execution of business processes and takes process embedding into account. It provides a process portal that visualizes an employee's running processes in which he or she plays a role in. The process portal guides the employee step by step through his or her processes. As individual process steps are carried out, the process portal automatically informs other involved employees, who then find their tasks in their individual task lists.

3.1 Process Modeling

The process model consists of two levels. On the upper level, the involved subjects and the messages they potentially exchange are described in the *Subject Interaction Diagram*. On the lower level, the detailed process is specified for each subject. Figure 1 shows the subject interaction diagram of a vacation approval process. The *Employee* sends a vacation request to his *Manager*. The *Manager* then approves or rejects the request. If it is approved, then the *Manager* also informs the human resources department (*HR*) for bookkeeping.

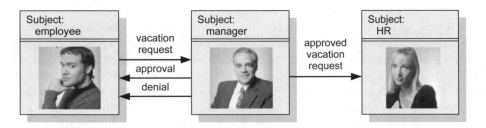

Fig. 1. Subject Interaction Diagram of Vacation Approval Process

Figure 2 shows the internal behavior of subject *Manager*. It is based on the language *Parallel Activities Specification Scheme* (PASS) [7], which is an implementation of subject-oriented modeling. At the basic level, PASS only distinguishes between three basic types of activities: *send message*, *receive message*, and *function*. The *Manager* receives a vacation request from an *Employee*, then approves or rejects it. To demonstrate a loop, the manager waits for a corrected vacation request from the *Employee*, in case he has rejected it in the first place.

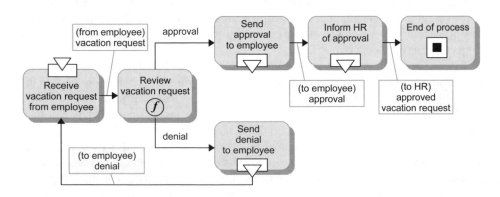

Fig. 2. Process model for subject *Manager*

4   Formal Description of PASS Processes

PASS is founded on top of the process algebra CCS [16] (Calculus of Communicating Systems) and all language constructs of PASS can be transformed down to pure CCS.

Process algebras provide a suitable means for modeling distributed systems. They offer well-studied algorithms for verification and for determining behavioral equivalences. In addition, the CCS composition operator facilitates a hierarchization and modularization of the model, allowing to handle business processes of arbitrary size.

4.1   Calculus of Communicating Systems (CCS)

Labeled Transition System: Let ACT be a fixed set of actions. A labelled transition system [11] $LTS = (\text{PROC}, \rightarrow)$ over ACT consists of

- A set PROC of states and
- A set $\rightarrow \subseteq \text{PROC} \times \text{ACT} \times \text{PROC}$ of transitions between states. Instead of $(s, a, s') \in \rightarrow$ we use the more suggestive notation $s \xrightarrow{a} s'$.

Syntax of CCS: Let $\mathcal{L}$ be a set of labels and let $Act = \{\tau\} \cup \mathcal{L} \cup \{\bar{a} | a \in \mathcal{L}\}$ be the set of all actions. Then the syntax of process P is given by:

$$P ::= 0 \ \Big| \ A \ \Big| \ a.P \ \Big| \ \sum_{i \in I} P_i \ \Big| \ P_1 | P_2 \ \Big| \ P \backslash L \ \Big| \ P[f]$$

with $a \in Act$, $L \subseteq \mathcal{L}$, $f : \mathcal{L} \to \mathcal{L}$, and $P, P_i \in \mathcal{P}$ where $\mathcal{P}$ is the set of processes. 0 is the inactive process that does nothing.

Semantic of CCS: The semantic of the CCS operators is given by rules of the type:

$$\frac{Pre_i, \dots, Pre_n}{Imp}$$

The Pre_i are the premises that are met if the implication Imp is satisfied. If $n = 0$ then there are no premises and Imp holds always. This kind of rules are called *Structural Operational Semantic* rules and were introduced by Plotkin [18].

Name	Sym.	Structural Operational Semantic
action	.	$\dfrac{}{a.P \xrightarrow{a} P}$
process identifier	:=	$\dfrac{P \xrightarrow{a} P'}{A \xrightarrow{a} P'} \ if \ A := P$
choice	Σ	$\dfrac{P_j \xrightarrow{a} P'_j}{\sum_{i \in I} P_i \xrightarrow{a} P'_j} \ j \in I$
parallel composition			$\dfrac{P \xrightarrow{a} P'}{P \mid Q \xrightarrow{a} P' \mid Q} \quad \dfrac{Q \xrightarrow{a} Q'}{P \mid Q \xrightarrow{a} P \mid Q'} \quad \dfrac{P \xrightarrow{a} P', \ Q \xrightarrow{\bar{a}} Q'}{P \mid Q \xrightarrow{\tau} P' \mid Q'}$
restriction	\	$\dfrac{P \xrightarrow{a} P'}{P \backslash L \xrightarrow{a} P' \backslash L} \ a, \bar{a} \notin \mathcal{L}$
renaming	f	$\dfrac{P \xrightarrow{a} P'}{P[f] \xrightarrow{f(a)} P'[f]} \ where f(\tau) = \tau, f(\bar{a}) = \overline{f(a)}$

4.2 Mapping PASS to CCS

There are three basic symbols to model the internal behavior of subjects in PASS: *send*, *receive* and *function*. Send and receive manage the interaction among different subjects and we denote them as communication activities. They are the equivalent to the send and receive actions of CCS. In the example below, receiving a vacation request is denoted as $vacation\_request$. Send actions are marked with an overline, e.g., sending the approval is denoted as $\overline{approval}$.

The function symbol of PASS is used to describe the call of an internal function, which may be implemented by a software service or it may require a user interaction. Such invokes are modeled by sending and receiving messages to a function library, which is specific for each subject. The following CCS code describes the behavior of subject *Manager*:

$$Manager_{Interface} := \overline{vacation\_request.int\_vacation\_request}.$$
$$(int\_approval.Manager^1_{Interface}$$
$$+ int\_denial.Manager^2_{Interface})$$
$$Manager^1_{Interface} := \overline{approval.approved\_vacation\_request}.0$$
$$Manager^2_{Interface} := \overline{denial}.Manager_{Interface}$$
$$Manager_{Library} := int\_vacation\_request.(\overline{int\_approval}.Manager_{Library}$$
$$+ \overline{int\_denial}.Manager_{Library})$$
$$Manager := Manager_{Interface} \mid Manager_{Library}$$

4.3 Hiding the Internal Behavior

All internal communication can be hidden by applying the restriction operator:

$$Manager := (Manager_{Interface} \mid Manager_{Library})$$
$$\backslash \{int\_vacation\_request, int\_approval, int\_denial\}$$

Inserting the process descriptions of $Manager_{Interface}$ and $Manager_{Library}$ and resolving the internal behavior afterwards, leads to a simpler term. This is shown in Figures 3 and 4 by an example of a simple subject A. A consists of the interface A_1 and the function library A_L. Using the simplification of equation 1, the behavior of subject *Manager* can be rewritten as:

$$Manager := vacation\_request.\tau.(\tau.Manager^1 + \tau.Manager^2)$$
$$Manager^1 := \overline{approval.approved\_vacation\_request}.0$$
$$Manager^2 := \overline{denial}.Manager$$

This describes the behavior of subject *Manager* which is visible externally. In an inter-business scenario, this allows the interacting parties to keep the details about their internal processes private.

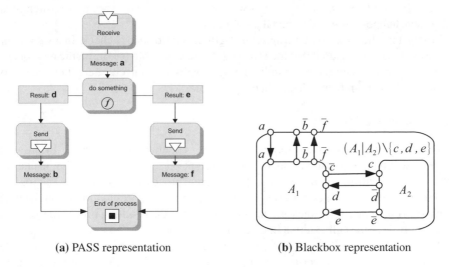

(a) PASS representation   **(b)** Blackbox representation

Fig. 3. The internal behavior of a subject $A = (A_1|A_2)\backslash\{c, d, e\}$ in two different representations

$$A_1 := a.\bar{c}.(d.\bar{b}.0 + e.\bar{f}.0)$$
$$A_2 := c.(\bar{d}.A_2 + \bar{e}.A_2)$$
$$A := (A_1 \mid A_2)\backslash\{c, d, e\}$$
$$\rightarrow (a.\bar{c}.(d.\bar{b}.0 + e.\bar{f}.0) \mid c.(\bar{d}.A_2 + \bar{e}.A_2))\backslash\{c, d, e\}$$
$$\rightarrow a.(\bar{c}.(d.\bar{b}.0 + e.\bar{f}.0) \mid c.(\bar{d}.A_2 + \bar{e}.A_2))\backslash\{c, d, e\}$$
$$\rightarrow a.\tau_c.((d.\bar{b}.0 + e.\bar{f}.0) \mid (\bar{d}.A_2 + \bar{e}.A_2))\backslash\{c, d, e\}$$
$$\rightarrow a.\tau_c.(\tau_d.(\bar{b}.0 \mid A_2) + \tau_e.(\bar{f}.0 \mid A_2))\backslash\{c, d, e\}$$
$$A' = a.\tau_c.(\tau_d.\bar{b}.(0 \mid A_2) + \tau_e.\bar{f}.(0 \mid A_2))\backslash\{c, d, e\}$$

$$\implies A' = a.\tau_c.(\tau_d.\bar{b}.0 + \tau_e.\bar{f}.0) \qquad (1)$$

Fig. 4. After the reduction of the subject equation of the subject A the process library A_2 is at its initial point again. A further solving of the equation is not possible without interactions to the environment of A.

4.4 Verifying Process Compatibility

The overall vacation approval process is given by combining all subjects using the parallel composition operator:

$$Vacation := (Employee \mid Manager \mid HR)\backslash\{L\}$$

where L denotes the set of all free messages of $Vacation$

We currently use the CWB-NC Workbench [5] for running verifications on the resulting CCS code. CWB-NC supports various behavioral equivalences as well as model checks. The model checker determines whether systems satisfy formulas written in an expressive temporal logic, the modal μ-calculus.

Firstly, this allows us to perform a choreography conformance check. In a valid composition, it must be ensured that the involved services are able to communicate properly with each other. Secondly, reachability analysis is used to ensure that all end states of the subprocesses can be reached, where applicable.

4.5 Distributed Modeling

In a scenario where multiple different businesses cooperate, the processes for different subjects will typically also be modeled in different places. In addition, the businesses are usually not willing to fully disclose their internal processes. As shown in section 4.3, the internal behavior can be removed from the full process specification using the CCS restriction operator and businesses only have to expose the resulting process description which only describes all external interactions of a subject.

The process compatibility can also be verified in a peer-to-peer fashion. For example, if the Employee wants to verify if his process is compatible with that of the Manager, then the Manager would only expose the parts of his process that are relevant for the interaction with the Employee. Hence, he would remove all communication with third parties using the restriction operator:

$$Manager_{Emp} := Manager \backslash \{approved\_vacation\_request\}$$

which yields:

$$Manager_{Emp} := vacation\_request.(\overline{approval}.0 + \overline{denial}.Manager_{Emp})$$

As described in section 4.4, the employee can now verify the following expression:

$$Vacation_{Emp} := (Employee \mid Manager_{Emp}) \backslash \{L\}$$

where L denotes the set of all free messages of $Vacation_{Emp}$

5   Process Execution

PASS processes can be directly executed on a suitable execution engine. From the process model to the final execution of a process instance the following two additional steps are necessary: *embedding* and *instantiation*.

5.1 Embedding

First, the process must be embedded into the organization and into the IT. This means that the subjects in the process are mapped to roles or services. If the tasks of a subject are executed by a software service, then a mapping from the subject to the service is defined. If the tasks are fulfilled by a human, then the subject is mapped to a *role*.

For example, the subject *Manager* is handled by the role *Area Head* or *Director* (Figure 5). Which role is the correct one, depends on the context: Employees direct their vacation requests to their manager, which is their Area Head. Area Heads direct their vacation requests to their manager, which is the Director of the lab.

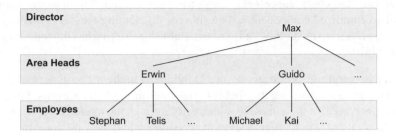

Fig. 5. Organigram of the Telecooperation Lab

We model the embedding information as a separate aspect apart from the process itself. Compared to that, BPEL does not have a mechanism to handle such embedding. Dynamically choosing between services at runtime must be explicitly coded into the process. Another approach would be to use proxy services, which decide at runtime to which other service they should forward requests. In contrast to that, the embedding concept reduces the number of process variants that would otherwise have to be modeled explicitly and it does not require additional proxy services.

5.2 Instantiation

Instantiation denotes the creation of a new process instance for a concrete subject carrier. For example, a message is sent to the subject *HR*, which is mapped to the role *Secretary*. *Elke* and *Birgit* have that role and therefore they can accept this message. Now, if *Elke* accepts the message, then a new process instance is created. From this time on, she takes over the subject *HR* / the role *Secretary* for this concrete process instance.

6 Message Routing

When such processes are executed in a distributed system on multiple communicating engines, then the question arises how to correctly route messages from a process instance to remote process instances, while taking embedding information into account. Because this requires a communication abstraction that supports dynamic endpoints and multicast, we use publish/subscribe.

6.1 Publish/Subscribe

A publish/subscribe system consists of a set of clients that asynchronously exchange messages, decoupled by a message broker. *Clients* can be characterized as *producers* or *consumers*. Producers *publish* messages, and consumers *subscribe* for messages by issuing *subscriptions*, which are essentially stateless message filters. Consumers can have multiple active subscriptions, and after a client has issued a subscription, the notification service delivers all future matching notifications that are published by any producer until the client cancels the respective subscription. The message broker is a logically centralized component responsible for distributing messages arriving from multiple publishers to its multiple subscribers. Publish/subscribe has the following characteristics [6]:

- **Space decoupling:** producers do not individually address consumers while publishing messages. Instead, they publish messages through the message broker, and subscribers receive these messages indirectly through the message broker. Publishers do not usually hold references to the consumers and they are not aware of how many consumers are participating in the interaction.
- **Time decoupling:** producers and consumers do not need to actively participate in the interaction at the same time. In particular, a subscription causes messages to be delivered even if producers join after the subscription was issued. In a plain publish/subscribe system, notifications are retained only as long as it takes to distribute them to current subscribers. Some brokers deliver messages to consumers through a queue. This allows consumers to temporarily disconnect from the system. All messages stored while the consumer was offline are dispatched upon reconnect.

The simplest publish/subscribe addressing scheme is based on the notion of *channels* or *topics*. Participants explicitly publish notifications to one or more channels, which are identified by a name (e.g., a string or an URL-like expression). The concept of channels is very similar to the concept of *groups* as defined in *group communication*. Subscribing to a channel can be viewed as becoming a member of the group, and publishing is performed by broadcasting the notification to all members of the group. The part of the notification that is visible to the event service is the identifier of the channel. Since there is no interplay between different channels, each channel can be considered as an event service of its own. A subscription-based Publish/Subscribe system with channel-based addressing supports the following operations:

$\mathbf{sub}(X, C)$ Client X subscribes to channel C
$\mathbf{unsub}(X, C)$ Client X unsubscribes from channel C
$\mathbf{notify}(X, n)$ Client X is notified about n
$\mathbf{pub}(X, n)$ Client X publishes n

Clients register their interest in specific kinds of notifications by issuing subscriptions via the $\mathbf{sub}(X, C)$ operation. From that time on, all notifications matching the channel C are delivered to the client. The client receives notifications through the notify operation, which is an output operation and often implemented as a call-back. Each client can have any number of active subscriptions. A client can revoke subscriptions individually by issuing the $\mathbf{unsub}(X, C)$ operation.

6.2 Communication between Subjects

Figure 6 shows the publish/subscribe channels involved in the vacation approval process. When Stephan, Erwin, and Elke use separate process execution engines, they issue the following subscriptions:

sub(Stephan, users.stephan)	**sub**(Erwin, users.erwin)	**sub**(Elke, users.elke)
sub(Stephan, roles.employee)	**sub**(Erwin, roles.areahead)	**sub**(Elke, roles.secretary)

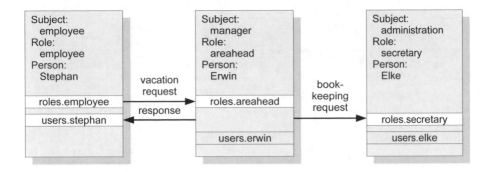

Fig. 6. Communication between subjects using Publish/Subscribe

Each process engine subscribes two channels from which it can receive messages. The first channel name is constructed from the role name and is used to receive messages when the subject *manager* of a process instance is not bound yet. It is best practice to send messages to roles whenever possible instead of addressing messages directly to specific persons. For example, an employee of area *SE* would send his vacation request to *areahead.se*. This indirection allows to put multiple persons in charge for a role or it allows to temporarily assign the role to another person, e.g., if Erwin takes vacation.

The second channel name is constructed from the name of the person. This allows to send messages to a specific person and is typically used for reply messages. When Erwin accepts or declines the vacation request from Stephan, then Stephan is already bound for subject *employee* in the process instance and it makes only sense to send that reply directly back to Stephan.

6.3   Embedding

Two use cases are particularly interesting with respect to embedding: *context resolution* and *anycast*.

Context Resolution: For example, Stephan issues a vacation request and thereby creates a new process instance. It is clear that he is the subject *employee* in the process. The overall process can only start at this subject, because it is the only subject that does not start with a receive action. The process engine of *Stephan* is configured with all roles he has. Hence, it can be determined from this information that his role is *employee*. Next, he sends the vacation request message to his *manager*.

The message flow is shown in Figure 7. Sending the message to his manager means that he broadcasts it to all *areaheads*. The process engine of each area head now passes the received message to the *resolver* service. The resolver service returns a boolean value indicating if the message should be accepted or not. The resolver of Guido returns false, because Guido is not responsible for Stephan. Hence, Guido silently discards the message. The resolver of Erwin returns true, because Stephan is in his area. Erwin now calls *accept* on the engine of Stephan to acknowledge the successful reception of Stephan's request.

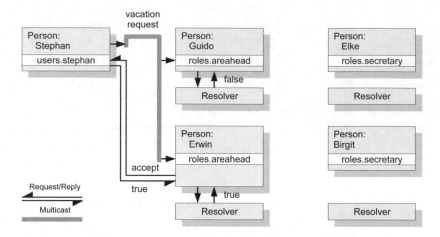

Fig. 7. Routing of a message to a single destination based on context

Anycast: The first example demonstrated how messages can be routed to a role, by selecting a specific responsible person based on the context. It is also possible that more than one person has the requested role and is able to process the message. This is shown in the anycast scenario in Figure 8. Here, Elke and Birgit both have the role *secretary* and it does not matter if Elke or Birgit handles the bookkeeping request.

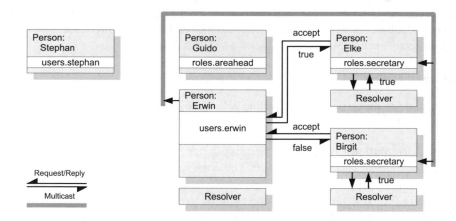

Fig. 8. Routing of a message to multiple destinations having the same role and equal status

The interaction goes as follows. Erwin sends the bookkeeping request to the channel *roles.secretary* which means that it will be multicasted to both, Elke and Birgit. Elke's engine asks the resolver if the message should be accepted, which returns true. Now, she calls *accept* and Erwin's engine returns *true*. Erwin now has the information that Elke has accepted the message and will continue with the process. If somebody else calls *accept*, then Erwin's engine will always respond with *false*. Birgit's resolver also re-sponds true. Now, when she calls *accept*, then Erwin's engine returns *false* and Birgit's engine silently drops the request.

7 Implementation

In the following, the implementation of our process choreography engine is described.

7.1 MundoCore

We used the communication middleware MundoCore [2] as Publish/Subscribe system. MundoCore is a flexible communication framework that allows to integrate service-oriented systems spanning multiple platforms and programming languages. It supports different communication abstractions, such as Publish/Subscribe and Remote Method Calls, over different transport and invocation protocols. MundoCore provides a common set of APIs for different programming languages (Java, C++, .NET) on a wide range of different devices. With a minimal footprint of approximately 42 KB, MundoCore can be run on a broad spectrum of computing devices, ranging from servers down to mobile phones or sensors. The Publish/Subscribe implementation of MundoCore operates fully peer-to-peer and does not require any centralized components for message routing.

7.2 Process Execution Engine

Our engine executes subject-oriented business process management (S-BPM) models created with the jPASS modeling tool and has a functionality that is similar to jFLOW. Each started engine executes a subset of the subjects defined in the process. Through

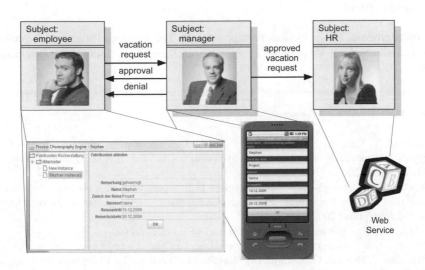

Fig. 9. Screenshots of the process execution engine on PC and Android mobile phone

interconnection of several engines, the whole process can be executed. The engine supports PCs and mobile devices, i.e., Android-based phones.

Figure 9 shows screenshots of the PC and Android versions of the process execution engine. For example, the employee uses the PC version, the manager uses the engine on his mobile phone, and the HR department uses an automatized process.

8   Conclusion

We have described an approach for the distributed execution of business processes, based on subject-oriented process modeling and a Publish/Subscribe communication middleware. Our system provides several benefits in the following two important use cases:

- A process model can be split up along its subjects and be executed in a distributed manner on several process execution engines. This is suitable for use within an enterprise and allows to execute processes on servers of different departments. In addition, employees can execute processes on their mobile devices and work on processes even when the do not have Internet connectivity.
- If cooperating processes are modeled in a distributed manner, which is often the case when different businesses cooperate, then we can still perform the same model checks as if the overall choreography was modeled as a single, centralized process. In addition, the businesses do not have to disclose their detailed internal processes.

The presented concepts have been implemented in our process choreography engine, which runs on PCs, servers, and Android-based mobile phones.

In our future work we plan to investigate how our approach can be applied to process models of the upcoming BPMN 2.0 standard and how BPMN 2.0 models could be transformed to PASS.

Acknowledgments. This work was supported by the Theseus Programme, funded by the German Federal Ministry of Economy and Technology under the promotional reference 01MQ07012.

References

[1] Agarwal, S., Rudolph, S., Abecker, A.: Semantic Description of Distributed Business Processes. In: Proceedings of AAAI Spring Symposium – AI Meets Business Rules and Process Management (2008)
[2] Aitenbichler, E., Kangasharju, J., Mühlhäuser, M.: MundoCore: A Light-weight Infrastructure for Pervasive Computing. Pervasive and Mobile Computing 3(4), 332–361 (2007), doi:10.1016/j.pmcj.2007.04.002
[3] BMWi: TEXO – Business Webs in the Internet of Services (2009), http://theseus-programm.de/scenarios/en/texo.html
[4] Bordeaux, L., Salaün, G., Berardi, D., Mecella, M.: When are Two Web Services Compatible? In: Shan, M.-C., Dayal, U., Hsu, M. (eds.) TES 2004. LNCS, vol. 3324, pp. 15–28. Springer, Heidelberg (2005)

[5] CWB-NC: The Concurrency Workbench of the New Century (2000),
    http://www.cs.sunysb.edu/~cwb/

[6] Eugster, P.T., Felber, P.A., Guerraoui, R., Kermarrec, A.M.: The many faces of pub-
    lish/subscribe (2003)

[7] Fleischmann, A.: Distributed Systems: Software Design and Implementation. Springer, Hei-
    delberg (1994)

[8] Fleischmann, A., Lippe, S., Meyer, N., Stary, C.: Coherent task modeling and execution
    based on subject-oriented representations. In: England, D., Palanque, P., Vanderdonckt, J.,
    Wild, P.J. (eds.) TAMODIA 2009. LNCS, vol. 5963, pp. 78–91. Springer, Heidelberg (2010)

[9] Guidi, C., Lucchi, R., Gorrieri, R., Busi, N., Tennenholtz, M.: SOCK: A Calculus for
    Service Oriented Computing. In: Dan, A., Lamersdorf, W. (eds.) ICSOC 2006. LNCS,
    vol. 4294, pp. 327–338. Springer, Heidelberg (2006)

[10] Huangfu, X., Shu, Z., Chen, H., Luo, X.: Research on Dynamic Service Composition
    Based on Object Petri Net for the Networked Information System. In: Fifth International
    Joint Conference on INC, IMS and IDC, pp. 1075–1080 (2009), http://ieeexplore.
    ieee.org/lpdocs/epic03/wrapper.htm?arnumber=5331528

[11] Keller, R.M.: Formal verification of parallel programs. Communications of the ACM 19(7),
    384 (1976), http://portal.acm.org/citation.cfm?id=360248.360251

[12] Koning, M., Sun, C., Sinnema, M., Avgeriou, P.: VxBPEL: Supporting Variability for Web
    Services in BPEL. Information and Software Technology 51(2), 258–269 (2009)

[13] Lapadula, A., Pugliese, R., Tiezzi, F.: A Calculus for Orchestration of Web Services. In: De
    Nicola, R. (ed.) ESOP 2007. LNCS, vol. 4421, pp. 33–47. Springer, Heidelberg (2007)

[14] Markovic, I., Pereira, A.C., Stojanovic, N.: A Framework for Querying in Business
    Process Modelling. In: Multikonferenz Wirtschaftsinformatik, pp. 1703–1714 (2008),
    http://ibis.in.tum.de/mkwi08/23_Semantic_Web_Technology_in_
    Business_Information_Systems/03_Markovic.pdf

[15] Metasonic: Welcome to the Future of BPM: S-BPM (2010),
    http://www.metasonic.de

[16] Milner, R.: Communication and Concurrency. Prentice Hall PTR, Englewood Cliffs (1995)

[17] Muthusamy, V., Jacobsen, H.-A.: BPM in cloud architectures: Business process manage-
    ment with sLAs and events. In: Hull, R., Mendling, J., Tai, S. (eds.) BPM 2010. LNCS,
    vol. 6336, pp. 5–10. Springer, Heidelberg (2010)

[18] Plotkin, G.D.: A structural approach to operational semantics (1981)

[19] Puhlmann, F.: On the Application of a Theory for mobile Systems to business process man-
    agement. Ph.D. thesis, University of Potsdam, Germany (2007),
    http://frapu.de/pdf/diss.pdf

[20] Puhlmann, F., Weske, M.: Interaction soundness for service orchestrations. In: Dan, A.,
    Lamersdorf, W. (eds.) ICSOC 2006. LNCS, vol. 4294, pp. 302–313. Springer, Heidelberg
    (2006)

[21] Schmidt, W., Fleischmann, A., Gilbert, O.: Subjektorientiertes Geschäftsprozess-
    management. HMD - Praxis der Wirtschaftsinformatik (266), 52–62 (2009)

[22] Wu, Z., Deng, S., Li, Y., Wu, J.: Computing Compatibility in Dynamic Service Com-
    position. Knowledge and Information Systems 19(1), 107–129 (2008), http://www.
    springerlink.com/index/10.1007/s10115-008-0143-5

[23] Wutke, D.: Eine Infrastruktur für die dezentrale Ausführung von BPEL-Prozessen. Ph.D.
    thesis, Universität Stuttgart (2010)

Interaction Choreography Models in BPEL: Choreographies on the Enterprise Service Bus*

Oliver Kopp, Lasse Engler, Tammo van Lessen,
Frank Leymann, and Jörg Nitzsche

Institute of Architecture of Application Systems, University of Stuttgart,
Universittsstraße 38, 70569 Stuttgart, Germany
lastname@iaas.uni-stuttgart.de

Abstract. Interactions between services may be globally captured by choreographies. We introduce BPEL^{gold} supporting modeling interaction choreography models using BPEL. We show the usage of BPEL^{gold} in an enterprise service bus to ensure an executed message exchange complies with a pre-defined choreography.

Keywords: BPMN, BPEL, BPELgold, Business Process Execution, Choreography.

1 Introduction

Choreographies capture the interaction between services on a global perspective [39]. The behavior of services taking part in the choreography may be expressed by an abstract process, which in turn models the public visible behavior. A choreography model interconnects the communication activities of each abstract process and hence forms an *interconnection model*. The second paradigm offered to model choreographies is the *interaction model* paradigm. Here, a send/receive message exchange is modeled as an atomic activity. The public visible behavior of each participant is not shown any more. Details are presented in Sect. 2.

BPEL [37] and BPEL4Chor [16] are currently the only two choreography approaches tightly integrated in the Web service stack. In this paper, we present BPEL^{gold} as a complement to BPEL4Chor: BPEL4Chor supports the interconnection-based modeling approach and BPEL^{gold} supports the interaction-based modeling approach. "gold" is an abbreviation for **glo**bal **d**efinition emphasizing the global process consisting of interactions. We show that BPEL^{gold} fulfills all requirements put on a choreography language. Subsequently, we show how BPEL^{gold} can be integrated in an enterprise service bus to make it choreography-aware. By aligning BPEL^{gold} with established standards in the field of Web service (e.g., BPEL, WSDL, XML), existing tooling as well knowledge may be reapplied in a BPEL^{gold} setting.

* This work was supported by funds from the European Commission (contract no. 215175 for the FP7-ICT-2007-1 project COMPAS).

A. Fleischmann et al. (Eds.): S-BPM ONE 2010, CCIS 138, pp. 36–53, 2011.
© Springer-Verlag Berlin Heidelberg 2011

On the one hand, choreographies capture the interaction between services on a global perspective. On the other hand, an enterprise service bus (ESB) is an standard-based integration platform [11]. For instance, all messages sent by a service are routed through the ESB, which selects the appropriate endpoint. Typically, an ESB is not aware of the choreography the service implementers agreed upon before executing the services. This paper introduces the concept of a choreography-aware enterprise service bus. A choreography-aware enterprise service bus can detect violations of the choreography and can react accordingly. Possible reactions include the interruption of the message transfer and informing the participants that an error occurred in the choreography. For that purpose, an extended choreography model can be modeled, which specifies reactions to erroneous situations.

Consequently, this paper is structured as follows: Section 2 presents an overview on the two choreography modeling paradigms. Subsequently, Sect. 3 introduces the choreography language BPEL^{gold}. It is evaluated against requirements on choreography languages in Sect. 4. The concept and implementation of a choreography-aware enterprise service bus is presented in Sect. 5. Section 6 presents an overview on related work in the field of compliance with respect to choreographies. Finally, Sect. 7 concludes and provides and outlook on future work.

2   Choreography Modeling Paradigms

We use a choreography dealing with investment proposals as illustration. A customer talks to a financial consultant. The consultant recommends an investment and hands over an investment proposal including information material. Governmental regulations require a time-window of at least 24 hours for the customer to decide on the investment. After 24 hours have passed, the customer may sign a contract. It is not allowed to receive a signature from the customer beforehand. Figure 1 models the choreography using the interconnection model paradigm. The notation used is the Business Process Model and Notation BPMN 2.0 [38]. The public visible behavior of each participant is modeled using a BPMN pool. The communication elements are connected by message flows. The intermediate event with the arrow label denotes that the choreography continues in the case the customer votes for the investment. The choreography may also be expressed using the interaction model paradigm. Figure 2 presents the choreography using the BPMN 2.0 choreography notation. Here, pairs of sending and receiving elements are collapsed into one choreography task. The gray shaded participant is the participant receiving the message. The event-based gateway denotes that the decision whether to accept or reject the proposal is made available to the consultant by the respective message.

The expressiveness of the two modeling paradigms "interaction-based modeling" and "interconnection-based modeling" is different [14]. On the one hand, interconnection models allow modeling of incompatible processes or even processes for which no partner exists [43]. For instance, service A waits for a message, but service B never sends that message. Decker and Weske [20] identified 8

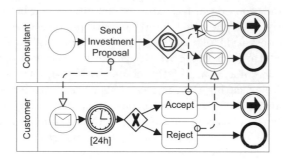

Fig. 1. Investment Choreography: Interconnection Model (BPMN 2.0 Collaboration)

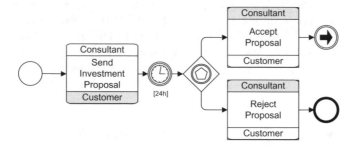

Fig. 2. Investment Choreography: Interaction Model (BPMN 2.0 Choreography)

anti-patterns which can be expressed by interconnection models, but not in interaction models. Wolf [43] studies the existence of partners for services, which is called "controllability". On the other hand, interaction models may introduce constraints, which need to be locally enforced in interconnection models by adding additional communication that is not captured in the original interaction model [44]. This property is called "local enforceability". For instance, if service A sends a message to service B and the interaction model demands that *subsequently* service C sends a message to service D, service C has to know when service B has received the message. "Realizability" is an even stronger requirement, which demands that all conversations produced by the interaction model must also be produced by the corresponding interconnection models [19]. Lohmann and Wolf [34] showed that the property of realizability is equal to the property of controllability.

Although the expressiveness of the two modeling paradigms is not equal, there exist mappings from interaction models to interconnection models and vice versa: Zaha et al. [44] present an approach of mapping interaction models to interconnection models. As shown above, not all interaction models can be mapped to interconnection models. Kopp et al. [30] show that sound and safe BPMN models following the interconnection style and containing control flow without exception handling can be mapped to interaction BPMN models (iBPMN [13]). Having

BPEL^{gold} at hand, the approaches may be adapted to map BPEL4Chor models to BPEL^{gold} models and thus being able to switch between the two modeling paradigms.

Decker et al. [17] show 10 requirements put on choreography languages. An evaluation using this requirements shows whether a language is suitable for choreography modeling. Decker et al. [17] use these requirements to evaluate current choreography languages including WS-CDL [28] and BPEL4Chor [16]. The result is, that WS-CDL fails in modeling an a priori unknown number of participants and that the integration with orchestration languages such as BPEL [37] is not given. BPEL4Chor on the other hand, fulfills all requirements. These requirements themselves are mainly based on the service interaction patterns [6]. These patterns list possible interactions between business processes. We use the requirements to evaluate BPEL^{gold} and present them together with the evaluation of BPEL^{gold} in Sect. 4.

BPMN 2.0 offers both the interconnection model paradigm ("BPMN collaborations") and the interaction model paradigm ("BPMN choreography"). Decker et al. [15] show the integration of BPMN interconnection models and BPEL4Chor. There is currently no study about the integration of BPMN 2.0 interaction models and BPEL4Chor or BPEL^{gold}. This study is out of scope of this paper as we focus on BPEL^{gold} and its integration in an enterprise service bus. A first evaluation of BPMN 2.0 showed that it still does not support the exchange of participant references between partners. Thus, BPEL4Chor and BPEL^{gold} are ahead of BPMN 2.0 in this regard. A detailed evaluation of BPMN 2.0 and a comparison to BPEL^{gold} are our ongoing work.

3   BPEL^{gold}

BPEL4Chor extended BPEL to a choreography language supporting interconnection models. Thereby, a participant topology and a grounding artifact has been added. We re-use these extensions to create a interaction choreography modeling language based on BPEL.

A *participant topology* provides a view on the participants and the connections between them. It consists of a list of participant types, a list of participants, and a list of message links. Each participant type is associated with a BPEL process describing the public visible behavior of this type. Thus, this artifact is called "participant behavior description". Concrete participants are listed subsequently. Each is linked to a participant type and thus specifying its behavior. BPEL4Chor also supports sets of participants, which enables modeling of an a priori unknown number of participants in a choreography. Each participant in a set is merely a reference to a concrete participant. In case a message is received from a participant not being in the set, it is added to the set. Finally, the message links connect communication activities of two participant behavior descriptions. It also lists the name of the message being sent and the participant references contained in the message (which may be empty).

BPEL4Chor is not bound to concrete WSDL service definitions: `partnerLinks`, `portTypes`, and `operations` are not specified in the communication activities. Instead, the message links establish the connection to the partner. When a BPEL4Chor choreography is executed, the choreography description itself is not executed, but services implementing the behavior described by the participant behavior descriptions. The services may be realized using BPEL, but they are not required to do so. Nevertheless, the service needs to know about WSDL information to be able to communicate with the partner service. This information is provided by the *grounding* document. Here, a mapping from a message link to a `portType/operation` pair is provided. This is then used to generate an abstract BPEL process for each participant behavior description, where the required `partnerLinks` are generated [17]. The abstract BPEL processes are not executable by themselves. Internal activities such as assign activities or invokations of internal services have to be added.

3.1   Participant Topology

BPEL^{gold} reuses the concept of the participant topology, but changes the way of the description of the interaction. Instead of specifying the behavior of each participant separately, an abstract BPEL process providing the interaction is used. A reference to the process is provided in the topology by the attribute `gld:interactionDescription`.

Figure 3 presents the topology for the investment choreography. First, the different participant types "Consultant" and "Customer" are enumerated. Subsequently, the concrete participants "consultant" and "customer" of the respective types are declared. In the `participants` element, multiple `participantSet` elements may occur. Here, additional participants can be listed. The semantics is that the participant are contained in the set. Here, a participant is merely a reference to a participant in the set instead of a concrete participant. In case a message is received from one participant out of a possible set of participants, the reference to this participant is added to the set at the receivers' side. The list of participants and participant sets is followed by a list of message links. In the investment choreography, there are three send/receive message exchanges leading to three message links. Each message link takes a `name`, a `sender`, and a `receiver` attribute. The name is unique and required for identification in the interaction description. Additionally, a message link can take a `participantRefs` attribute enabling the transfer of participant references. The attribute `sender` may be replaced by the attribute `senders`, where a set of possible senders may be specified. This enables modeling of an a priori unknown set of participants. The sender may send a reference to himself to enable a reply back to him. In case the reference is included in a set, this reference is added to the set at the receiver's side.

The `participantSet` element may be annotated with a `forEach` attribute. This attribute indicates, that the referenced `forEach` iterates over the respective sets. The current iterator is provided by a `forEach` attribute at a participant reference contained in the set. This enables sending a message to multiple

```
<topology name="investment" gld:interactionDescription="inv:interactions">
  <participantTypes>
    <participant name="Consultant" />
    <participant name="Customer" />
  </participantTypes>
  <participants>
    <participant name="consultant" type="Consultant" />
    <participant name="customer" type="Customer" />
  </participants>
  <messageLinks>
    <messageLink name="investmentProposal"
        sender="consultant" receiver="customer" />
    <messageLink name="acceptance"
        sender="customer" receiver="consultant" />
    <messageLink name="rejection"
        sender="customer" receiver="consultant" />
  </messageLinks>
</topology>
```

Fig. 3. Investment Choreography: BPEL^{gold} Participant Topology

participants. `forEach` is an activity of BPEL, which is used for iterating over a set in a sequential or parallel way. The concrete action has to be modeled as activity nested in the `forEach` activity. In case of BPEL^{gold} this is the `gld:interaction` activity.

3.2 Interaction Description

The main building block of the interaction description is the `gld:interaction` activity. This activity is embedded as an `extensionActivity` in the BPEL process. BPEL^{gold} uses one abstract BPEL process to capture the interactions between the participants. An abstract BPEL process always follows an abstract process profile. BPEL^{gold} introduces two profiles: (i) The "Abstract Process Profile for Basic Interaction Models" and (ii) the "Abstract Process Profile for Extended Interaction Models". The basic profile enables specification for the interactions between the participants and hence provides a true global view. The extended profile allows additional communication starting from or targeted to the global observer. A global observer observes the interactions made by the participants of the choreography. In our case, this *global observer* is the enterprise service bus.

The "Abstract Process Profile for Basic Interaction Models" forbids the usage of BPEL's standard communication activities and only allows `gld:interaction` as communication activity. Hence, only the interaction between participants can be modeled and the modeled process does not require an active global observer. As the global observer has to track the choreography and uncertainty should not be modeled, the profile requires that the expressions of conditions must be based on data derived from exchanged messages and that all modifications from the message receipt to the condition are modeled. For instance, required variable assignment activities have to be modeled. The requirement ensures that the global observer can evaluate the conditions for itself and thus properly keeps track of the choreography. Opaque activities and attributes are allowed as long as they do not infer with that requirement.

The "Abstract Process Profile for Extended Interaction Models" allows for modeling the interactions between participants. In addition, the global observer may actively participate in the choreography. Reasons include a communication of faults in the choreography execution to participants, which are not notified of the faults otherwise. Besides gld:interaction activities, the common BPEL communication activities are allowed. BPEL4Chor's rules forbidding partnerLink, portType, and operation still apply. In addition, the sender or receiver of such a communication activity must be the GOLDobserver, which also must be listed as participant in the participant topology. For these communication activities, the message links specified by BPEL4Chor have to be used. The GOLDobserver participant must not be used in message links referred to in gld:interaction activities. As a consequence, this profile mixes interaction models and interconnection models together: The interaction between the participants is modeled using the interaction paradigm and the interaction between the global observer and the participants is modeled using the interconnection paradigm. The reason is that the global observer takes a special role in the choreography as it knows the status of the choreography and can also react accordingly if a participant does not comply with the choreography or even disappears. A detailed discussion is provided in Sect. 5.

The extended interaction models defines three standard faults: gld:interactionInitiationFault, gld:interactionCompletionFault, and gld:choreographyViolation. A gld:interactionInitiationFault is raised if the interaction cannot be initiated by the sending participant. Reasons include that the participant itself crashed and does not recover, or that message sending activity is on a dead path in the process and will never be executed. A gld:interactionCompletionFault is raised if the message cannot be received by the targeted participant. Reasons include that the participant crashed and does not recover, a communication fault to the receiver occurred, or that the message receiving activity is on a dead path in the process and will never be executed. Finally, a gld:choreographyViolation fault is raised if the CSB detects a violation of the choreography. The reason is a message which is sent but not allowed in the choreography definition.

A gld:interaction activity itself refers to a message link by the messageLink attribute. The referred message link in turn states from which participant to with other participant the message is sent. This indirection is inherited from BPEL4Chor, where the connection between participants is also made at the participant topology. The reuse enables a seamless integration with BPEL4Chor described in Sect. 3.3. The child element correlations denotes the correlations used in the interaction. Both the sender and the receiver use the same correlation set. Each set may be initiated (yes) or an initiation may be forbidden (no). In case it is unsure, whether the set has already been initiated, the value join may be used. These options are derived from the BPEL specification, where the same values are specified. BPEL^{gold} introduces the attributes senderInitiate and receiverInitiate to enable a specification of the sender's and the receiver's behavior according to correlation. The attribute value

```
<process>
  <sequence>
    <extensionActivity>
      <gld:interaction messageLink="investmentProposal">
        <correlations>
          <correlation set="cor" gld:senderInitiate="yes"
                                 gld:receiverInitiate="n/a" />
        </correlations>
      </gld:interaction>
    </extensionActivity>
    <wait for="P1D" />
    <pick>
      <gld:onInteraction messageLink="acceptance">
        <correlations>
          <correlation set="cor" gld:senderInitiate="n/a" />
        </correlations>
      </gld:onInteraction>
      <gld:onInteraction messageLink="rejection">
        <correlations>
          <correlation set="cor" gld:senderInitiate="n/a" />
        </correlations>
      </gld:onInteraction>
    </pick>
  </sequence>
</process>
```

Fig. 4. Investment Choreography: BPEL^{gold} Interaction Description

is transformed to the `initiate` attribute of the respective communication activity in the respective participant behavior description. The attribute may take the additional value `n/a` to indicate that the correlation set is not used at the respective participant. For instance, in our scenario, the customer is not required to use a correlation set as he executes a receive/send message exchange only. Finally, an `gld:interaction` activity may take the attribute `variable` to specify the message format (by the type of the variable) and to enable choreography tracking by the global observer.

Figure 4 presents the interaction description of the investment choreography using the basic profile. The correlation set used for communication is named `cor`, initiated at the sender only. In our scenario, the customer executes a receive/send message exchange only. If one regards the full choreography, the customer has to send initiate a correlation set on his own at the acceptance interaction. This ensures that the consultant reaches him to negotiate the details of the contract. The `pick` activity uses `gld:onInteraction` branches, which replace BPEL's `onMessage` branches.

3.3 From BPEL^{gold} to Executable BPEL Processes

Going from BPEL^{gold} to executable BPEL processes is one way to enact the choreography. Other ways include that each participant uses the choreography description and implements the services in his favorite language. Nevertheless, the created endpoints must be made available to the other participants in order to enable them to reach the participant.

When using BPEL as implementation language, the way starting from BPEL^{gold} is depicted in Fig. 5: A choreography is modeled using a BPEL^{gold}

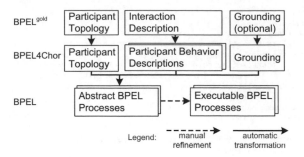

Fig. 5. From a BPEL^{gold} Choreography Description to Executable BPEL Processes

participant topology, a BPEL^{gold} interaction description and optionally a grounding. A grounding provides a mapping from the message links to their concrete WSDL implementation in the form of one concrete `portType` and one concrete `operation` for each message link.

The BPEL^{gold} participant topology is transformed to a BPEL4Chor participant topology, where names for sending and receiving activities have to be generated. This generation is necessary as BPEL^{gold} has no knowledge of the activities used at the participants. The process interaction description is transformed to participant behavior descriptions following the ideas presented in [44]. The main idea is to split an `interactionActivity` into an `invoke` and `receive` activity. A `pick` is translated into an `if` at the sender's side and to a `pick` at the receiver's side. For each `gld:onInteraction` branch, a condition branch in the `if` activity is generated. The first activity in the condition branch is an `invoke` activity. On the receiver's side, each `gld:onInteraction` branch is transformed to an `onMessage` branch. A detailed description of the transformation is out of scope of this paper and will be presented in our future work. In case the grounding description does not exist, it has to be created in order to gain a full BPEL4Chor choreography description. This choreography description can now be used to generate abstract BPEL processes as shown in [17]. These abstract BPEL processes contain `partnerLinks`, `portTypes`, and `operations` at each communication activity. The processes are abstract as they do not contain the internal behavior of each participant. The abstract BPEL processes have to be expanded in order to get executable BPEL processes. This is the only manual refinement step.

4   Evaluation of BPEL^{gold}

In this section, we evaluate BPEL^{gold} using the requirements on choreographies [17], which in turn are based on the service interaction patterns [6]. Other approaches to compare modeling languages are not tailored towards choreography languages, but towards orchestration languages. These approaches include the workflow patterns [1], process instantiation patterns [18], correlation patterns [5], data handling patterns [42], exception handling patterns [41], and a discussion regarding block-structured and graph-based modeling styles [32]. As these patterns are not centered around choreographies, an evaluation using these patterns is out of scope of this paper, but part of our future work.

In the following, we list each requirement of [17] and evaluate BPEL^{gold} according to its fulfillment.

R1. Multi-lateral interactions   A choreography language has to support more than two participants in a choreography. This is directly enabled by the BPEL^{gold} topology.

R2. Service topology   A choreography language should provide a structural view, where the types and number of participants involved is provided. This is directly supported by the `participant` and `participantSet` elements in BPEL^{gold}'s topology. In case the concrete number of instances are known from a participant, it is listed multiple times as `participant`. A priori unknown numbers are supported by the `participantSet` element.

R3. Service sets   A choreography language must support modeling of an a priori unknown arbitrary number of services. This is directly supported by the `participantSet` element.

R4. Reference passing   A choreography language must provide support for passing references to participants to enable distribution of knowledge about participants. BPEL^{gold} supports this requirement by the attribute `participantRefs` of a message link.

R5. Message formats   It is possible to agree on concrete message formats when agreeing on a choreography. Thus, a choreography language should support the specification of message formats. BPEL^{gold} supports specification of message formats by the `variable` attribute in the `interactionActivity`.

R6. Interchangeability of technical configurations   Concrete WSDL `portTypes` and WSDL `operations` typically vary from implementation to implementation even if the implementation itself offers the same functionality. Thus, a choreography language should support changing the concrete identifiers. BPEL^{gold} enables this by the concept of grounding.

R7. Time constraints   A choreography has to offer constructs for modeling time constraints. This is offered by BPEL's `wait` activity and the `onAlarm` branch of a `pick` activity and the event handler of a `scope`. Hence, this requirement is supported by BPEL^{gold}.

R8. Exception handling   Typically, there is a separation of the "happy path" through a process and the exception path. BPEL^{gold} allows using the `scope` construct of BPEL thus enables explicit modeling of exception handling.

R9. Correlation   A process may be instantiated multiple times, each taking part in different choreographies. Thus, a choreography language has to be able to specify the identifiers used for correlation. This is enabled by the `correlationSet` specification at the `interactionActivity`.

R10. Integration with service orchestration languages   BPEL is the de-facto standard to implement business processes based on Web services. Therefore, choreography languages must allow an integration with BPEL, including generation of

BPEL processes out of choreographies. Section 3.3 showed that BPEL processes can be generated out of a BPEL^{gold} choreography description.

5   Choreography-Aware Enterprise Service Bus

A traditional ESB does not know whether the message it currently routes is part of a conversation. Thus, it cannot react on messages out of band. In contrast, a choreography-aware enterprise service bus (CSB for short) is aware of the choreography and can react accordingly. A CSB should act transparent to the participants. There are use-cases, however, where participants with knowledge about the choreography-awareness of the bus allow enhanced solutions. We refer to such participants as choreography-aware participants (CAP for short). A CAP offers an interface to the CSB, where the CSB may request information or inform the CAP of events not captured in the choreography definition. For instance, a CSB may ask the CAP whether it still runs. In case a CAP is not running any more, the whole choreography cannot be enacted further. Thus, the CSB informs the other CAPs that the choreography faulted. The CAPs in turn can take appropriate fault handing actions including a termination of the process taking part in the choreography. A CAP can also push information on interactions to the CSB. Thus, it can inform the CSB whether an interaction has been skipped. The CSB can then check whether this complies with the choreography definition and take appropriate actions.

We implemented a prototype of an choreography-aware enterprise service bus based on Apache ServiceMix 3.3.1 [4] and call it CASmix—**C**horeography-**A**ware **S**ervice**mix**. We did not change any of ServiceMix code. All extensions were implemented through the extension mechanisms and Java Business Integration components. For tracking the state of the choreography, we extended the Apache ODE engine [3] to ODE^{gold}. The overall architecture and the message flow of one message in CASmix from a participant A to a participant B denoted by the steps 1 to 8 in the diagram.

A binding component provides connectivity to services located outside of the bus. Thus, the message of participant A is received by the binding component (step 1), transforms the message to a normalized message and puts it on the normalized message router (step 2). All communication internal of ServiceMix is based on normalized messages. The *CASmix Message Interceptor* is plugged into the normalized message router and inspects each message being put on the bus (step 3). It checks whether the message belongs to a choreography instance. This is done by checking with the *CASmix Choreography Manager*, which stores and provides information about the currently deployed choreography descriptions. The CASmix Choreography Manager also keeps track of currently running choreographies and is responsible for the fault propagation to choreography-aware participants. In case the message does not belong to a choreography, the CASmix Message Interceptor releases the message unchanged to the normalized message router (step 4). The message then is handed over to the binding component of participant B (step 5'), where it is sent to participant B (step 6'). In

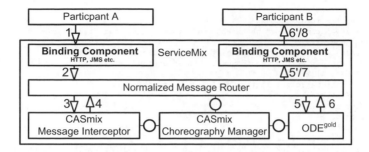

Fig. 6. CASmix: Components and Message Routing

case the message belongs to a choreography, the target endpoint is changed to ODE^{gold} and the original endpoint is stored at a message property. The message is put back to the normalized message router (step 4), where it is forwarded to ODE^{gold} (step 5). ODE^{gold} checks whether there is a matching active `receive` activity. In case there is no such activity, the choreography is violated and a `gld:choreographyViolation` fault is thrown in the outermost `scope` of the respective choreography instance. In case an explicit fault handler is modeled, the specified activities are executed. In case no explicit fault handler is modeled, the choreography is terminated and (by using the CASmix Choreography Manager), all choreography-aware participants are notified. In case ODE^{gold} finds a matching choreography instance for the message, the message is routed to the instance and processed there. Otherwise, ODE^{gold} identified a choreography model which can be instantiated with the message and the message can be processed there. After processing, the message is put pack to the normalized message router with the original recipient (step 6). A flag in the message indicates that the CASmix Message Interceptor is not required to redirect the message to ODE^{gold} again. Thus, the message flows via a binding component (step 7) to the participant B.

We have identified three ways to provide support for the `gld:interaction` activity and the `gld:onInteraction` branch in Apache ODE. (i) ODE's mechanism for implementing the behavior of an `extensionActivity`, (ii) implementing the extension directly in the runtime, and (iii) transforming each `gld:interaction` activity and `gld:onInteraction` branches into native BPEL activities. As ODE does not support extensions for the behavior of `pick` activities, the `gld:onInteraction` branch cannot be implemented using an extension mechanism. Thus, approach (i) cannot be taken. Implementing the extensions directly in Apache ODE is a change in ODE's internals and leads to code duplication as the sending and the receipt of messages have to be re-implemented. Therefore, we dropped option (ii). Finally, we opted for option (iii) and transform the BPEL^{gold} model to a standard BPEL model.

Figure 7 shows how a `gld:interaction` activity is transformed to standard BPEL. The `onMessage` element on line 3 is used to receive the specified message.

```
1   <pick>
2     <!-- regular interaction -->
3     <onMessage partnerLink="inboundPL" operation="opName" variable="varName">
4       <sequence>
5         <assign><!-- copy original target epr to outboundPL --></assign>
6         <invoke partnerLink="outboundPL" operation="opName" variable="varName">
7           <catchAll>
8             <throw>gld:interactionCompletionFault</throw>
9           </catchAll>
10          <invoke>
11        </sequence>
12      </onMessage>
13      <!-- notification from ChoreographyManager -->
14      <onMessage partnerLink="chorManagerInbound" operation="opNameInteractionFailed" />
15        <throw>gld:interactionInitiationFault</throw>
16      </onMessage>
17  </pick>
```

Fig. 7. `gld:interaction` mapped to Standard BPEL Activities (without correlation, simplified)

The operation name `opName` and the variable name `varName` is a uniquely name within the choreography definition. The CASmix Message Interceptor changes the destination of a message accordingly. In line 5 the endpoint reference of the original recipient from the message header is assigned to the partner link. In line 5 the message to the recipient is sent. ODE also propagates communication faults into the process [31], thus a fault occurring at the `invoke` activity denotes a communication fault. This fault is propagated by throwing an `gld:interactionCompletionFault` (line 8). In case the CASmix Choreography Manager detects that a participant cannot initiate the interaction any more, it sends a message to ODE^{gold}. This message is received by the `onMessage` in line 14 and leads to a propagation in the `gld:interactionInitiationFault`. A similar transformation is done for a `gld:onInteraction` element. Opaque activities are deleted from the process and opaque assignments, too. As the profile definition itself ensures that values for variables are available for conditions, these deletions do not alter the behavior of the choreography. The other elements of the process are transformed one by one.

When a fault occurs and no explicit exception handling is modeled, the CSB has to inform all participants. They can then trigger their individual error handling. Propagating a fault to CAP is achieved using the interface offered by the CAP. For non-choreography aware participants we have to distinguish three possibilities: (i) fault messages may be sent, (ii) erroneous messages may be sent, and (iii) future interactions may be blocked. In case the participant is expecting a message and the respective operation supports fault messages, one of them may be sent by the bus. If no fault message is expected, the bus may send a message of the expected type and fill all parameters with erroneous values (such as empty strings or 0), which in turn leads to a fault in the participants process. In case the participant is currently expecting no messages, we just block any further messages of it and reply with faults or faulty messages, respectively.

6   Related Work

WS-CDL has been introduced to capture choreographies in the field of Web services. It follows the interaction modeling approach. It has been criticized for not supporting all service interaction patterns [21], for the impossibility to specify an a priori unknown number of participants [21], and for not being integrated with BPEL [7]. Based on WS-CDL, Fredlund [23] present a tool for debugging WS-CDL specifications and to check WS-CDL models against a property formulated as safety automaton. It is not possible to use his tool for runtime checking during the execution of a choreography. Kang et al. [27] extended WS-CDL to support its execution. They mainly added variable initialization to WS-CDL and called it WS-CDL$^+$. As messages are received and sent, WS-CDL$^+$ is a kind of orchestration language without the full capabilities of BPEL. An overview on current available choreography language and an evaluation is presented by Decker et al. [17]. There is no language based on BPEL following the interaction modeling paradigm.

We sketched the concept of a choreography-aware service bus in [29]. This paper extends the work in (i) providing a concrete language for choreography modeling and (ii) presenting a proof-of-concept implementation of a choreography-aware enterprise service bus.

Conformance between a choreography and an orchestration can be checked at design time [10, 33, 26, 35]. The approaches assume that at least the public behavior description of each service *used* is available. That might not be possible in case services provided by other companies not offering the code of the deployed implementations. Thus, the approaches cannot prove whether the opaque service implementation adheres to the choreography specification.

Alberti et al. [2] present an approach based on a computational logic for runtime conformance verification. The language does not support an a priori unknown number of participants and the concrete integration to the ESB is not shown. Rozinat and van der Aalst [40] show a conformance approach based on Petri process models. They provide metric definitions of the degree of conformance to the specified model. The support of an a priori unknown number of participants and the integration to the ESB is not shown.

Gheorghe et al. [25] combine enforcement capabilities of a BPEL engine with the ones of an enterprise service bus (ESB). Gheorghe et al. monitor the execution of the process and the message exchange using events, which trigger actions if a certain rule is matched. The actions include altering the process instance and modification of messages. Thus, the possible violations are modeled in a declarative way. This is similar to the approach taken by Montali et al. [36], which offer a declarative way to specify choreographies. In our approach, we opt for the explicit way of specifying choreographies. Once a choreography is explicitly specified, it is not required any more to specify additional declarative properties to ensure compliance: The modeled choreography artifact can directly used to check compliance and take necessary actions.

The work of Gheorghe et al. [25] builds on the work presented by Gheorghe et al. [24]. There, the ESB part of [25] is detailed. The work of Birukou et al. [8]

also describes a solution for compliance checking at an ESB. Here, the events produced by a BPEL engine are put to the ESB, where the events are logged and analyzed by a business intelligence engine and by a complex event processing engine. That approach also does not rely on a choreography description to check for compliance with the service interaction to the choreography model.

Daniel et al. [12] survey on business compliance checking, where runtime compliance is a part of. No work uses a choreography description language supporting all choreography requirements by Decker et al. and uses the choreography description itself at the ESB to check for compliance.

A survey on the history on protocol design is provided at by von Bochmann [9]. Although the authors do not explicitly mention the modeling style used, the models presented there follow the interconnection modeling approach.

The S-BPM language PASS (as presented by Fleischmann [22]) builds on the interconnection model paradigm. There currently is no evaluation whether the interaction modeling paradigm is suitable for the S-BPM approach, too.

7   Conclusion and Outlook

This paper presented $BPEL^{gold}$ as alternative to WS-CDL and BPEL4Chor tightly integrated in the Web service stack. Similar to WS-CDL it supports the interaction modeling approach, but supports all common requirements on choreography languages. Similar to BPEL4Chor it builds on the control flow constructs of BPEL, but follows the interaction modeling paradigm instead of the interconnection modeling paradigm.

After presenting $BPEL^{gold}$ and an evaluation of it, we gave an overview on CASmix, a choreography-aware service bus. We have shown how a $BPEL^{gold}$ choreography description can be deployed on CASmix enabling tracking of the choreography and reacting on derivations of the choreography. Neither we measured the efficiency choreography design using $BPEL^{gold}$ nor measured the cost of the additional message flow through the ODE^{gold} component and leave that as future work.

The current limitation of CASmix is the missing enforcement of choreographies. For instance, if messages are sent out of order, it may be the case that CASmix puts the choreography in a faulting state instead of holding the message back until it can be handled by the choreography. Thus, future work is a detailed investigation on possible implementation strategies for choreography-aware enterprise service buses. This includes a transformation of $BPEL^{gold}$ models to state machines, where a choreography-aware enterprise service bus can keep track the changes without the need of a customized BPEL engine.

Acknowledgments. This work was supported by funds from the European Commission (contract no. 215175 for the FP7-ICT-2007-1 project COMPAS, http://www.compas-ict.eu).

References

[1] van der Aalst, W.M.P., ter Hofstede, A.H.M., Kiepuszewski, B., Barros, A.P.: Workflow patterns. Distributed and Parallel Databases 14(1), 5–51 (2003)

[2] Alberti, M., Chesani, F., Gavanelli, M., Lamma, E., Mello, P., Montali, M., Storari, S., Torroni, P.: Computational logic for run-time verification of web services choreographies: Exploiting the *SOCS-SI* tool. In: Bravetti, M., Núñez, M., Tennenholtz, M. (eds.) WS-FM 2006. LNCS, vol. 4184, pp. 58–72. Springer, Heidelberg (2006)

[3] Apache: ODE website, http://ode.apache.org/

[4] Apache: ServiceMix Website, http://servicemix.apache.org/

[5] Barros, A., Decker, G., Dumas, M., Weber, F.: Correlation Patterns in Service-Oriented Architectures. In: Dwyer, M.B., Lopes, A. (eds.) FASE 2007. LNCS, vol. 4422, pp. 245–259. Springer, Heidelberg (2007)

[6] Barros, A., Dumas, M., ter Hofstede, A.H.M.: Service Interaction Patterns. In: van der Aalst, W.M.P., Benatallah, B., Casati, F., Curbera, F. (eds.) BPM 2005. LNCS, vol. 3649, pp. 302–318. Springer, Heidelberg (2005)

[7] Barros, A., Dumas, M., Oaks, P.: A Critical Overview of the Web Services Choreography Description Language (WS-CDL), bPTrends (March 2005)

[8] Birukou, A., et al.: An integrated solution for runtime compliance governance in SOA. In: Maglio, P.P., Weske, M., Yang, J., Fantinato, M. (eds.) ICSOC 2010. LNCS, vol. 6470, pp. 706–707. Springer, Heidelberg (2010)

[9] von Bochmann, G., Rayner, D., West, C.H.: Some notes on the history of protocol engineering. Computer Networks 54(18), 3197–3209 (2010)

[10] Busi, N., Gorrieri, R., Guidi, C., Lucchi, R., Tennenholtz, M.: Choreography and Orchestration Conformance for System Design. In: Ciancarini, P., Wiklicky, H. (eds.) COORDINATION 2006. LNCS, vol. 4038, pp. 63–81. Springer, Heidelberg (2006)

[11] Chappell, D.A.: Enterprise Service Bus. Theory in Practice, 1st edn. O'Reilly Media, Sebastopol (2004)

[12] Daniel, F., et al.: Business Compliance Governance in Service-Oriented Architectures. In: Proceedings of the IEEE Twenty-Third International Conference on Advanced Information Networking and Applications (AINA 2009), pp. 113–120. IEEE Press, Los Alamitos (2009)

[13] Decker, G., Barros, A.: Interaction modeling using BPMN. In: ter Hofstede, A.H.M., Benatallah, B., Paik, H.-Y. (eds.) BPM Workshops 2007. LNCS, vol. 4928, pp. 208–219. Springer, Heidelberg (2008)

[14] Decker, G., Kopp, O., Barros, A.: An Introduction to Service Choreographies. Information Technology 50(2), 122–127 (2008)

[15] Decker, G., Kopp, O., Leymann, F., Pfitzner, K., Weske, M.: Modeling Service Choreographies Using BPMN and BPEL4Chor. In: Bellahsène, Z., Léonard, M. (eds.) CAiSE 2008. LNCS, vol. 5074, pp. 79–93. Springer, Heidelberg (2008)

[16] Decker, G., Kopp, O., Leymann, F., Weske, M.: BPEL4Chor: Extending BPEL for Modeling Choreographies. In: International Conference on Web Services, IEEE Computer Society, Los Alamitos (2007)

[17] Decker, G., Kopp, O., Leymann, F., Weske, M.: Interacting services: From specification to execution. Data & Knowledge Engineering 68(10), 946–972 (2009)

[18] Decker, G., Mendling, J.: Process Instantiation. Data & Knowledge Engineering 68, 777–792 (2009)

[19] Decker, G., Weske, M.: Local enforceability in interaction petri nets. In: Alonso, G., Dadam, P., Rosemann, M. (eds.) BPM 2007. LNCS, vol. 4714, pp. 305–319. Springer, Heidelberg (2007), http://www.springerlink.com/content/602146845nt31197/

[20] Decker, G., Weske, M.: Interaction-centric Modeling of Process Choreographies. Information Systems 36(2), 292–312 (2011)

[21] Decker, G., Zaha, J.M.: On the Suitability of WS-CDL for Choreography Modeling. In: EMISA 2006 – Methoden, Konzepte und Technologien für die Entwicklung von dienstbasierten Informationssystemen. LNI, vol. 95. GI (2006)

[22] Fleischmann, A.: What is S-BPM? In: Buchwald, H., Fleischmann, A., Seese, D., Stary, C. (eds.) S-BPM ONE 2009. CCIS, vol. 85, pp. 85–106. Springer, Heidelberg (2010)

[23] Fredlund, L.R.: Implementing WS CDL. In: Proceedings of JSWEB 2006 (II Jornadas Científico-Técnicas en Servicios Web) (2006)

[24] Gheorghe, G., Neuhaus, S., Crispo, B.: xESB: An enterprise service bus for access and usage control policy enforcement. In: Nishigaki, M., Jøsang, A., Murayama, Y., Marsh, S. (eds.) IFIPTM 2010. IFIP Advances in Information and Communication Technology, vol. 321, pp. 63–78. Springer, Heidelberg (2010)

[25] Gheorghe, G., et al.: Combining enforcement strategies in service oriented architectures. In: Maglio, P.P., Weske, M., Yang, J., Fantinato, M. (eds.) ICSOC 2010. LNCS, vol. 6470, pp. 288–302. Springer, Heidelberg (2010)

[26] Hongli, Y., Xiangpeng, Z., Chao, C., Zongyan, Q.: Exploring the Connection of Choreography and Orchestration with Exception Handling and Finalization/Compensation. In: Derrick, J., Vain, J. (eds.) FORTE 2007. LNCS, vol. 4574, pp. 81–96. Springer, Heidelberg (2007)

[27] Kang, Z., Wang, H., Hung, P.C.: WS-CDL+ for web service collaboration. Information Systems Frontiers 9(4), 375–389 (2007)

[28] Kavantzas, N., Burdett, D., Ritzinger, G., Lafon, Y.: Web Services Choreography Description Language Version 1.0 (November 2005)

[29] Kopp, O., van Lessen, T., Nitzsche, J.: The Need for a Choreography-aware Service Bus. In: YR-SOC 2008, pp. 28–34 (2008)

[30] Kopp, O., Leymann, F., Wu, F.: Mapping interconnection choreography models to interaction choreography models. In: Central-European Workshop on Services and their Composition, ZEUS 2010. CEUR-WS.org (2010)

[31] Kopp, O., Leymann, F., Wutke, D.: Fault handling in the web service stack. In: Maglio, P.P., Weske, M., Yang, J., Fantinato, M. (eds.) ICSOC 2010. LNCS, vol. 6470, pp. 303–317. Springer, Heidelberg (2010)

[32] Kopp, O., Martin, D., Wutke, D., Leymann, F.: The Difference Between Graph-Based and Block-Structured Business Process Modelling Languages. Enterprise Modelling and Information Systems 4(1), 3–13 (2009)

[33] Li, J., Zhu, H., Pu, G.: Conformance Validation between Choreography and Orchestration. In: TASE (2007)

[34] Lohmann, N., Wolf, K.: Realizability is controllability. In: Laneve, C., Su, J. (eds.) WS-FM 2009. LNCS, vol. 6194, pp. 110–127. Springer, Heidelberg (2010)

[35] Bravetti, M., Tennenholtz, M.: Towards a Unifying Theory for Choreography Conformance and Contract Compliance. In: Lumpe, M., Vanderperren, W. (eds.) SC 2007. LNCS, vol. 4829, pp. 34–50. Springer, Heidelberg (2007)

[36] Montali, M., Pesic, M., van der Aalst, W.M.P., Chesani, F., Mello, P., Storari, S.: Declarative specification and verification of service choreographiess. ACM Trans. Web 4(1), 1–62 (2010)

[37] OASIS: Web Services Business Process Execution Language Version 2.0 – OASIS Standard (2007)

[38] Object Management Group (OMG): Business Process Model and Notation (BPMN) Version 2.0 (2010), http://www.omg.org/cgi-bin/doc?dtc/09-08-14, http://www.omg.org/cgi-bin/doc?dtc/10-06-04

[39] Peltz, C.: Web Services Orchestration and Choreography. IEEE Computer 36(10), 46–52 (2003)

[40] Rozinat, A., van der Aalst, W.M.P.: Conformance checking of processes based on monitoring real behavior. Inf. Syst. 33(1), 64–95 (2008)

[41] Russell, N., van der Aalst, W.M.P., ter Hofstede, A.H.M.: Workflow Exception Patterns. In: Martinez, F.H., Pohl, K. (eds.) CAiSE 2006. LNCS, vol. 4001, pp. 288–302. Springer, Heidelberg (2006)

[42] Russell, N., ter Hofstede, A.H.M., Edmond, D., van der Aalst, W.M.P.: Workflow Data Patterns: Identification, Representation and Tool Support. In: Delcambre, L.M.L., Kop, C., Mayr, H.C., Mylopoulos, J., Pastor, Ó. (eds.) ER 2005. LNCS, vol. 3716, pp. 353–368. Springer, Heidelberg (2005)

[43] Wolf, K.: Does my service have partners? In: Jensen, K., van der Aalst, W.M.P. (eds.) Transactions on Petri Nets and Other Models of Concurrency II. LNCS, vol. 5460, pp. 152–171. Springer, Heidelberg (2009)

[44] Zaha, J.M., Dumas, M., ter Hofstede, A., Barros, A., Decker, G.: Service Interaction Modeling: Bridging Global and Local Views. In: EDOC. IEEE, Los Alamitos (2006)

BPM 2.0: Business Process Management Meets Empowerment

Matthias Kurz[1] and Albert Fleischmann[2]

[1] University of Erlangen-Nuremberg, Information Systems II,
Lange Gasse 20, 90403 Nuremberg, Germany
[2] Metasonic AG, Münchner Straße 29 - Hettenshausen, 85276 Pfaffenhofen, Germany
matthias.kurz@wiso.uni-erlangen.de, albert.fleischmann@metasonic.de

Abstract. Traditional approaches for business process management assume that process models remain unchanged. However, businesses today have to adapt their business process models to new market changes instantaneously. Current methods for business process management approaches and their supporting information systems turn out to be too time-consuming and costly. This contribution suggests a new business process management concept (BPM 2.0) along with a corresponding software system that increase the flexibility of businesses by allowing employees to improve "their" business processes. A case study at a large European construction firm critically examines the feasibility both of the concept as well as the software system.

Keywords: BPM 2.0, Business Processes, Web 2.0, Enterprise 2.0, Empowerment.

1 Introduction

With businesses being forced to adapt themselves to continuously changing business environments, business process management is confronted with an ever increasing demand for flexibility. Due to the declining predictability of complex processes, the border between designing and executing business processes is blurring rapidly. Therefore, business processes have to be adapted to new business conditions more quickly and more cost-efficiently.

This contribution suggests a new business process management concept – BPM 2.0 – along with a corresponding software system that increase the flexibility of businesses by allowing employees to improve "their" business processes. A case study critically examines the feasibility both of the concept as well as the software system.

The article is structured as follows: In chapters two, requirements for increased flexibility in business process management (BPM) are identified. In chapter three, classical BPM is examined with regard to the level of flexibility it provides. Based on this analysis, self-organization is introduced as an instrument to increase the flexibility of BPM. Based on this foundation, chapter four presents the BPM 2.0 approach which applies self-organization to BPM. A brief

A. Fleischmann et al. (Eds.): S-BPM ONE 2010, CCIS 138, pp. 54–83, 2011.
© Springer-Verlag Berlin Heidelberg 2011

overview of a corresponding software platform shows how IT systems can support BPM 2.0. Chapter five describes a case study which has been conducted at an industry partner in order to assess the practicability of the new approach.

2   BPM and Flexibility

2.1   Business Services and Susiness Process Management

Business services and business processes have a close relationship. Business services define an interaction between a service requestor (customer) and a service provider. A service provider executes activities on behalf of a service requestor. These activities produce a certain result which is handed over to the service requestor. In order to produce the corresponding result, various resources and suppliers are involved. These suppliers can be considered service providers which produce contributions to the overall result (output) for the customer. This output has a business value for the service requestor [1].

Services are implemented with business processes, because a business process is "a structured, measured set of activities designed to produce a specific output for a particular customer or market. It implies a strong emphasis on how work is done within an organization, in contrast to a product focus's emphasis on what. A process is thus a specific ordering of work activities across time and space, with a beginning and an end, and clearly defined inputs and outputs: a structure for action. [...] Taking a process approach implies adopting the customer's point of view. Processes are the structure by which an organization does what is necessary to produce value for its customers." [2]. Many similar definitions of the term process can be found in literature (e.g. [3]–[6]).

Based on the definitions of the term process in [2]–[5], the following list of characteristics of a business process is compiled [7]:

- Definability: It must have clearly defined boundaries, input and output. The input is the request from the customer and the output the outcome of the process. In general, between the initial input and the final output additional interactions between the service requestor and the service supplier organization can be necessary.
- Customer orientation: There must be a recipient of the process outcome, a customer.
- Value-adding: The transformation taking place during the process must add value to the recipient.
- Sequence: It must consist of activities that are ordered according to their position in time and space. These activities are executed by the participants of a process who belong to different functions, organizations, or companies.
- Embedding: A process cannot exist in itself; it must be embedded in an organizational structure. In a global economy most processes span multiple functions or even companies. Embedding a process into an organization or a company means assigning the process tasks to corresponding executors. Executors can be humans or machines like enterprise resource planning software.

– Cross-functionality: In typical processes, several functions or organizations
  are involved.

Any holistic business process management approach has to consider these
characteristics as well as the entire lifecycle of business processes: "Business Process Management (BPM) includes concepts, methods, and techniques to support
the design, administration, configuration, enactment, and analysis of business
processes." [6]. In other words, BPM offers a service for managing processes
delivering services.

2.2 Flexibility

Flexibility means that a process can be adapted easily and in a short period of
time to new business conditions. During these adaptations, the processes' characteristics described above may change. There are various reasons for processes
to be modified: Customers expect new service features or better quality, management expects to reduce the costs for providing a service, competition offers new
products and services, etc. All these changes in the business environment require
corresponding adaptations to existing business processes. Based on the previously introduced characteristics of business processes, flexibility-requirements to
BPM approaches can be summarized as follows:

– Definability: In many cases, these requirements induce changes to the interfaces of processes, e.g. new output specifications. In other words, BPM
  approaches have to assist in modifying process interfaces.
– Customer-orientation: Businesses are increasingly confronted with new requirements from existing or new customers. Therefore, processes need to be
  adapted to these new requirements.
– Value-adding: With customer requirements changing the input and output
  of business processes, the focus of value-adding changes as well. Thus, BPM
  approaches have to assist stakeholders and process owners in determining
  the new focus of a processes' value generation.
– Sequence: New customer requirements typically impact the order of process
  activities. For example, new activities may be added or unnecessary activities
  may be removed. In many cases, the efficiency of processes can be improved
  by altering the sequence of activities. Consequently, BPM approaches have
  to provide instruments for rearranging the activity sequence of processes.
– Embedding and cross-functionality: The embedding of processes within the
  organizational context changes frequently. Participants like suppliers are replaced or the organizational structure is changing due to new customer requirements. A widely used instrument for improving process performance is
  outsourcing processes and sub processes to specialized outsourcing providers.
  BPM approaches have to be prepared for changing the embedding of business
  processes.

A business process management infrastructure must provide an environment
that allows adapting business processes to new business conditions in an efficient and effective way. Based on a case study at two large European firms, the

following flexibility-related requirements for business process management have been identified [8]:

- Up-to-date: The business process models must correspond to the actual process instances.
- Level of detail: Business processes must exhibit a sufficient level of detail.
- Accelerate: Process improvement cycles need to be accelerated.
- Coordinate: Requirements for process improvements have to be easily collected and coordinated across multiple organizational units or companies.
- Communicate: Adapted business processes have to be easily communicated to all involved parties.

These two requirement lists will be referred to below when assessing the practicability and use of the BPM 2.0 approach which is introduced in section four.

3   Employees as Drivers for Flexibility

3.1   Motivation

As elaborated in the previous section, the flexibility of business processes and the corresponding changes to these processes have a significant impact on the people involved in a process: Customers, employees, subcontractors, etc. must change their behavior. This means they execute new activities, they have to execute activities in a different order, they replace a subcontractor or delegate their work to subcontractor, etc.

Changes always have the highest impact on the parties involved in a process, because they drive a process. Therefore, in order to adapt processes to new business conditions quickly, efficiently, and effectively, people involved in this process should participate in these changes. Their familiarity with hidden knowledge like best practices allows adapting a process quickly and efficiently to new requirements (see the golden rules of change management defined by Lewin, described in [9]).

Therefore, BPM approaches emphasizing the flexibility aspect should support the participation of the people involved in a process to be changed. In the next section, the predominant organizational theories will be examined with regard to the role of the individuals in creating organizational structures.

3.2   Organizational Theory and BPM

Organizational theories offer a model for describing what organizations are, how they function, how they evolve, and which factors influence the evolution of an organization [10]. An overview of organizational theories can be found in [9]–[11]. Organizational theories consider the following aspects [9] which have a close relationship to the process characteristics described above.

- Structure of the activities to be executed. This corresponds to the process characteristics value-adding and sequence.

- Integration of individuals into organizations. This is related to the process characteristics embedding and cross-functionality.
- Relationships of organizations to its environment. This corresponds to the process characteristics definability and customer-orientation.
- Informal structures and processes are not part of BPM.
- Change management: This management concept is a major driver for flexibility.

A well-known organizational theory is Taylorism (also known as Scientific Management) which is major inspiration to Fordism. The principles of Taylorism are [12]:

- Centralization: The decision-making power is transferred from employees to managers.
- Standardization: Work procedures are highly standardized in order to improve efficiency.
- Selection: Workers are carefully selected according to the requirements each job has.
- Training: Workers are extensively trained to adhere the highly standardized procedures.
- Planning: The work procedures are planned in great detail by specialists.
- Motivation: Wages depend on the productivity of each worker and therefore are an incentive for improved output.

Fordism extends Tailorism with the idea of an assembly line: In order to coordinate the work of employees, Ford introduced assembly lines for producing cars. At each workplace of the assembly line the tasks sequences are defined in great detail. Managers (so-called white collars) define the task sequences and blue collar workers execute the task sequences as defined by the white collars. The task sequences at each workplace are synchronized by the assembly line. Management defines the sequences of tasks and defines the layout of the assembly line.

Today, the same pattern inspires almost all BPM approaches: Business and process analysts define the processes and employees execute these processes. Thereby, processes are typically defined like assembly lines. The following figure shows a process specification using event-driven process chains (EPC) which are a wide-spread method for defining business processes.

EPC-like specification of business processes have a management focus: If an employee wants to know his tasks in a process he/she has to go through the whole description in order to find the tasks he/she has to execute.

In general, necessary changes to a process are first defined by white collar employees and then communicated to the corresponding blue collars. Yet, is a cumbersome and time-consuming way of responding to changes in the business environment, as white collar employees can become a bottleneck for process maintenance and adaptations. Experience shows that companies which have more than thousand business processes, have BPM departments with about 15 employees. In order to bypass this bottleneck, process owners are assigned the

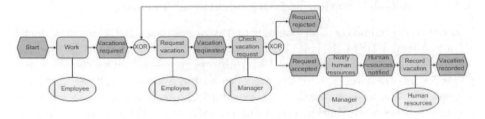

Fig. 1. EPC Example

responsibility for a process. This has the advantage, that process owners typically have more knowledge about the processes than a central department. This allows them to communicate and implement process changes. Process consultants support process owners in cases of methodical questions. Because business processes are-cross functional there is a conflict between the process and the corresponding functional managers. Process managers define which tasks have to be executed in a function and the responsibility for the performance of that organization has another person. Clarifying such conflicts proves to be time-consuming.

With classical BPM approaches being based on assembly line philosophy, they are confronted with similar critics like the original assembly lines:

- Structure of the activities to be executed: Sequences of activities are the focus of assembly line-oriented BPM methods. The structure of the work is defined by "white collars" and executed by the "blue collars". Usually, "blue collars" can influence the activity structure only during periodical reviews.
- Integration of individuals into organizations: There is a tendency to regard blue collar workers as uninformed and their ideas and suggestions are ignored. This way, valuable knowledge is lost to the decision-making process.
- Relationships of organizations to its environment: The environment is not considered deeply. Instead, most BPM approaches primarily focus on highly standardized process models. Therefore, it is difficult to modify these process models to a changing environment.
- Informal structures and processes: These structures and processes are an important aspect of any organization and serve as an alternative to the hierarchical organization in cases which are not covered by the organization, they are not considered by classical BPM approaches.
- Change management: White collar managers change processes and communicate these changes to the blue collar workers. This way, the knowledge of blue collar employees is lost for the creation of a changeimplementation plan.

In general, classical BPM approaches are optimized for highly standardized processes and rely on the strict distinction between white collar and blue collar workers. Most individuals within an organization have little influence on the development and improvement of "their" business processes.

3.3   Subject-Orientation and Organizational Theories

In order to overcome the shortcomings of Taylorism-based BPM, we introduced
subject-oriented BPM [13][14]. In this approach to BPM, the parties involved
in a process are in the center of BPM. Subjects represent active elements in a
process – in other words, subjects are roles within a process [14]. Subjects are
not special persons, organizations, or machines. Subjects are abstract resources
acting in a process. During the transformation of a process model into a workflow
concrete resources (persons, organizations, etc) are assigned to subjects. These
subject providers execute the actions according to the specified behavior of the
subject.

While subjects can be found in nearly all methods for BPM, their importance
in process specifications is varying. Figure 2 depicts three ways how subjects can
be introduced in process specifications.

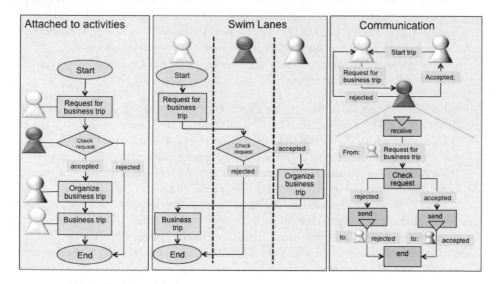

Fig. 2. Integrating Subjects in Process Models

In assembly line-oriented specification methods, subjects are added to the activity sequence specifications like people at a real assembly line. The disadvantage of this approach is that the employees who take over a certain role (subject
provider) have to go through the whole process to find out what they have to
do when. In order to solve that problem, swim lanes are introduced. Each swim
lane represents a subject. This way, the tasks of each subject are much easier to
determine. In both ways of representing subjects in a process model, the focus
of the process specification is on activity sequences. Therefore, the communication between the subjects is "implemented by an assembly line". Thus, these
two methods can be considered semi subject-oriented. With both semi subject-
oriented approaches having their roots in Fordism, both methods do not allow

to describe the behavior of each subject independent from the other subjects. The assembly line paradigm introduces a tight coupling between subjects.

The subject-oriented approach is based on the communication between the subjects. A process is considered to be a structured communication between the subjects of a process. Subjects send messages, receive messages, and execute actions which are not visible to other subjects. In order to simplify communication, subjects expect a certain behavior from other subjects with whom they communicate. This behavior describes which messages a subject sends or accepts as well as their sequence.

This approach for defining business processes fits well with the organizational theory based on Luhmann's sociological system theory [11]. This theory focuses on three major concepts [15][16]:

1. System theory
2. Communication theory
3. Evolution theory

Luhmann's theory is based on communication which is the basis for social systems. A social system is defined by a boundary between itself and its environment. Communication within a system operates by selecting only a limited amount of all information available in the system's environment. After that, systems interact by sending and receiving messages.

This has several implications for organizations:

- Organizations are social systems
- Organizations are systems of communication
- Communication is the smallest unit of an organization
- Communication takes place between two information processing processors (systems)
- An organization is a system which is coupled with other systems
- People do not belong to an organization
- People are systems which are coupled with an organization
- Organizations reduce complexity

In Luhmann's theory systems exist by communicating and observing. Continuous communication keeps systems alive. Additionally, systems observe themselves and their environment. Observing the environment allows systems to adapt themselves to their environment. Thus, learning is an integral part of Luhmann's systemic organizational theory.

Applying Luhmann's organizational theory to process management increases the independence of the parties involved in a process. These process participants describe their behavior (the sequence of interactions and actions) and coordinate their behavior with their neighbors (direct communication partners). White collar and blue collar tasks are not strictly separated any more. This implies that the task of this process owner is not to define task sequences. Instead, his or her task is to coordinate and moderate the communication between subject providers who autonomously adapt the processes to new business requirements. This communication yielding the definition of the communication (a process) can be seen as meta communication. Social software can assist and structure this meta communication. The combination of self-organization and social software is a major property of the Enterprise 2.0 concept [17].

In the following sections a BPM approach leveraging self-organization and the corresponding meta communication is presented.

4   BPM 2.0: Empowering Employees

4.1   Overview

Although the previous sections presented management approaches leveraging self-organization, they offer no comprehensive BPM methodology. The BPM 2.0 approach described in [8][18] aims at offering such a methodology by providing a procedure model encompassing all phases of the BPM life cycle. The term BPM 2.0 refers to applying the Enterprise 2.0 concept to BPM. The suffix 2.0 indicates that integrating employees who execute business processes as part of their day-to-day tasks into the design of business processes is the core idea of BPM 2.0. In other words, in this paper, BPM 2.0 is defined as follows:

> BPM 2.0 is a business process management approach which encourages employees to improve "their" business proccsscs. Wcb 2.0 tcchnologics are utilized to enable contributions from employees with little BPM expertise. [19]

This definition is extended by the definition given in [14] which requires that the developed process models are immediately executable by IT systems without requiring any programming. Thus, BPM 2.0 requires an integrated BPM suite "that automates, integrates, and monitors process execution end-to-end." [14].

Besides business processes (BP), process innovations (PI) are the key artifact of BPM 2.0. PI are improvements to BP which are initiated and collaboratively developed by stakeholders like employees who are involved in executing the respective processes.

The BPM 2.0 approach comprises multiple components: (1) A role concept for implementing BPM 2.0 in the organization, (2) a procedure model detailing how these roles interact during the lifecycle of a process, (3) a software platform which allows business users to contribute to PI, and (4) an IT-based execution environment which provides almost instant IT support for business processes and therefore mitigates the gap between business and IT.

The focus of this publication is presenting components one to three. Like any new organizational approach, BPM 2.0 is likely to encounter challenges when being implemented. These challenges are discussed in the next section. In the following sections, the BPM 2.0 components one to three are derived from these challenges. IT-based execution support is not within the scope of this publication. However, examples for computer-based execution support of BPM 2.0 are given in [14][19].

Two case studies are currently being conducted in order to test whether the promises of BPM 2.0 hold true in a real-world business environment. With the focus of BPM 2.0 being the development of new PI, these case studies examine in greater detail how employees can be enabled and motivated to contribute to developing new PI using the example of several process innovations each. One of these case studies along with its implications on the BPM 2.0 approach is presented in greater detail in chapter 1.1. This chapter presents the final BPM 2.0 approach which was substantially influenced by the findings of the case studies.

4.2   Challenges

In order to be successful, BPM 2.0 has to address the challenges it is likely to meet. This section summarizes the challenges which have been identified during a literature review. The BPM 2.0 approach and its components have been designed with these challenges in mind. For simplified referencing, each challenge is assigned an identifier.

New organizational concepts are frequently met with skepticism with regard to their feasibility [20] (Challenge ChA). This especially applies to those managers who enjoy substantial power in the current organizational structure.

Among other implications, self-organization questions the well-established power structure of a company. Decisions which previously were reserved to managers are transferred to employees. Like any form of power loss, this triggers the resistance of those mangers who previously had the decision power [21] (Challenge ChB).

This resistance is reinforced by the fact that in BPM 2.0, managers remain responsible for the process performance. Therefore, they are likely to fear that self-organization at least partially takes away hierarchical power as an instrument to manage processes successfully [22] (Challenge ChC).

Traditionally, middle management uses the selection of information which is relayed to the upper management as an instrument to influence decisions which middle management cannot make itself [23]. The value of this instrument is endangered by the information transparency which comes with Enterprise 2.0-related concepts [23] like BPM 2.0. As the benefit of process-related self-organization increases with the availability of information about the processes, it is likely that managers opposing single innovations or the entire approach may use the selection of information as a weapon against BPM 2.0 as long as a sufficient degree of information transparency is not yet achieved (Challenge ChD).

Individuals are not always acting in the best interest of their respective organization. Instead, particular interests and hidden agendas play a key role in company politics [24]. With such politics typically being intransparent [25], it is difficult to predict resistance from individuals whose interests conflicts with single process innovations or the entire approach (Challenge ChE).

While taking away power from managers is likely to provoke resistance, transferring this power to employees is problematic as well:

A major source for innovation is the willingness to question and improve existing structures. This implies that employees are ready to critically question their actions, accept critique, and thereby extend their own capabilities [26] (Challenge ChF).

The accustoming of employees to a small degree of influence on decision finding is a major barrier for successful implementations of self-organization [22]. After all, hierarchical environments with their very limited decision-making freedom reduce individual risks [22] (Challenge ChG).

While soft factors like social competence play an important role in organizational concepts which rely on a greater degree of self-organization [26], sufficient domain and methodic knowledge remain important success factors [26]. Typically, trainings for employees who execute BP focus on how processes are expected to be conducted and provide little guidance for designing or improving BP (Challenge ChH).

Besides insufficient methodical knowledge, employees who fulfill only single functions within a process often possess no holistic perspective on large processes and their environment (Challenge ChI). Therefore, process innovations are prone to local optima which are not necessarily beneficial to the entire processes. This is especially true for processes that are embedded in complex scenarios and therefore feature a high degree of complexity (Challenge ChO).

Therefore, managers have to ensure that PI are compatible with the company's goals and strategy. However, self-organization requires sufficient freedom for making own decisions [23]. If the management rejects PI too often, the employees' motivation for contributing to PI is diminished (Challenge ChJ).

Similar to extensive management intervention, a high workload makes encouraging employees to handling even more work difficult as well [27] (Challenge ChK). Even in cases where the innovation teams have sufficient time for working on a PI, further – often external – resources are required [28]. External experts for developing new or adapting existing IT systems are just one example for such external resources (Challenge ChL).

Enterprise 2.0-related concepts like BPM 2.0 require supporting software systems which are easy to use [23]. Widely used systems like ARIS Business Designer focus on BPM experts and therefore confront employees with limited expertise with too much complexity (Challenge ChM). Along with insufficient methodical knowledge, this provides a strong initial barrier for occasional contributions (Challenge ChN).

4.3   Procedure Model

Classical BPM lifecycle models like [6] or [29] distinguish between designing, implementing, executing, and analyzing BP. Innovation management lifecycle models like [30] exhibit a similar structure: Innovations are identified, selected, implemented, and finally evaluated. The main difference between management lifecycle models for innovations and business processes is that the former assume that a larger quantity of individuals is involved in creating innovations than in creating business process improvements. Therefore, it is necessary to implement review mechanisms for innovations.

However, both lifecycle models have to be adapted before being applied to BPM 2.0: Selecting PI requires a sufficient degree of maturity of these innovations in order to adequately assess their potentials and costs. Therefore, the BPM 2.0 lifecycle model must allow developing PI before and after the selection of process models. Figure 3 depicts the BPM 2.0 lifecycle which combines the innovation [30] and BP management lifecycles [6] previously mentioned.

During the design phase, employees involved in the respective BP create and refine (develop) PI. By using a web based platform, options are discussed in discussion boards, documented in wikis, and formalized as graphical process models.

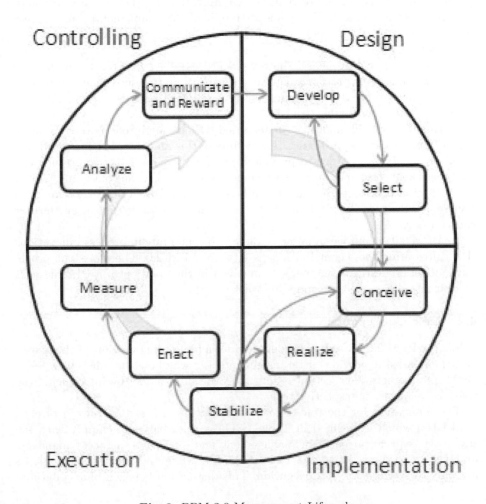

Fig. 3. BPM 2.0 Management Lifecycle

By including potentially all stakeholders in this early stage, the risk of failing implementations as well as Challenge ChI – the lack of a holistic perspective – are mitigated. Transferring design tasks to the employees allows fulfilling multiple requirements: First, business processes are improved continually, because it is in the best interest of the employees to change business processes which impede their daily work. Second, they can swiftly and autonomously create answers to new challenges like changing market requirements [8]. Because multiple PI may be created in parallel, these innovations have to be selected: First, stakeholders and employees evaluate proposed innovations during a collaborative assessment. In the next step, the process owner reviews promising innovations and – if accepted – triggers its implementation.

The implementation phase is about realizing PI both organizationally and technically. During this phase, PI are refined and change plans are conceived first. Then, these change plans are realized: Organizational structures are adapted, stakeholders trained, and IT systems are modified. The implementation progress is measured and – if necessary – the change plan is adapted to unforeseen challenges.

During the execution phase, the revised processes are brought to life by employees who enact the processes. During the execution, the enactment component of the business process management system (BPMS) records key performance indicators (KPI) for further analysis.

During the controlling phase, the recorded KPI are analyzed in order to assess the performance of the processes. The results of this analysis are then published to all stakeholders in order to provide input for further PI. By comparing the KPI recorded before and after the implementation of a PI, the contribution of PI to the overall process performance can be estimated. Based on this estimation, rewards for the contributors to a PI are determined in order to encourage further contributions.

As BPM 2.0 encourages a larger audience to contribute in process innovations (PI), integrating these contributions is vital for BPM 2.0. Therefore, the procedure model orchestrates the persons involved in the creation of a PI. The next section introduces the corresponding roles in detail.

4.4   Role Concept

While the BPM 2.0 procedure model provides a high-level overview of the phases and their tasks, it provides little insight into the way how the different roles in BPM 2.0 interact. This section refines the procedure model by introducing the roles as well as their respective tasks.

The foundation for the role concept of BPM 2.0 is the role concept of classical BPM which is outlined in Table 1. These roles basically comply with the tayloristic separation between management and employees: Process managers and process owners define the tasks to fulfill, while the process participants are only responsible for task execution. This distinction between blue collar and

Table 1. Roles in classical BPM [29]

BPM project manager	Responsible for the introduction of business process management	Introduction
Process consultant	Conceptual and methodic support during introduction	Introduction
Process manager	Responsible for improving and integrating the BPM framework	Operation
Process owner	Responsible for achieving the goals of a BP and improving the BP	Operation
Process controller	Responsible for improving BP and conducting the process controlling	Operation
Process participant	Responsible for task execution	Operation

white collar workers is only marginally blurred by the definition of process teams consisting of blue- and white collar workers who are assigned to solve specific challenges [29].

BPM 2.0 is based on a substantially different distribution of tasks and responsibilities:

Blue collar workers like process participants take over many tasks and responsibilities of the white collar managers. They are empowered to define and rework definitions for processes which they participate in every day. Because they repeatedly switch between managing and executing roles, they are changing from blue collar workers to "checkered blue/white collar workers".

Instead of prescribing tasks and process execution in detail, white collar managers provide frameworks, tools, and guidelines for creating and improving business process models. With process governance and process compliance being vital for large enterprises, management has to ensure that the processes which have been designed by blue-color workers are compatible with the company's frameworks and guidelines. Thus, managers have to mediate between the mandatory rules and the empowered employees.

Table 2 provides an overview of the roles involved in BPM 2.0 as well as their interaction among each other. Each role and its corresponding tasks have been introduced in order to mitigate the challenges presented in section 4.2. Therefore, the table includes a column indicating which challenges the tasks of each role address. With BPM 2.0 being an extension of classical BPM, the roles in Table 1 are also part of the BPM 2.0 role concept. Because the tasks of these roles – with the exception of the process owner – are not substantially changed by BPM 2.0, they are not listed in Table 2.

Table 2. BPM 2.0 roles

Role	Description	Challenges addressed
Process contributors	Employees executing BP as part of their day-to-day work (process participants) possess extensive domain knowledge and experience with their processes. Process contributors are process participants who, due to their limited methodical know-how, primarily contribute non-formal information to process innovations by taking part in discussions, adding comments to process models, or editing wikis pages. Due to the intuitive use of these Web 2.0 instruments, little training is required. Process contributors typically will not change BP models directly. Instead, they provide non-formal contributions that are refined by process innovators.	ChH, ChN
Process innovator	Graphical process models are a vital instrument for BPM, because they provide a clear and intuitive way to visualize processes. A brief training provides process innovators with sufficient methodical expertise for directly modifying process models. Therefore, they are able to transform the informal input from process contributors to formal process models. Like process contributors, process innovators are employees who regularly participate in the execution of a BP. With the most important instrument of BPM 2.0 being the inclusion of a broad range of contributors and innovators in the creation of a PI, no specialized knowledge or experience besides elementary BP modeling capabilities are required for process innovators. Instead, the specialists and experts described below assist process innovators and contributors in developing a PI.	ChH, ChN
Modeling specialist	With process innovators typically only possessing limited knowledge about the formalities of business process modeling, they are likely to make syntactic or semantic errors. Thus, modeling specialists ensure the formal correctness of process models that are part of PI. While modeling specialists can assist any time during the development of PI upon request, their inclusion is mandatory during the review of a process innovation. With increasing experience of process innovators, the importance of modeling specialists is expected to diminish over time. Modeling specialists require moderate knowledge in BP modeling. Experience in process design projects is advisable.	ChH

Table 2. (*continued*)

Role	Description	Challenges addressed
Method mboxexpert	In complex scenarios, simply adhering to the modeling guidelines and being compliant to the syntactic rules of the modeling notation used is insufficient. With the modeling specialist focusing on the modeling techniques, methodical knowledge is not part of his expertise. Instead, it is the method expert who answers questions regarding the BPM methodology. Important questions the method expert has to address are: – How are complex business processes structured? What are the respective best practices? – What guidelines and rules have to be considered in PI? – How are process governance and compliance affected by a PI? – How should business processes be aligned to the overall process framework? For example, how are PI integrated in the company's reference process house? The method expert requires extensive methodical BPM knowledge which for example employees of BPM policy units posses. It is recommended that the method expert has extensive BPM experience.	ChH
Domain expert	Process innovation teams may predominantly consist of members who are involved in a particular part of a BP. This may cause PI to achieve local optima which may have a negative impact on the overall process performance. The holistic perspective of the domain expert allows him to identify incompatible interfaces between processes. Thus, it is mandatory to include the domain expert in the review of a PI. However, it is advisable to include domain experts already during the development of process innovations. Domain experts preferably are members of middle management: These managers have wide reaching responsibilities in order to ensure a holistic perspective and still are close enough to the processes in order to possess sufficient domain expertise.	ChI

Table 2. (*continued*)

Role	Description	Challenges addressed
Process owner	The process owner is responsible for the process performance and therefore reviews process innovations and decides whether to accept or reject them. While the process owner has the final word about releasing a PI for implementation, he is expected to seriously consider PI because unnecessarily rejecting PI will discourage employees to contribute to process innovations. Process owners require substantial knowledge about the processes they are responsible for. With the respective experts and specialists being available for consultation, possessing methodical, domain, or modeling knowledge is helpful, yet not mandatory.	ChC
Mediator	The mediator assists two challenges PI teams are likely to encounter: (1)Insufficient organizational power of the PI team and (2) insufficient resources. First, the mediator assists in resolving conflicts between PI teams and management that may arise from conflicting perspectives or interests. By reporting directly to the top management (e.g. the process manager), he or she can back PI teams with organizational power when necessary and thereby decrease the risk that a PI is unnecessarily rejected. In cases where certain aspects of a PI are not likely to be successful – e.g. due to political processes within the company – he can proactively consult the PI team accordingly. Based on the collaborative assessment of PI, the mediator provides PI teams with training, a network of experts, or resources. With the lack of available time being a major barrier to substantial contributions, the mediator can partially exempt selected employees for a limited time. In order to avoid resistance from the exempted employee's organizational unit, this unit is financially compensated for the temporary loss of a resource. A network of experts helps PI teams tackling the complexity of highly complex processes. Innovators and participants of a successful PI are rewarded in order to encourage further innovations and to compensate rot taking the risk of taking more responsibility. In order to back up PI teams in case of conflicts, the mediator needs to be equipped with sufficient organizational power. Similarly, providing PI teams with resources or training implies an adequate budget.	ChB, ChE, ChH, ChO, ChK, ChG, ChJ, ChD
Champion	Implementing BPM 2.0 in a company requires the support both of employees and managers. Therefore, it is vital to convince key stakeholders within the organization of the benefits and potentials of BPM 2.0. Champions win and retain the goodwill towards this concept. With the regularly interacting with high-ranking executives, he or she should be a member of middle or – preferably – top management.	ChB, ChA

All process participants are offered basic training. Therefore, all process participants potentially are contributors and/ or innovators. The membership to the group of contributors or participants is predominantly based on the personal affinity. The long-term goal is to develop a large pool of process innovators.

Table 2 shows a fine-grained role concept. Introducing a large number of roles for BPM 2.0 is not likely to be beneficial in smaller environments. Instead, the roles are expected to be overlapping. For example, the process owner (or one of his assistants) can fulfill the roles of the modeling specialist, domain expert, and modeling expert. With the process manager often being a high-ranking manager, he or she is a good candidate for being the champion of the BPM 2.0 concept.

4.5   Platform

The BPM 2.0 concept is complemented with a corresponding BPM 2.0 software system which supports the approach by providing platform that allows combining the informal contributions of process contributors like comments, discussions, and wiki pages with formal process models which are enhanced by process innovators.

The platform serves as an instrument for testing and refining the BPM 2.0 approach. The software was used in case studies at three industry partners, one research project which is not related to the BPM 2.0 research, and several smaller scenarios with information systems students. It was extensively used in the case study presented in chapter 1.1.

In order to allow as many employees as possible to improve "their" processes, the platform is web-based and thereby requires no software installation on the users' computers. It provides a separate workspace for every business process. This workspace assembles all information related the respective process and the innovations which are developed for this processes. Thereby, workspaces assist in communicating new process innovations as well as in coordinating the development of PI spanning multiple departments.

The platform is based on a customized Microsoft SharePoint installation which is extended by several WebParts (re-usable user interface components). Among other functionalities, these WebParts allow collaboratively editing business process models. Using WebParts allows process owners to conveniently customize workspaces. For example, one industry partner chose to display multiple process models on one workspace in order to reduce the number of navigation steps. Workspaces will be adapted during the phases of the BPM 2.0 procedure model. For example, during conceiving an implementation plan for a PI, a WebPart for displaying new task responsibilities is added to the workspace.

The platform offers four major components: (1) a modeling tool for graphical BP, (2) an annotation function that allows adding comments to graphical process models in a post-it-like manner, (3) a wiki, (4) a discussion board, and (5) a push messaging system.

Contributors can deliver their input by using a variety of informal instruments: The wiki allows complementing and thereby detailing process models with text and graphics. That way, employees can develop and/or refine process innovations without requiring formal expertise. Problems, hints, or questions

72   M. Kurz and A. Fleischmann

regarding specific parts of a process model can be added using the comment functionality. Contributions can be coordinated by using the discussion board.

Over time, many contributors will extend their expertise and finally become process innovators who are capable of designing formal process models. The web-based modeling tool allows these process innovators to design and improve formal business processes models without requiring locally installed software.

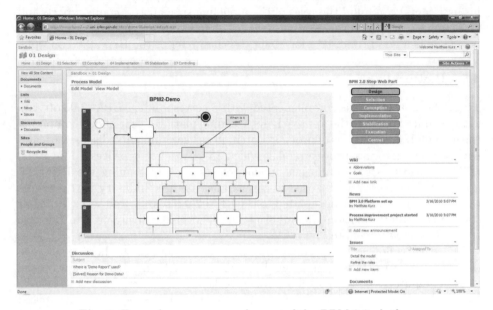

Fig. 4. Exemplary process workspace of the BPM 2.0 platform

Figure 4 depicts an exemplary workspace of the BPM 2.0 platform which shows a graphical process model along with a comment, important wiki links, sent push news and the discussion board.

A precondition for encouraging contributions is a push component that allows proactively notifying the participants and other stakeholders about updates of a process innovation by email messages or news feeds. This is realized by using standard SharePoint functionality.

In order to reduce the costs of the trainings that explain the BPM 2.0 platform and the first modeling steps to potential process contributors and innovators, an online video tutorial has been created and integrated in the platform.

4.6   Summary

The BPM 2.0 approach and its components promise to increase the flexibility of business processes by allowing employees and operational departments to define and improve "their" business processes (ChF). The following list demonstrates how BPM 2.0 assists in achieving this goal by examining the impact this approach has on the flexibility requirements laid out in section 1.

- Customer-orientation: Operational departments are enabled to swiftly adapt processes to new customer requirements.
- Definability: Changes to process interfaces can be efficiently coordinated between the process owners and participants of the neighboring processes by using the BPM 2.0 approach and platform.
- Value-adding: Coordinating the decision for a new focus of value creation as well as communicating this new focus is simplified by the collaborative BPM 2.0 approach.
- Sequence: One of the key aspects of BPM 2.0 is to allow process innovation teams to collaboratively develop PI. With a key aspect of BP models being the control flow of business processes, BPM 2.0 radically improves adapting the activity sequence of BP to new requirements.
- Embedding and cross-functionality: Enabling operational departments to embed processes in new contexts ensures that these processes are fit for implementation in their new environment.
- Up-to-date: Assuming that the process compliance is ensured, employees following these process models are highly motivated to ensure that process models are executable and up-to-date. Otherwise, they waste valuable time in finding workarounds.
- Level of detail: As the employees executing BP as part of their daily tasks possess intimate knowledge about these processes, they are likely to ensure that the processes are sufficiently detailed.
- Accelerate: With employees being among the first who are confronted with new market demands, they can adapt the affected process models to these new requirements – assuming that the process compliance is ensured.
- Coordinate: The BPM 2.0 approach provides both a procedure model as well as a platform for teams spanning multiple functions which collaboratively develop PI.
- Communicate: The BPM 2.0 platform allows communicating changes related to PI in an early stage of a PI. Push mechanisms ensure that the stakeholders are informed.

The role concept and the web-based platform address all challenges except challenge ChF – the ability to critically reflect the own actions. This challenge cannot be addressed by a software solution or a procedure model. Instead, this ability requires an environment that encourages employees to cultivate their own capabilities and knowledge. All in all, BPM 2.0 promises to overcome the challenges which have been identified during a literature review.

However, BPM 2.0 is a new approach to BPM that has not yet been extensively tested in practice. Therefore, the case study presented in section 1.1 is an important first step in proving the practicability of this approach.

5   BPM 2.0 Applied: A Case Study

5.1   Scenario

In order to verify that the BPM 2.0 concept achieves its goals, the concept has been tested in a real-world corporate environment. Between March 2010 and July 2010, a project for improving eight business process models has been conducted at a large European plant construction firm as part of the company's initiative to improve the management of its business processes. This project used the BPM 2.0 approach as the overall framework and the BPM 2.0 platform as the underlying software platform.

In order to ensure that the case study has been conducted according to scientific requirements and that the findings are reusable for further research, the canonical action research (CAR) methodology served as a framework for conducting this case study ("project" in the CAR terminology).

With CAR being an iterative methodology, CAR projects consist of multiple iterations that exhibit the same structure (see Figure 5). The researcher-client agreement (RCA) is the foundation of each CAR project: In order to efficiently conduct a project, the tasks and responsibilities both for the researchers in the project as well as the industry partner ("client") have to be defined and agreed upon. By including information about the project like goals, the analysis methods, and mutual guarantees, it serves as a foundation for building trust.

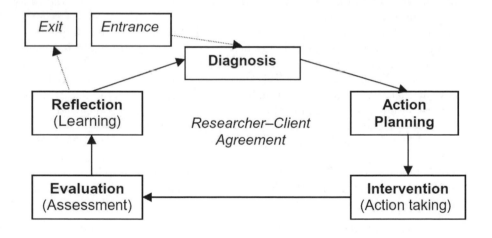

Fig. 5. Canonical action research process model [31]

At the start of the project, the respective process owners presumed that the current process models were partially incorrect, not up-to date, and not detailed enough in order to be implemented in the day-to-day routine. Therefore, their practical use as a management instrument was questioned. Accordingly, the industry partner's ("client") project goals were: (1) Ensure that the process models are accurate, (2) sufficiently detailed, and (3) fit for implementation. The goal of the researchers was to test whether BPM 2.0 provides an adequate solution for the problem at hand.

The project comprised three iterations: (1) Advertising the concept, preparing the platform, and conducting training sessions, (2) allowing the employees to familiarize themselves with the concept and the corresponding platform, and (3) introducing a support role (modeling specialist) for improving the quality of the business processes models as well as providing self-learning material in order to lessen the workload for the modeling specialist.

Four groups played a vital part in the project: (1) Two managers who are responsible for BPM at the industry partner, assisted in convincing key stakeholders and ensuring management support. In other words, these managers were BPM 2.0 champions. (2) The employees executing the business processes participated in the process innovations by improving the models of "their" processes. Depending on their interactions, these employees were either process contributors or process innovators. (3) The owners of these processes ensured the quality of the respective process innovations. Furthermore, they served as domain experts. (4) The researchers were responsible for analyzing the situation at hand and providing guidance for implementing BPM 2.0. Thus, they served as method experts and mediators. In the third iteration, one of the researchers overtook the tasks of the newly specified modeling specialist role.

5.2 Iteration 1: Preparation

Diagnosis. At the beginning of the project, the client already had identified the BPM-related challenges given in section 1.1. In order to get a better understanding of the problems, an in-depth as-is analysis of the client's BPM approach was conducted. For this analysis, semi-structured expert interviews with a process manager, several process owners, and other stakeholders like high-ranking IT representatives were conducted. This analysis revealed the following challenges regarding process models:

1. The process models were rarely updated.
2. The process models were partially inconsistent.
3. The process models frequently exhibited an insufficient level of detail.
4. In many cases, the actually executed processes significantly differed from the process models.
5. The client's change management processes were rarely triggered by input from employees executing these processes. This was predominantly attributed to the observation that employees saw little use in contributing to improvements of process models which had only limited relevancy to the day-to-day work.
6. Regular mandatory reviews initiated only minor changes like renaming activities or processes.

These results are consistent with a case study that examined challenges at two different large European companies [8].

Action planning. The diagnosis confirmed that the client's challenges are very similar to the challenges BPM 2.0 strives to solve. Therefore, the BPM 2.0 approach promised to be an adequate solution candidate.

In order to be able to execute this case study, key stakeholders had to be identified and addressed by both process managers who served as BPM 2.0 champions. Once the key stakeholders have been convinced to participate in the project, several processes had to be selected for inclusion in this project. These processes had to fulfill several criteria: (1) They must not be trivial, (2) they must not be extraordinarily complex, (3) they should not have an above average number of interfaces to other processes, and (4) the respective process owners agree to take part in the pilot project. While criteria (1) and (4) are obvious, (2) and (3) were intended to ensure that the project will not require too much resources.

With an adequate modeling environment being a prerequisite for the successful implementation of BPM 2.0, a concept for integrating the BPM 2.0 platform in the client's infrastructure had to be conceived. Previously, the company used a derivate of event-driven process chains (EPC) as a modeling notation. In order to minimize the learning curve for the potential contributors, the platform was extended to support this EPC derivate as well.

Finally, a training concept for workshops has been designed. These trainings were geared towards employees who previously had little or no expertise in business process modeling. Therefore, only basic modeling elements and guidelines were introduced. In order to familiarize the workshop participants with the platform, all training was conducted using the platform.

As workshops are time-consuming to prepare and conduct, web-based training material was considered to be the most cost efficient way of providing the process innovation teams with sufficient training. Therefore, the majority of the process innovation teams was designated to rely on web-based training. That way, the researchers were able to test whether the web-based training is sufficient.

Intervention. The first intervention was to address the process owners of processes fulfilling the selection criteria conceived during the planning phase and ask for contributions. The owners of eight suitable processes agreed to participate in the project. In this contribution, the process improvement sub projects are referred to as process innovations PI1 to PI8.

In the next step, the BPM 2.0 platform was installed within the organization's intranet. A major goal of this project was to ensure that the platform can be used without any preparations. Integrating the platform with the company's identity management system allowed seamless access to the platform by any employee with sufficient authorization. The web-based training material comprising a brief overview of the modeling language as well as a more in-depth introduction to the modeling concept was included into every process workspace. For each PI a workspace was created.

Once the technical preliminaries have been concluded, an initial workshop was conducted for PI1. During this workshop, this team could make its first steps with process modeling. The teams participating in PI2-PI8 were simply provided with a hyperlink to their respective workspaces along with a pointer to the online training material.

Evaluation. Within weeks, a number of process owners indicated their willingness to participate in the project.

The results of the training workshop for PI1 were evaluated by analyzing the feedback of the participants. This feedback indicated the presence of two groups within the process innovation team: Employees who expressed interest in the platform as well as the approach and a second group which demonstrated little interest in refining the models after the workshop. However, during the workshop, both groups provided extensive input to the workshop instructor who transformed this input in a new process model. When being asked for the reason of their unwillingness to use this platform, the members of the first group suggested that their generation (the average age was above 45 years) is not used to web-based tools.

Reflection. The champion role is vital for the initial success of BPM 2.0. In this project, the champions were successful in ensuring management goodwill and convincing process owners to participate. Thus, the approach was swiftly accepted within the organization.

The limited enthusiasm of one half of the team participating in PI1 is hardly surprising, as using Web 2.0 services for private purposes is rare among members of this age group as well [32].

5.3   Iteration 2: Encouraging Contributions

Diagnosis. So far, the organization has changed very little during the preparation iteration. With management support being available and the initial training carried out, the stage was set for the process innovation teams to improve their process models.

Action planning. In this phase, the researchers intentionally restrained themselves from extensive interaction. Instead, monitoring the progress of the process innovations was the goal of the next phase. That way, the researchers strived to understand how the BPM 2.0 concept is used in real-world environments.

Intervention. The platform's versioning functionality provided an instrument for monitoring the intensity of the interaction as well as the development of the process models' maturity. If no contributions were made, the process owners were asked for reasons periodically. If necessary, assistance was provided. With participation in the project being voluntary, the management support was intentionally not leveraged for encouraging contributions.

Evaluation. During observing the activities of the process innovation teams, two classes became apparent: First, the team responsible for PI8 showed little activity. When asked for the reasons, the process owner explained that the current workload currently makes contribution difficult. Second, all innovation teams except that of PI8 substantially extended the process models: In three cases (PI1, PI6, and PI7), the need for splitting one process into distinct processes became apparent. The process of PI1 was split into two processes with the corresponding process innovations PI1a and PI1b. Similarly, it became apparent that the PI6 process had to be split into three processes. For two of those processes, the process innovations PI6a and PI6b were initiated. Finally, the PI7 process was split into seven processes. The process innovations PI7a-PI7d were initiated for four of these processes.

While informal comments were the primary instrument for contributions, the process models were modified extensively as well. This fits well with BPM 2.0 distinguishing between contributors who provide informal contributions and process innovators who transform this informal input into formal changes to the process model.

On the other hand, wikis and discussion boards were only rarely used. In an expert interview, both process managers involved in the project suggested that these functions are likely to be used once the innovation teams are more familiar with the platform.

Brief interviews with the process owners confirmed that the quality of the process models of PI1a-PI3 and PI5-PI7d was substantially improved with regard to the project's goals. Although the pragmatics of these process models was clear, the models of PI1a-PI1b and PI7a-PI7d exhibited several syntactical and semantical errors.

While the process model of PI4 initially showed substantial improvement, these improvements were lost during later contributions which introduced extensive syntactical errors that rendered the model difficult to understand. When analyzing this surprising development, insufficient modeling knowledge of some team members and a large number of interfaces to other processes were identified as the reasons for this development.

Reflection. In this project, the contributions obviously depend on the willingness to work with the tool and the perceived priority of the process innovations. When these preconditions have been fulfilled, the BPM 2.0 approach yielded process models with substantial improvements. In three cases, the processes were even completely redesigned.

As expected, the employee's modeling knowledge proved to be insufficient. This deficit manifested itself in frequent errors and extensive use of non-formal comments.

5.4   Iteration 3: Improving the Formal Model Quality

Diagnosis. The introduction of BPM 2.0 allowed employees to improve "their" business process models. However, varying degrees of contributions were observed and the amount of formal errors in the process models had to be reduced.

Action planning. As the participation in the project was voluntary, enforcing contributions to process innovations was considered an inadequate solution. Instead, assistance was offered to the team of PI8 which showed only limited activity.

Compensating the lack of modeling knowledge was determined to be the key task for this iteration. Three options were considered: (1) Conducting further workshops, (2) improving the training material, and (3) providing assistance to modeling. With empowering a large number of employees being the key instrument of BPM 2.0, conducting further workshops might have been too time-consuming for employees whose primary tasks are not related to process modeling. Therefore, options (2) and (3) have been chosen for enactment in this iteration. Due to the exceptional situation of process PI4, a workshop for re-moving errors was planned.

The training material was extended with improved modeling guidelines that considered frequent errors which occurred in iteration 2. Furthermore, an on-line video tutorial covering the basic interaction with the BPM 2.0 platform was conceived and integrated in the platform as well as the improved training material.

The most important intervention in this iteration was introducing a modeling specialist who removes syntactical errors from the process models. That way, employees can contribute their domain expertise while ensuring that the process models exhibit a high quality with regard to formal correctness. In this project, one of the researchers served as a modeling specialist.

Intervention. Similar to iteration 2, the process owner of process PI8 has been contacted periodically and offered assistance. A workshop for innovation team PI4 was conducted in order to eliminate the errors within the process model.

The modeling specialist proactively removed syntactical errors from the pro-cess models. This was done in consent with the respective process owners. That way, the modeling specialist basically became a new process innovation team member who focuses on the formal aspect of the process innovation.

Evaluation. With the process models of PI2-PI3 and PI5-6 already exhibiting sufficient syntactical correctness, little improvement could be measured. In a final workshop, the innovation team of PI1 accepted the new processes models of PI1a and PI1b for introduction into the company's process house. The process models of PI2-PI3 have been accepted by the process owner and incorporated in the process house as well.

The syntactical correctness of the process models PI1a-b and PI7a-d improved substantially after the intervention. Therefore, they were soon used for internal purposes. Later, they have been imported into the process house as well. While the improved and advertised training material had a positive impact on the frequency of the errors, removing errors remained to be a time-consuming task for the modeling specialist.

Process PI8 which had little contributions in the previous iteration remained unchanged in this iteration as well.

The workshop for process innovation team PI4 revealed that the syntactical errors within the model were not the only challenge this innovation team had to face. It became obvious that the team members had different understandings of this process and therefore could not agree on a common model during this workshop.

Reflection. This iteration succeeded in further improving six process models (PI1a-b and PI7a-d) with regard to the project's goals while maintaining the formal correctness. The latter aspect is a significant improvement compared to the previous iteration. However, the workload of the modeling expert turned out to be considerable. Therefore, the work coming with this task has to be carefully distributed in order to ensure that the approach scales well. This can be achieved by ensuring that each process innovation team has one well-trained member who can take over the tasks of the modeling specialist. The mediator described in section 1.1 can assist in providing this training to the modeling specialist.

Complex issues like that one of the PI4 team apparently cannot be resolved by process innovation teams possessing limited modeling knowledge. In such cases, assistance by a process management expert is advisable.

5.5 Summary

The process owners confirmed that the process models of PI1-PI3 and PI5-PI7 are more accurate than before, have a higher level of detail, and thus are better suited for implementation. Therefore, the project can be considered a success.

All in all, the BPM 2.0 approach was received very well within the industry partner's organization. The project started with process innovations for eight process models. Three of these process models were significantly improved. Another three process models were completely restructured into eight process models. In total, eleven substantially reworked process models have been released to the company's process house.

Only two process innovations yielded little success: One proved to be too complex for the process innovation team. The second one experienced little contributions. With BPM 2.0 relying on contributions of the process innovation teams, an incentive concept and objectives from the management can assist in increasing the motivation for employees to participate in process innovations.

During the case study, the role concept was extended: The mediator was split up into the three roles mediator, champion, and modeling specialist. As expected, the mediation aspect of the mediator had little relevancy in this case study, as the process innovations were not radical enough in order to cause resistance within the organization.

This project was the very first attempt within the client's organization to empower employees to improve "their" processes. Therefore, insufficient modeling knowledge was to be expected. It is likely that – over time – the modeling capabilities of the process innovation teams improve. Thereby, the workload of the process innovator will decrease. Meanwhile, the combination of improved training and assistance of modeling specialists promises to compensate the insufficient modeling know-how.

The contributions of BPM 2.0 to the flexibility of business processes which are outlined in section 1.1, were observed as follows:

- Customer-orientation: The customers did not introduce new requirements during the case study.
- Definability: The process interfaces were extensively modified in PI1, PI6 and PI7 due to splitting them into distinct processes. The other processes' interfaces remained largely unchanged.

- Value-adding: The focus of the business processes did not change during the case study.
- Sequence: Six process models received substantial improvements during the project. All six improvements came with substantial changes to the activity sequence.
- Embedding: The process embedding remained unchanged during the project.
- Cross-functionality: The BPM 2.0 approach and platform assisted in coordinating PI spanning multiple organizational units.
- Up-to-date and level of detail: During the reviews of the PI, the process owners ensured that the new process models created during PI1a-PI3 and PI5-PI7d were up-to-date and are sufficiently detailed for real-world use.
- Accelerate: The improvement cycles were substantially reduced: Before the project, the processes received little improvements for several years. By giving the users direct and simplified access to the process models, they were enabled to identify and realize the above-mentioned potentials. During this project, the processes of PI1-PI3 and PI5-PI7 were improved in a matter of weeks.
- Coordinate: The PI teams of the above-mentioned processes made extensive use of the BPM 2.0 platform.
- Communicate: In all above-mentioned processes, especially the platform's informal mechanisms for communication and coordination were used.

These observations indicate that the case study did not leverage all potential contributions of BPM 2.0 to the flexibility of business processes, as this was not necessary within the case study. However, these observations confirm that BPM 2.0 significantly benefitted the aspects definability, sequence, cross-functionality, up-to-date, level of detail, accelerate, coordinate, and communicate.

6 Conclusion

Empowerment and especially its younger derivate Enterprise 2.0 are currently en vogue in the scientific community, as they promise to bring the flexibility of self-organization and Web 2.0 to the business environment. BPM 2.0 starts with similarly ambitious goals. The case study presented in this contribution confirms that many of these goals can be fulfilled. Currently, the results of the case study are being analyzed with regard to the accumulated costs. In order to determine the monetary improvements, the accumulated costs of utilizing the BPM 2.0 approach will be compared to the costs of a classical approach for improving business process models which has been conducted in parallel to the project outlined in this article.

BPM 2.0 is not limited to modeling business processes. With IT systems being more important to executing business processes than ever, extending BPM 2.0 to IT systems is vital for the adoption of this approach. [14] and [19] suggest concepts for including IT systems in the BPM 2.0 approach.

References

[1] Kindermann, K.: Identifikation und Potenzialbeurteilung interner Business Services zur Service Externalisierung. Diploma Thesis. Friedrich-Alexander-Universität Erlangen-Ntürnberg, Ntürnberg (2010)

[2] Davenport, T.H.: Process innovation. Reengineering work through information technology. Harvard Business School Press, Boston (1993)

[3] Hammer, M., Champy, J.: Reengineering the corporation. A manifesto for business revolution. Harper Business, New York (1993)

[4] Rummler, G.A., Brache, A.P.: Improving performance. How to manage the white space on the organization chart. Jossey-Bass, San Francisco (1995)

[5] Johansson, H.J.: Business process reengineering. Breakpoint strategies for market dominance. Wiley, Chichester (1993)

[6] Weske, M.: Business Process Management. Concepts, Languages, Architectures. Springer, Heidelberg (2007)

[7] Wikipedia: Business process, `http://en.wikipedia.org/wiki/Business_process` (last checked: July 18, 2010)

[8] Kurz, M.: BPM 2.0. Kollaborative Gestaltung von Geschäftsprozessen. In: Schumann, M., Kolbe, L.M., Breitner, M.H., Frerichs, A. (eds.) Multikonferenz Wirtschaftsinformatik 2010, pp. 729–740. Univ.-Verl. Göttingen, Göttingen (2010)

[9] Schreyögg, G.: Organisation. Grundlagen moderner Organisationsgestaltung. Mit Fallstudien. Gabler, Wiesbaden (2008)

[10] Crowther, D., Green, M.: Organisational theory. CIPD, London (2008)

[11] Kieser, A., Ebers, M.: Organisationstheorien. Kohlhammer, Stuttgart (2006)

[12] Taylor, F.W.: The principles of scientific management. Dover, Mineola (1998)

[13] Schmidt, W., Fleischmann, A., Gilbert, O.: Subjektorientiertes Geschäftsprozessmanagement. HMD - Praxis der Wirtschaftsinformatik, 52–62 (2009)

[14] Fleischmann, A.: What is S-BPM? Accepted. Communications in Computer and Information Science 85 (2010)

[15] Berghaus, M., Luhmann, N.: Luhmann leicht gemacht. Eine Einführung in die Systemtheorie, Böhlau, Köln (2004)

[16] Wikipedia Foundation: Niklas Luhmann, `http://en.wikipedia.org/wiki/Niklas_Luhmann` (last checked: July 27, 2010)

[17] McAfee, A.P.: Enterprise 2.0. The Dawn of Emergent Collaboration. MIT Sloan Management Review 47, 20–28 (2006)

[18] Kurz, M.: BPM 2.0. Organisation, Selbstorganisation und Kollaboration im Geschäftsprozessmanagement. Bamberg, Erlangen-Nürnberg, Regensburg (2009)

[19] Billing, G., Kurz, M., Hettling, K., von Jouanne-Diedrich, H.: Applying BPM 2.0 in IT centric environments. Accepted paper. In: Hull, R., Mendling, J., Tai, S. (eds.) BPM 2010. LNCS, vol. 6336, Springer, Heidelberg (2010)

[20] Stamer, S.: Enterprise 2.0. Learning by Doing. In: Buhse, W., Stamer, S. (eds.) Enterprise 2.0 - die Kunst, loszulassen, Rhombos, Berlin, pp. 59–87 (2008)

[21] Cacaci, A.: Change Management. Widerstände gegen Wandel. Deutscher Universitäts-Verlag/ GWV Fachverlage GmbH Wiesbaden, Wiesbaden (2006)

[22] Randolph, A.W.: Re-thinking Empowerment. Why Is It So Hard to Achieve? Organizational Dynamics 29, 94–107 (2000)

[23] McAfee, A.: Eine Definition von Enterprise 2.0. In: Buhse, W., Stamer, S. (eds.) Enterprise 2.0 - die Kunst, loszulassen, Rhombos, Berlin, pp. 17–35 (2008)

[24] Kotter, J.P., Schlesinger, L.A.: Choosing Strategies in Change. Harvard Business Review 86, 130–139 (2008)

[25] Neuberger, O.: Mikropolitik und Moral in Organisationen. Herausforderung der Ordnung. Lucius & Lucius, Stuttgart (2006)

[26] Picot, A., Reichwald, R., Wigand, R.T.: Die grenzenlose Unternehmung. Information, Organisation und Management. Gabler, Wiesbaden (2001)

[27] Böhle, F., Bolte, A.: Die Entdeckung des Informellen. Der schwierige Umgang mit Kooperation im Arbeitsalltag. Campus-Verl, Frankfurt/Main (2002)

[28] Hauschildt, J., Salomo, S.: Innovationsmanagement. Vahlen, München (2007)

[29] Schmelzer, H.J., Sesselmann, W. (eds.): Geschäftsprozessmanagement in der Praxis. Kunden zufrieden stellen, Produktivität steigern, Wert erhöhen. Hanser, München (2008)

[30] Reichwald, R., Möslein, K., Huff, A.S., Kölling, M., Neyer, A.-K.: Service Innovation, Leipzig (2008)

[31] Davison, R.M., Martinsons, M.G., Kock, N.: Principles of Canonical Action Research. Information Systems Journal 14, 65–85 (2004)

[32] Busemann, K., Gscheidle, C.: Web 2.0: Communitys bei jungen Nutzern beliebt. Ergebnisse der ARD/ZDF-Onlinestudie 2009. Media Perspektiven 7, 356–364 (2009)

Dynamic Catenation and Execution of Cross Organisational Business Processes - The jCPEX! Approach

Nils Meyer, Thomas Feiner, Markus Radmayr,
Dominik Blei, and Albert Fleischmann

Metasonic AG, Münchner Str. 29 - Hettenshausen,
85276 Pfaffenhofen, Germany
{nils.meyer,thomas.feiner,markus.radmayr,dominik.blei,
albert.fleischmann}@metasonic.de

Abstract. In order to meet today's business needs, companies using business process workflow engines not only demand to span their business processes across organizational borders but also to have the flexibility to dynamically select their partners to be able to react adequately to change.

This paper explores the requirements arising from this need, followed by an evaluation of existing approaches regarding cross organizational process modelling and –execution. Finally we introduce our solution for dynamic connection of business processes between organizations, which is based on a subject-oriented business process modelling language.

Keywords: Cross company, business process management, subject-oriented business process modelling.

1 Introduction

Traditionally, businesses often operated in stand-alone mode. Cooperation with other organizations was rather static and lasted for a longer period of time. Nowadays, due to globalization and increased market transparency, competition has become more intense. Fast technological developments cause shorter life cycles of products and services with increasingly frequent modifications and replacements. In addition, products and services have become more complex. Therefore, dynamically established cooperation among organizations is becoming much more of a requirement to meet market demands [6] [10].

But not only cooperation is crucial under present business conditions. Moreover, organizations have to be more flexible and be able to quickly adapt to change – also in the choice of collaboration partners. Partners are more and more selected just for a short to medium period of time [11].

Organizations that want to come up with those requirements and already are using workflow management systems for their internal processes, therefore want to expand their business processes to their business partners, whereby processes are executed across organizational boundaries. However, much of the existing workflow management technology only supports intra-organizational workflows,

A. Fleischmann et al. (Eds.): S-BPM ONE 2010, CCIS 138, pp. 84–105, 2011.

assuming a homogeneous workflow management system in the context of a single organization. When workflow management is extended across organizational boundaries, the complexity is heavily increased [8].

Support is needed for modelling such inter-organizational cooperation as well as for executing these business processes between organizations and across – maybe even heterogeneous - workflow engines. But, as we have stated at the beginning of the introduction, cross organizational business processes and their execution not only have to be defined once – frequent partner changes shall be enabled without the need to invest much time and cost in adapting the IT infrastructure. Because business goals often dynamically determine which partner to use in the enactment of the business process to achieve those goals, organizations shall be enabled to select the appropriate business partners even at runtime. Additionally, those decision criteria often can be formalized, so that mechanisms should be found to allow the configuration of which partner should be selected in specific circumstances in advance (e.g. dependent on the content of a business object).

With the advent of cross-organisational IT-supported communication questions arise regarding security and possibilities to hide process internal issues of involved partners. Therefore mechanisms have to be found to make only those aspects of internal processes available which are necessary for cross-organisational process definition.

In summary it has to be stated that cross organizational business process definition is an urgent need within the economy. Increasing efforts in developing choreography standards (e.g. WS-CDL) prove this assumption. Therefore business process modelling has to operate across organizational borders. The connection of these processes cause different problems to solve. First of all, experience has shown that the connection of processes is very expensive and time consuming. Given that internal processes cross organizational boundaries, new aspects of information hiding have to be defined in order to hide sensitive data and processes within an organization. Furthermore, responsibility for modelling is distributed between the participating companies.

In the next section we will introduce an example which considers the stated business needs to link business processes between organizations and which we will refer to in the upcoming sections. Requirements related to the global objective and the deduced goals are described in section 3, before existing approaches are evaluated in section 4. Finally we will introduce our jCPEX! approach to model, connect and execute cross organizational business processes in section 5.

2   Example

In this section, we illustrate the above mentioned business needs with the help of a concrete but simplified example.

This use case is modelled with S-BPM – a subject-oriented business process management methodology. S-BPM is a "semantic paradigm, modelling and implementation approach" [5] and was invented by Albert Fleischmann. The used process description method is taking its cue from the theoretical concepts of Milner [9] and Hoare [7].

Just as subject, predicate and object in the grammatical context, the approach here focuses on the behaviour of the individual participant in the process. This participant can be a human being as well as an EDP system. Participants exhibiting this behaviour pattern within a process are called "subject". Subjects are active. In drawing parallels to German grammar, the subject is identified by answering the question on "who or what does something". By contrast, the object is passive and represents something involved in the subject's performance like data or databases.

The advantage of S-BPM is its focus on the individual process participant and behaviour, its decentralized modelling, and that the modelled processes are directly executable as workflow.

Conventional BPM focuses on modelling (with analyzing and optimizing the resulting models) and subsequent execution. Business processes "define at what point in time process participants execute individual activities on related objects" [5]. Nowadays business requirements are changing rapidly and therefore business processes have to be adopted "with the same speed".

There is an urgent need for a new generation of BPM, which is combined with SOA and Web 2.0 and is therefore called BPM 2.0. It is considered less technology oriented (like old BPM approaches with syntactical analyzing and optimizing of models) and should include more human aspects. S-BPM is a "new BPM methodology which combines all of these various properties of BPM 2.0, from a technical perspective as well as with regard to human interaction". The focus is put on "acting elements within a process, the so called subjects". Accordingly to natural languages, subjects "execute and synchronize their activities by exchanging messages" [5].

Figure 1 shows two Subjects "Applicant" and "Approver", which are exchanging the messages "proposal" and "accepted"/"rejected". It is obvious, that this type of modelling is closer to human perception of everyday processes.

Within Subjects there are activities, which form the behaviour of the subjects (like the predicate of a sentence). These activities are divided into send messages (Figure 2), receive messages (Figure 3) and actions (Figure 4). Every send- and receive message has a corresponding message exchange description between Subjects (like "proposal" in Figure 1).

Actions/Activities like "Check Proposal" in Figure 4 are executed within a Subject. These internal actions are defined on internal data like business objects. They can change business objects, check the values of business objects or both. The action is executed within the state and can end in several results (in this example the results can be "accept" or "reject").

In the following we want to introduce a travel application example that implies cross organizational cooperation. In this scenario an employee of a company is required to go on business travel. She sends a business travel application to her line manager, who either accepts the application or rejects it. In case of approval, the manager is responsible for forwarding the employees application to the in-house travel office.

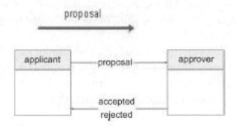

Fig. 1. Subjects and Messages

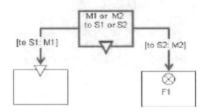

Fig. 2. Send Message

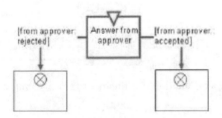

Fig. 3. Receive Message

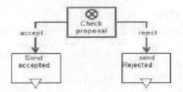

Fig. 4. Actions/Activities

The travel office then searches for an appropriate travel agent to book the required railway tickets and the hotel accommodation.

The travel agent here is another company that executes the requested services. After having booked rail and hotel, the travel agent sends a confirmation back to the customer travel office.

Figure 5 shows a cross organizational process model of this scenario in PASS, a subject-oriented business process modelling language. The subjects Employee, Manager and Travel Office are part of the customer in this business trip booking process, Travel Agent, Rail and Hotel comprise the company that provides the booking service.

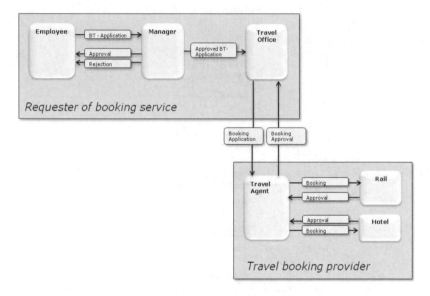

Fig. 5. Process model of a business trip booking application

The description of the process flow and the message exchange in detail:

- An Employee commits a business-trip application to a "subject" Manager, which returns an Approval or a Rejection.
- In case of an Approval, Manager commits the Approved BT-Application to the in-house Travel Office.
- The Travel Office sends the Booking Application to one external Travel Agent
- Dependent on the message passed to the Travel Agent, the Travel Agent sends messages to Rail and/or Hotel.
- Rail and Hotel return Approval messages to the Travel Agent
- The Travel Agent finally returns a Booking Approval to the Travel Office of the requesting company.

If we want to invite more than one travel agent to submit an offer for that service, we have to introduce a so called multi-subject to support that one-to-many relation:

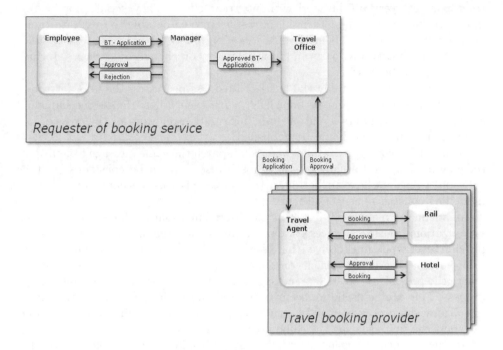

Fig. 6. Process model of a business trip booking application with multi-subject

Figure 6 shows the same business case with the use of a multi-subject. The customer Travel Office now sends requests for quotation to several Travel Agents (realized as multi-subject). The travel office then decides by means of the returned offers which travel agent to instruct and sends it the booking application.

3   Requirements

In the introductory section we explained and motivated the global objective of this paper and identified several goals to achieve this global objective. In this chapter we want to derive requirements arising out of these goals.

Requirements can be divided into modelling and execution aspects. Additionally there should be no gap between those two, no further transformation of the model must be required to execute it.

When modelling cross-organizational processes, time and effort for partners to coordinate each other should be minimized. Therefore it is crucial that organizations should be able to model their processes for themselves, with interfaces for the communication to other organizations. Only those interfaces have to fit to each other and have in some cases to be synchronized. Not only the message exchange has to be defined in such an interface, also the sequence of the messages and possible decisions are of great importance.

The high dynamic of today's business demands that organizations can change their partners very quickly and without great effort. They should not be required to intricately adapt their IT infrastructure to be able to integrate their new partner's workflow. If mechanisms can be found to determine compatible processes automatically, easy and fast selection or change of partners during runtime would be possible.

If companies cooperate on the basis of business processes, they do not want to share their internal process knowledge with each other. Hence, mechanisms are needed to hide internal matter, only information relevant for the cross organizational cooperation should be published.

Situations where organizations want to dispatch the same message to multiple recipients - i.e. one-to-many relationships – also have to be considered in the solution. Concepts have to be found to realize this case without cumbersome modelling constructs as workaround.

An adequate role concept has to be considered in a solution for executing cross organizational business processes. On the one hand organizations may want to provide several possible receivers for a message of a certain service and map those to an internal user management, on the other hand scenarios shall be supported where the possible receivers of a message are defined in the model of the sending process. This can be useful for security reasons to restrict possible receivers in a scenario where processes shall be dynamically connected within an organization (i.e. between units sharing the same user management).

At execution time it is important that no central instance is needed to coordinate and/or execute the cross organizational message exchange. This would raise questions about who is responsible for operating this central instance or what to do if the central instance is ceased (see UDDI). A decentralized architecture has the advantage that partners can connect to each other very dynamically and that no third party is required as mediator.

Furthermore, as mentioned above, potential partners should be identifiable at runtime so that the selection of the partner can depend on changing business goals or on the content of the message. If the partner selection can be formalized with certain criteria, there should be possibilities to statically define such rules for specific processes in advance.

In summary, the following points have to be considered for a solution of cross organizational business processes. Regarding modelling these are:

- Interfaces describe the observable behaviour of a process that cooperates with other processes.
- It not only considers in- and outgoing message exchange, but also the sequence of the messages and possible decisions that have an impact on the further message flow.
- Internal matter that is non-relevant for the cross organizational process is not part of the interface.

- Easy change of partners has to be enabled by automatic identification of compatible processes.
- One-to-many relations have to be supported.
- A role concept is needed that can restrict possible receivers and maps publicized to actual roles.

During runtime, the following requirements and constraints have to be considered:

- No central instance must be required to control the message flow
- Identification of potential partners at runtime
- Possibilities to automate the partner selection in respect of specific predefined conditions.

In the next section we will evaluate existing approaches regarding these requirements.

4   Evaluation of Existing Approaches

4.1   EPC (Event-Driven Process Chain)

The Event-Driven Process Chain (EPC) is one important part of ARIS (Architecture of Integrated Information Systems) developed by IDS Scheer . EPC was created in 1992 and is a model to depict business processes. EPC itself is a semi-formal language based on the theories of Petri-Nets.

Figure 7 shows the basic elements of EPC. Events are the passive elements of the model. These events can trigger functions, which can result to events in turn.

Functions are the active elements of EPC, hence only the can change business objects. Functions are triggered by events and lead to events in turn.

The Organization unit describes the person or organisation, which is responsible for a function.

Input data give basis information to a function, output data is produced by a function.

EPC is the main representative for control-flow oriented business model descriptions.

There exist approaches to use EPC for CBP (cross-organizational business processes. [14] gives an example for using EPC for modelling communication between organisations and government. They distinguish between global processes, process views and private processes. In order to hide internal data (like demanded from our requirements) private processes have to be transformed to process views, which describe the communication between two participants.

Global processes at the other hand describe the "global observable behaviour" between all participants of a specific process. Different approaches for modelling these three types of processes are shown: top-down, bottom-up and middle-out (we will later discuss that our solution is a middle-out approach depending on the organizational needs). The process communication occurs with the aid of input/output message exchange.

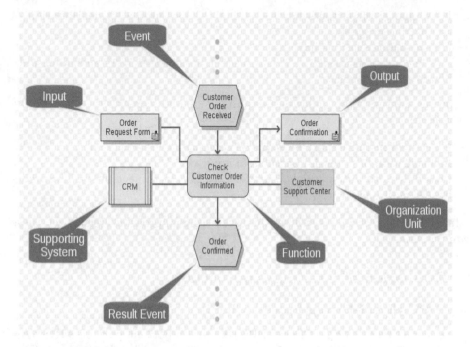

Fig. 7. Elements of Event-Driven Process Chain (from [12])

Despite this concrete attempt using EPC for CBP, there are a couple of steps from modelling to execution. Technical EPC has to be transformed from conceptual EPC, thereafter BPEL executable processes are derived. This raises the need of IT support to come from conceptual modelling to execution. This contradicts our requirement to assume responsibility for modelling and executing processes by functional departments. In our opinion this approach (in virtue of the Zachmann Framework) implies too many possibilities of semantic gaps and misinterpretation between the model-to-model transformation boundaries.

4.2 BPMN 2.0

BPMN (Business Process Modelling Notation) is a graphical business process and workflow modelling language. The building blocks are shown in Figure 9.
 These elements comprise

 – Activities: these are tasks within a business process), events (denotes that something happens, e.g. a message receive or a specific data is reached.
 – Gateways: decision points, where control flow can be split or merged.
 – Sequence and message flows
 – sequence flow connects activities, gateways and events. Message flow describes message exchange between independent partners.
 – Pools and lanes: Pools represent a participant in a workflow, this can be a role or a system. A lane divides a pool.

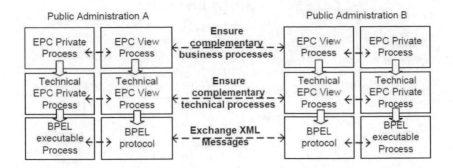

Fig. 8. Process types involved in protocol development (from: [14])

Though BPMN 2.0 tries to close the semantic gap and therefore should be executable, hindrances regarding cross-organizational are evident.

First of all there exist three different modelling types for partner process execution: Collaboration, Choreography and Conversation. This contradicts the need of just one meta-model to describe business processes. Inconsistencies between process models described with different model types can occur.

Multi-instance activities enable communication between two or more elements of same type. At present there exists no possibility to specify the exact execution semantics of this element. [1] describes an example, where the selection of a provider has to be modelled with the aid of timeouts, which clearly lacks of execution semantics afterwards.

4.3 WS-CDL

WS-CDL (Web Service Choreography Language) is a language which globally describes interaction between two or more participants. A WS-CDL document can be seen as a multi-party contract. The choreography is contained in a package (which describes the basic entities of the choreography like name, author, version, participants, etc.) and comprises name, relationship, activities, variables, etc. Activities can be sequential, parallel, choices, workunits and interactions.

Choreographies describe the globally observable behaviour of all participants. Thus choreography languages have a different scope compared to the view of a single organisation (behavioural interface). Nonetheless different weaknesses of WS-CDL can be identified and are described in "A critical overview of WS-CDL".

The identified problems are:

– Weak degree of formalism (that hinders validation like detection of deadlocks, livelocks and leak freedom)
– Choreography is statically bound to a specific WSDL interface, this hinders reusability
– Semantic consistency between WS-CDL and local (executable) process is complicated
– Explicit support for multi-party interactions is missing

Core Set of BPMN Elements

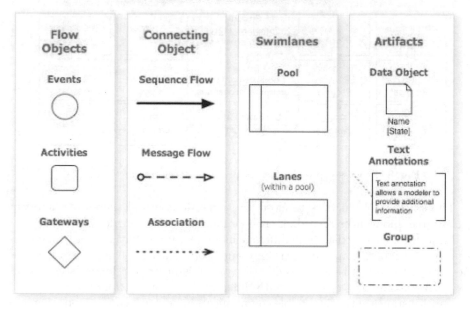

Fig. 9. Core Set of BPM

All in all WS-CDL is just one piece for enabling cross-organizational communication. It is a design-artefact and can be seen as a "contract" for all participants of such multi-lateral communication. Therefore each participant has to develop own solutions to verify the "fit" of own process description to this "contract". WS-CDL does not facilitate holistic approaches regarding modelling and execution.

4.4 Let's Dance

Let's dance is a language proposed by a consortium of Queensland University of Technology and SAP Research Centre in Australia. The main objective of Let's Dance is to provide a language which targets at behavioural aspects of service interactions (in addition to well-known structural aspect descriptions).

In the paper [13] common approaches are criticized regard treating service interactions as extension to a core language (like BPMN and BPSS). Furthermore these languages do "not provide an unique framework for capturing interactions both from a local and from a global viewpoint" [13].

The language "Let's Dance" is targeted at business analysts and software architects during the initial phases of service development. Nonetheless this language can be used to generate executable models (like BPEL).

Let's Dance tries to solve the issues not handled in a convenient way by other standards like WS-CDL (for example multi-instance activities, deferred choice, cancel activities). Furthermore Let's Dance is tightly coupled to the Interaction Patterns (described by [2]), which can be compared to traditional patterns within the software design domain. The value of these patterns lies in "their independence of specific languages and techniques" [2] and can be used to compare different approaches of service interaction design.

All in all Let's Dance is a very suitable proposal for service interaction patterns and there exists also a modelling tool [3]. Nonetheless the authors of Let's Dance differentiate between expressive and suitable languages, whereas our approach tries to be expressive and suitable simultaneously. With "Let's Dance" there also exists a "semantic gap" between modelling and execution, although Let's Dance models are executable at a certain level of abstraction and "can thus be used for simulation and verification" [4]. Nonetheless Let's dance is a research project and lacks of fulfilling requirements like "rule based selection of receiver" and "roles".

4.5   Execution

The execution of process models is typically realized by workflow engines (like Apache ODE, Bonita, FlowMind, Imixs, jBPM, etc.). Some of them are based on BPEL processes, which have to be modelled first. Classical control-flow oriented engines lack of support for cross-organisational process execution. If cross-organisational processes are executed in such control-flow oriented manner, services of participants have to be triggered (e.g. by the use of web services). This raises the question about the responsibility for the whole process.

UDDI has shown that this central accountability is a crucial point for all cross organisational concerns, since 2005 IBM, Microsoft and SAP cancelled their support for UDDI. Therefore decentralized execution engines are necessary, whereat each organisation retains control for own processes and cross-organisational execution semantics is covered by modelled protocols and bilateral agreements.

SAP Process Integration (PI) is a further development of SAP XI (Exchange Infrastructure) and a SOA-implementation for connecting SAP and foreign systems. It is a middleware part of SAP NetWeaver and serves as Enterprise Application Integration platform. SAP XI has a process engine which uses BPEL. With these technologies it is possible to define integration processes in order to connect cross-organisational business processes. This integration effort is defined, coordinated and supervised centrally by ccBPM (cross-component BPM). The centrally defined integration process is stateful and is persisted within the integration server. Messages are sent/received to/from connected workflow engines. Within the integration server rules can be defined for routing messages. Nonetheless ccBPM and SAP PI allow only centrally defined message exchange between workflow engines. The involved organisations in fact retain control over their own business processes but not over the connection to other processes. Furthermore the rules for routing messages are deposited within the central integration server and not divided into sender rules and receiver rules.

EDI (electronic data interchange) efforts at the other side focus on the data transmission between organisations. EDIFACT, RosettaNet, etc. try to describe data formats in order to ensure they are exchangeable between partners. Therefore all EDI approaches lack of process support for these participants. Furthermore implementing 1:n scenarios (like described within "Requirements") and dynamic connection between different organizations is not covered by EDI approaches.

5   Our Solution – jCPEX! Process Router

In this chapter we eventually present our approach that makes use of the potential of the S-BPM to provide a solution for connecting business processes between organizations and considers the requirements worked out in section 4. We go through the requirements and develop our idea step by step deduced from this demands.

5.1   Information Hiding

In chapter 2 we showed an example of a cross organisational business process for planning business trips described by means of subject-oriented modelling. Though this model is able to be executed on two distributed workflow management systems, some questions and problems arise regarding the requirements stated in chapter 3.

In the process model of our example the whole internal process flow is visible to all participating partners. This is opposed to the common demand of hiding internal process definitions. The use of subjects helps us to eliminate this dilemma. Usually there is one subject which is responsible for inter-company process message exchange. Therefore only this subject should be externally observable. Consequently, the message exchanges with internal subjects – subjects that do have no contact with the external process - have to be hidden from the public process. At the end of this operation a presentable "interface subject" is created, which can be seen as the observable behaviour of the whole process. Subsequently we will call this the Behavioural Interface (BI). Anyway it is important that the sequence of the message flow as well as contained decisions (turnoffs) is preserved. This is ensured by our way of deducing the behavioural interface from the complete process.

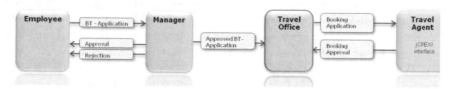

Fig. 10. Business Trip booking process definition

Figure 11 describes the generation of a "Behavioural Interface" for the travel agency booking process. As it can be seen in Figure 10, "Travel Office" is the subject which is responsible for the communication with other companies. Additional to this "Travel Office" subject an external subject "Travel Agent" is needed which acts as a placeholder for the potential partner in order to model the message exchange against this subject. This subject has to be marked as external jCPEX! interface.

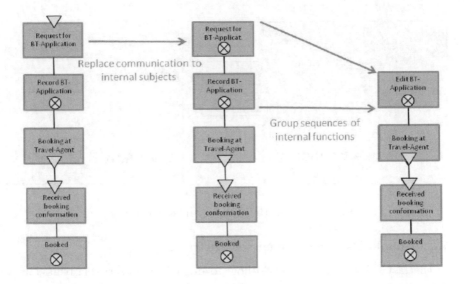

Fig. 11. Behavioural interface extraction from "Travel Office"

Figure 11 shows the internal process flow of this "Travel Office" subject. All internal message exchange has to be eliminated from this subject to retrieve the observable behaviour. For this reason, "Request for BT-Application" (which is the message coming in from subject "Manager") is changed to an "internal function" (left part of Figure 11). After all internal incoming and outgoing message exchange is altered this way, sequenced internal functions can be merged (right part of Figure 11).

After these steps a behavioural interface of the "Travel Office" subject is available and can be publicly released to other companies.

Figure 12 shows the modelling of the opposing travel agency's process view. The algorithm of deducing the external observable behaviour works the same way as described above. After all, both deduced behavioural interfaces have to fit to each other in order to be able to be connected (Figure 13).

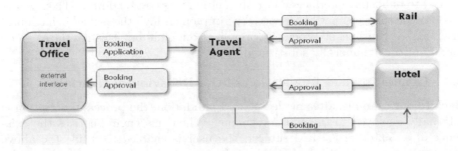

Fig. 12. Travel agency booking process

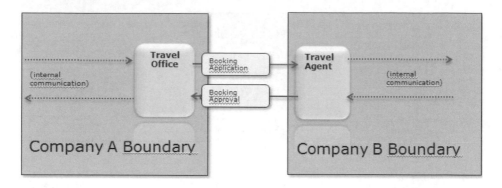

Fig. 13. Connecting inter-organizational processes

5.2   Enable Dynamic Change of Partners

In the last subsection we showed how to derive the observable behaviour of a whole process of an organization from the point of view of the involved partner. This behavioural interface can now be publicly announced in order to enable potential partners to model their process suitable to this interface.

When, for example, the travel agent from our example publishes the derived behavioural interface for its service (we will show where to publish the BI in a subsequent section), organizations demanding such a booking service can download the interface and model its internal process suitable to this external interface. But how is partner change enabled this way? How can organizations using the booking service dynamically change the travel agency for further bookings – for example depending on the travel destination?

Therefore, another concept is introduced additionally to deriving the observable behaviour for once service. We need the possibility for further organizations to offer their booking service so that the demanding organization can switch to those suppliers without adapting their internal process. That means that the processes of the additional providers have to satisfy the same observable interface as the initial offerer of the booking service.

To facilitate this we assign unique IDs in the form of unique resource identifiers (URIs) to published interfaces. With the help of this URIs, additional companies can provide their compatible services by "implementing" the primal behavioural interface. At runtime, all processes (organizations) fulfilling this interface can be found and/or dynamically substituted.

5.3   Generation and Publication of the Behavioural Interface

Back to our example, after modelling and validation, the process description is internally deployed to the runtime engine. When this engine notices the existence of an external jCPEX! subject, the user is enabled to define the above mentioned unique identifier (URI), in order to enable other companies to implement their services compatible to this "behavioural interface". Only if the travel

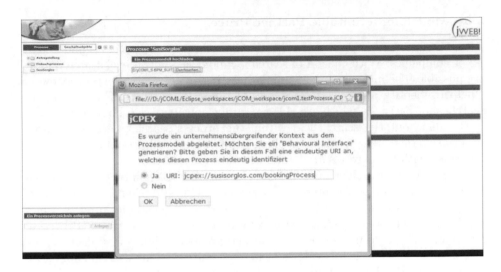

Fig. 14. Generation and Deployment of Behavioural Interface

agent assigns an URI to her interface, the "observable behaviour" of subject "Travel Agent" is calculated and published.

5.4   Adding Metadata to Behavioural Interface

After generation of the behavioural interface the user provides additional information about this behavioural interface in order to be better findable by other companies.

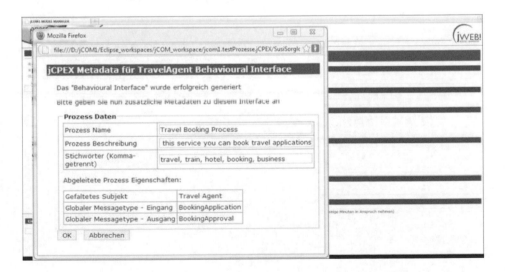

Fig. 15. Adding metadata to deployed behavioural interface

5.5   Modelling a Suitable Partner Process

After the deployment process described above, the service-process is findable by
other companies. With the aid of search technologies, multi-level search queries
are possible. The metadata and ontology description - given by the process owner
- help to identify appropriate processes of potential partners. E.g. a company
searches for partners, which are able to conduct business trip bookings.

By filling out the search field within the process search platform with appropriate terms (like "travel", "booking" and "hotel") all processes which were
described with these terms are found.

In opposite to search engines like Google, not an URL pointing to a web page
is returned, but an URI is presented which can be used during the modelling of
one's own processes. Figure 15 shows the model of the customer process, which
wants to use the "Travel Agent" process for booking a business travel (Process as
a Service). The customer models his internal process and uses a subject "Travel
Agent" which is marked as external interface subject. This external subject is
marked with the URI just found by the process search engine. To assist the
modeller, there should be support by the modelling tool to import the external
interface subject including the internal behaviour. This convenience function

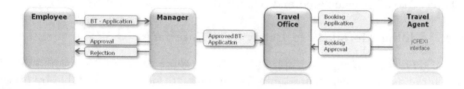

Fig. 16. Definition of Business Trip booking process

Fig. 17. Find appropriate processes with the aid of metadata

helps not only to model a suitable internal process, but also to validate the
fitting of the processes.

5.6   Process Execution and Decentralized Architecture

Due to problems, which arise with centralised architecture of information systems (e.g. single point of failure) the jCPEX! approach uses a decentralized
architecture. The main idea behind our solution was born during talks with a
big network solution provider. Parts of the jCPEX! software is already installed
on routers, which are able to compute subject oriented process models. Figure
19 shows the principles of this architecture, the grey rectangles show the process
model aware routers.

In chapter 5.3 we already described the deployment of the travel agent business process. The business trip booking process (customer) is also deployed to the
internal workflow engine, the customer can decide on publishing his own process
and thus is searchable by a process search engine. In either case the behavioural
interface of this process is calculated and validated against the behavioural interface of "Travel Agent" (like mutual process fit, dead lock detection, etc.). The
deployed process and interface descriptions reside on the own process engine and
process gateway.

Our solution entails pull-oriented techniques, because either (business process)
search engines, as well as other process gateways have to pull process information (process URI, etc.) from certain process gateways. In order to enable the
distribution of information about involved process engines, network theories like
Border Gateway Protocol (BGP) and Distributes Hashtables (DH) are used.

After deployment the customer is able to execute his business process. If
the workflow engine recognizes messages from or to external subjects (jCPEX!
subjects), these messages are not executed within the runtime anymore, but are
sent to the internal process router (Process Gateway within company A shown in
Figure 19). The usage of process dispatchers enables weak binding to minimize
hard references to other Process Gateways. With the aid of the URI of the
external subject retrieved from the process model, the process router is able to
search for appropriate implementations about this URI throughout the jCPEX!
net. One or more companies are able to "implement" an interface described by
an URI.

A process router is able to ask all known gateways or standalone routers
about possible implementations (bottom left side in Figure 19). These gateways and routers return know implementations and ask themselves other known
routers/gateways about implementations for the given URI. With the aid of this
decentralized approach, all possible implementations can be found within the
jCPEX! net. (in our example company B is found as an implementation of the
given URI).

After this decentralized searching process company A (the customer) and
company B (the travel agency) are able to communicate directly. At first, the
travel agency returns all possible receivers for the process which implements
the given URI. In Figure 18 just one receiver "Order Acceptance" is returned to

the customer. After this step the customer has to select a receiver either manually or by predefined rules (see section 5.7 for details). The workflow engine sends the message with the chosen receiver to his own process router, which communicates with the process router of company B (travel agency). The process router of company B forwards the message to the internal workflow engine and therefore triggers a business process within this company. Company B in turn is able to send an answer directly to company B (without the need of routing with the aid of other process router). Company's A process router forwards this answer message to its own workflow engine in order to continue the internal business process. The message send and receive actions can be implemented by virtue of Web Services. The main value of our approach (in opposite to bare Web Service solutions) is the distributed alignment of process interaction by the definition of Behavioural Interfaces.

By virtue of this approach, also one-to-many (multi-subject) communication is enabled, since there can be two or more companies, which implement a given interface (identified by an URI). Despite communicating with just one other company during process execution, there are also scenarios, where a certain message is sent to a couple of appropriate companies. The concept of a behavioural interface (in opposite to actual implementations of that interface) is the main principle to enable one-to-many communication.

The Gateways are responsible for process routing, process logic, data conversion and message exchange with other Gateways. Further vertical issues are e.g. security (integrity, availability, confidentiality, liability) and access rights issues. The Gateway is both responsible for retrieving all possible implementations for a given URI (either in specific intervals or on demand) and for sending messages to other known Gateways. It is obvious that the Gateway is responsible both for content and communication issues, where communication issues are delegated to the associated network router.

Our subject-oriented workflow engine is first of all qualified for executing cross organisational business processes modelled with the jCPEX! approach. Nevertheless also other workflow engines are able to be used to enable our technique (e.g. by virtue of invoke/receive in BPEL).

5.7   Process Rules

Sometimes rules can be useful either to restrict possible receivers or to select a particular service provider based on conditions like e.g. values from a business object. In our business travel booking process, the initiator of the process wants to select the supplier dependent on the destination of the travel. If the travel destination is within Germany, travel agency A shall be engaged to book the travel. If the destination lies outside of Germany, the booking order is sent to a travel agency platform. If, however, the travel destination is Japan, Tokyo Travel gets the job.

On the other side, receiver rules are able to act like "process firewalls" and reject messages based on different assumptions. E.g. a travel agent could reject all business trip applications coming from outside Europe.

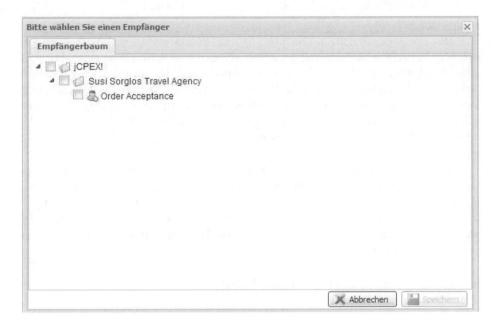

Fig. 18. Receiver selection

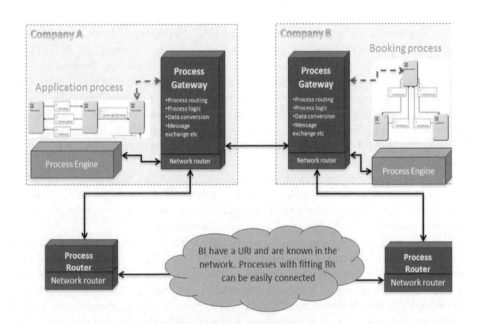

Fig. 19. Process Router Architecture

In summary rules enable lazy binding of cross organisational processes.

Rules are separated from the process model and reside within the process gateway. Therefore a front-end exists to create and edit these rules both at sender and receiver side. All sender rules deposited at the gateway are related to one or more behavioural interfaces. While retrieving all possible implementations for a specific interface an ordering relation between all rules decides which rule is executed first. The rules itself are very generic, so that the decisions can be based on different facts like "content of business object", time, ontology data of implementing organizations, etc..

Each rule is able to restrict the set of possible process receivers (implementation of interfaces). After applying all appropriate rules, the set of remaining implementing organisations is used to extract the receiver tree for displaying it to the message sending user. Figure 17 shows a receiver selection comprising just one implementing organization "Susi Sorglos Travel Agency" and one receiver "Order Acceptance".

6   Conclusions and Future Work

Based on the global objective and derived goals for today's business needs regarding cross-organisational process modelling and execution we deduced several requirements, which have to be fulfilled in order to support these businesses in an effective and efficient way. These requirements were divided into modelling and execution aspects, whereas we want to close the gap between those aspects.

We derived several requirements regarding modelling, like "observable behaviour", sequence of messages, non-relevance of internal behaviour, ease of partner change, multi-recipient communication and role concepts. During runtime our requirements are decentralized execution, identification of partners during runtime and automated partner selection in respect to pre-defined rules.

In the next chapter we evaluated some approaches for cross-organisational process modelling and execution support and observed at modelling level EPC, BPMN 2.0, WS-CDL, Let's Dance and at execution level typical BPEL runtime engines, SAP PI and EDI.

While it has to be stated that some of these approaches have specific strengths in specific areas, none of these are able to meet all of our requirements. It was apparent, that none of the solutions and approaches tries to reduce the gap between modelling semantics and runtimes semantics.

In the last chapter we introduced our jCPEX! solution, which fulfils all requirements we described in the second chapter. The "Subject Oriented" modelling helps to meet the requirements, because this modelling technique already gives the appropriate granularity in order to communicate with other organisations. Therefore the gap between modelling and execution is minimized.

Future work is necessary regarding security and effective search capabilities and appropriate description of organizations with the aid of Ontologies. Most notably Ontologies can be used to map different Business Objects of different companies, our current approach requires to use the same Business Object within a communication. Also the possibility of process capability description is part of future work and affects meta-data description of cross organisational processes models.

References

[1] Allweyer, T.: Kollaborationen, Choreographien und Konversationen in BPMN 2.0 - Erweiterte Konzepte zur Modellierung übergreifender Geschäftsprozesse. Fachhochschule Kaiserslautern (2009)

[2] Barros, A., Dumas, M., ter Hofstede, A.H.M.: Service Interaction Patterns. In: van der Aalst, W.M.P., Benatallah, B., Casati, F., Curbera, F. (eds.) BPM 2005. LNCS, vol. 3649, pp. 302–318. Springer, Heidelberg (2005)

[3] Decker, G., Kirov, M., Zaha, J.M., Dumas, M.: Maestro for Lets Dance: An Environment for Modeling Service Interactions. In: Dustdar, S., Fiadeiro, J.L., Sheth, A.P. (eds.) BPM 2006. LNCS, vol. 4102, Springer, Heidelberg (2006)

[4] Decker, G., Zaha, J.M., Dumas, M.: Execution Semantics for Service Choreographies (2006) (unpublished)

[5] Fleischmann, A.: What is S-BPM Rohrbach (2009)

[6] Grefen, et al.: Internet-Based Support for Process-Oriented Instant Virtual Enterprises. IEEE Internet Computing (2009)

[7] Hoare, C.A.R.: An axiomatic basis for computer programming. Communications of the ACM 12(10), 576–585 (1969)

[8] Mehandjiev, N., Grefen, P.: Dynamic Business Process Formation for Instant Virtual Enterprises. Springer, London (2010)

[9] Milner, R.: Communicating and Mobile Systems - the Pi-Calculus. Cambridge University Press, Cambridge (1999)

[10] Pieper, R., Kouwenhoven, V., Hamminga, S.: Behond the Hype - e-Business Strategy in Leading European Companies. Van Haren Publishing (2001)

[11] Timmers, P.: Electronic Commerce - Strategies and Models for Business-to-Business Trading. John Wiley & Sons, Chichester (1999)

[12] http://en.wikipedia.org/~wiki/Event-driven_process_chain (downloaded July 12, 2010)

[13] Zaha, J.M., Barros, A., Dumas, M., ter Hofstede, A.: Let's dance: A language for service behavior modeling. In: Meersman, R., Tari, Z. (eds.) OTM 2006. LNCS, vol. 4275, pp. 145–162. Springer, Heidelberg (2006)

[14] Ziemann, J., Matheis, T., Freiheit, J.: Modelling of Cross-Organizational Business Processes - Current Methods and Standards. Enterprise Modelling and Information Systems Architectures. 2, 23–31 (2007)

BPM and BPMN as Integrating Concepts in eGovernment - The Swiss eGovernment BPM Ecosystem

Konrad Walser and Marc Schaffroth*

University of Applied Sciences Bern
- Competence Center Public Management & E-Government,
Morgartenstrasse 2a/Postbox 305, 3000 Bern 22, Switzerland
konrad.walser@bfh.ch, marc.schaffroth@isb.admin.ch

Abstract. This article sets out a paradigmatic BPM framework of public administration developed on the basis of a pioneering organisational concept of public administration. In conjunction with the corresponding BPM framework, standardisations have been undertaken, for example with respect to the inventtory of services and for tools and platforms for the documentation of services and processes. Based on the underlying organisational concept, "black boxes" of local service production are combined with "white boxes" of cross-administrative processes. Production processes are set against communication processes with the end clients of the administration. In particular, communication with end clients (distribution) is to be simplified through the separation of production and distribution, with the result that the administrative workload is scaled down. At the same time, services in the production network are agreed on a cross-institutional basis by means of service level agreements.

Keywords: BPM, BPMN, Business Architecture, Enterprise Architecture, New Public Management, Public Services, Service Distribution, Service Production, Process Chains.

1 Introduction

1.1 Problem Definition

Administrations are typically made up of institutions or elements of a state which interact with one another in a collaborative (process-oriented) manner, whereby horizontal, vertical, and interoperable internal and external collaboration is regulated via a formal division of tasks ([18], p. 32 et seq.). The collaboration does not stop at the boundaries of the administration, but may be understood as extending from suppliers right through to the clients of the administration. The collaboration is typically effected via three or more federal levels (principle of federalism) and is contextually defined. The division of labour (principle of

---

* Marc Schaffroth is working for the eGovernment architecture department of the Federal Strategy Unit for IT (FSUIT).

A. Fleischmann et al. (Eds.): S-BPM ONE 2010, CCIS 138, pp. 106–120, 2011.

subsidiarity) determines the work carried out both in and between administrative units. In contrast to the private sector, public administration processes are more strongly determined by legislation, which is in turn based on the constitution. Constitutions themselves set out in detail this principle of subsidiarity in a particular country-specific or government-specific guise.

The topic of business process management is one that is discussed in both theoretical and practical terms in public administration ([1], [5], [6], [7], [8], [9], ([11], [12], [14], [15], [19], [23], [32], [33], [35]). This is based on the electronic support provided to the administration in the context of eGovernment and the modernisation of public administration, which is gaining currency in many administrations as a result of New Public Management approaches ([25], [26]). A question that arises here in relation to business management is how the corresponding process-oriented forms of collaboration are established, mapped in technology ([20]), and thereby supported. The process-oriented nature of administrative action is discussed and partially implemented in Switzerland both at the management level (strategic leadership, guidance, top-down) and by the operating administrative units themselves (execution, bottom-up)[1]. An example of this is the question of electronic business process execution as part of business administration and document management[2]. The BPM and BPMN instrument support in Switzerland is effected through the provision of a free and open-source-based BPM tool (BPM Starter Kit [32] provided by www.ech.ch)[3]. Among others through the incorporation of a web area for BPM Community Building, this facilitates the mapping of the business processes to be documented as well as a discourse on an exchange of BPM illustrations of partly generic administrative processes. Today, there is already a whole range of technical tools available for enabling the implementation of BPM outputs in application development [4][4]. An advantage of the BPM approach is the option of bundling or modularising business processes on the basis of readily available visualisations[5] and making an integrated conceptual working platform available to the different service-producing and -providing areas. This takes place on the basis of the service bundles and service provision procedures aimed at citizens and clients

---

[1] This is initiated at federal level by the Federal Strategy Unit for IT (FSUIT). The FSUIT holds shared responsibility for ICT strategy across the federal government. The FSUIT and other parties both inside and outside the Federal Administration are substantially involved in the service standardisations implemented via the eCH association that are bound up with business processes.

[2] Cf. GEVER, ELAK and DOMEA in the eCH-0073 standard found on http://www.ech.ch/vechweb/page?p−categoryList&site=/standards/nachNummer.

[3] Cf. BPM Object Management Group (www.omg.org) and the BPMN standard http://www.omg.org/spec/BPMN. The BPMN standard has been subsumed into the eCH-0073 standard (documentation of public services and processes).

[4] When transformed to the BPEL (Business Process Execution Language) code, the notation output of the corresponding tools can be used for the technical implementation of business processes in application systems and service-oriented architectures (SOA). This is an explicit goal in Switzerland ([20], [23]).

[5] Cf. the modularised enterprise and application architectures in eGovernment [26].

([18], p. 52 et seq.). Here, the use of BPM in public administration works only if the administration management, the different service-producing units involved, and the units responsible for the technology collaborate closely with one another. They may arrive also at a shared understanding of process-oriented collaboration in the administrative environment[6].

A number of further steps will need to be taken if a process-oriented administration is to be achieved, but an essential extra element is cultural change. This requires a boundary-less and new culture of collaboration while taking into account federal organisation and the subsidiary breakdown of tasks ([18], p. 60 et seq.). The following aspects need to be taken into account in the context of cultural change: organisational culture, employee culture, and business process management culture. Here, cultural change is governed by the primacy of service orientation and the cross-administrative networking of services, processes, distribution structures, and production structures. Technical support for information provision and administrative practices represents a key challenge in this respect, and also harbours potential for the ongoing efficiency-oriented development of public administration. The funds invested in eGovernment and BPM must lead to a qualitative and continual improvement of services as results of processes of the State.

1.2   Objective

The following objectives are pursued in this article: a sample mapping of BPM(N) perspectives in the context of public administration, administration modernisation [17], administration and management from the standpoint of New Public Management [26], management of interoperability, management of modularised administration services, processes and application components, and client orientation together with service orientation. In Switzerland, all these areas are factored in as part of the eGovernment strategy implementation[7] in a BPM framework or BPM ecosystem, which lies at the heart of this article. Independently from the chosen modeling approach, it seems to be important to implement an adequate ecosystem, in which the S-BPM- or Non-S-BPM-approach increases its benefits in an integrated manner.

1.3   Content of Article

The article illustrates also a sub-area and the status of standardisation as part of a federal business process management approach[8]. An evaluation is undertaken

---

[6] Cf. management of culture (of collaboration) ([15], p. 60 et seq.).
[7] Cf. eGovernment strategy Switzerland at
http://www.egovernment.ch/de/grundlagen/strategie.php
(accessible as of 2010-05-09)
[8] Cf. http://www.ech.ch/vechweb/page?p=categoryList&site=/standards/nachNummer as well as the following eCH standards that this sets out: eCH-0049, eCH-0070, eCH0073, eCH-0074, eCH-0096 in the narrower or wider context of business process management.

on the basis of the latest status of existing standardisations and documentation on the topic of BPM and the fleshing out of a BPM framework for Swiss eGovernment. Up until now, the basis of the BPM framework has lacked the conceptual view of Swiss eGovernment, which is now in place thanks to the organisational concept for eGovernment in Switzerland [18]. In addition, the development and differentiation of further development outlooks for standardisations on the basis of BPM and BPMN will be set out, starting with the above-mentioned organisational concept. The following components are then also positioned: a BPM documentation standard valid throughout Switzerland, the associated documentation tool (eCH-0096 BPM Starter Kit [32]), service inventory documentation, and the embedding of the directory of services and prescriptive elements relating to the documentation of public services.

2   BPM and BPMN

2.1   Administrative Issues and BPM / BPMN

BPM is a multi-faceted enterprise function and comprises among other things business process modelling that takes into account various dimensions such as organisational participations, documentation guidelines, the legitimacy of administrative action (modelling of law-making or law application ([3], [21], [22], [28], [29], [30], [34])), the adopting of roles and positions, the use of resources, temporal aspects and the dependencies of administrative action, document exchange and information exchange between the various role-bearers working together in processes, etc. BPM must be viewed and conceived independently of the applications that are typical to public administration, for example electronic business administration. In other words, BPM should not be determined by the application system types that happen to be in circulation. BPMN is a product-neutral notation language for the standardised specialist documentation of business processes.

On the basis of process modelling with BPM tools, new potential areas of discourse arise on the modelled aspects: e.g. with regard to "make or buy" decisions for administrative processes ([18], [27]) or with regard to a professional interface and interoperability management system that is more readily explained and conveyed thanks to process documentation. This might result, for example, in consequences for the application systems affected by the process structures. Viewed in this light, the BPM and BPMN instruments act as intermediary objects or instruments (boundary objects) between business and IT departments, also serving the alignment of business and IT. The operation and usage of BPM instruments represent a core capability of enterprise architecture management in the sense of providing a foundation for the application architecture design. Generally speaking, BPM is still not very widespread as a standard in public administration. Nonetheless, BPM can still be viewed as a de facto standard for process modelling. However, business process management in the context of the cross-administrative networking of services and processes [17] in eGovernment is increasingly and inexorably gaining in significance.

There are two pioneers with respect to the BPM approach in the Swiss administration: the Federal Department of Foreign Affairs FDFA ([11], [24]) and the Federal Office for Agriculture FOAG [16]. BPM on the basis of BPMN is an essential component if cooperation is to be assured both in and across administrative units (cf. [18], p. 21 et. seq. as well as Fig. 1. with respect to this point and the following).

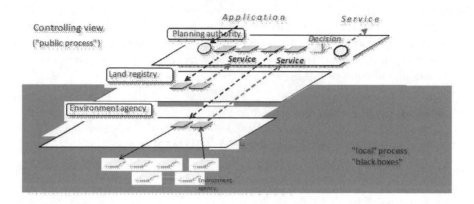

Fig. 1. Coupling of local processes through the exchange of services in cross-organisational administrative procedures ("public process") ([18], p. 33.)

Alongside the discourse on interoperability in the context of eGovernment, which is increasingly gaining importance in the context of enterprise architecture management, documentation techniques for business architecture management are also increasingly gaining in significance. The deployment of BPM in the sphere of business architecture management allows for the possibility of supporting and operating from the business architecture side in equal measure both service-oriented application architecture concepts and traditional component-based concepts. The prerequisites for BPM are considered to be administration strategies and the correspondingly derived central business or production models that are key components to administrations [10]. On the basis of business and production models, the features that exist between in-house and external services of the administration are defined, e.g. as part of service-oriented administrative action on the basis of so-called service inventtories. This has a direct connection to the service-oriented architecture principle as mentioned above [18][9]. Furthermore, it is via BPM and BPMN that the management and manageability of public administration and administrative operations is ensured in a new form as a result (Business and IT alignment). Also conceivable here is the supply of business figures for managing the corresponding business processes. As a result, the measurability of administrative operations becomes possible – where desirable –

---

[9] In the case of Switzerland, for example, this is the Swiss eGoverment strategy, cf.
http://www.egovernment.ch/de/grundlagen/strategie.php
(accessible as of 2010-05-09).

on the basis of business processes and BPM. The process documentation is also used for the training of administration staff in the execution of business. This was a key initial focus of the consular process modelling undertaken by the Federal Department of Foreign Affairs (FDFA), as consular staff change frequently. But process documentation also provides the opportunity to substantiate simplifications of business processes and explain changes through visualisation. Based on BPM reengineering aspects in the public administration context have so far been underemphasised in German-speaking regions.

2.2   Reasons for and Expansion of Standardisation Attempts on the Basis of BPM and BPMN

Standardisation of BPM and BPMN aspects is of particular importance given the federalism principle and the subsidiarity principle. The corresponding BPM and BPMN standardisations also have a significant role to play in the future development of the administration. Between BPM tools too, a certain degree of interoperability is required for the further use of BPM outputs on the basis of BPMN, as a number of different instruments are deployed in Swiss public administration, for example. Also of great importance is the connectivity of business process management to enterprise architecture management if across-the-board structuring – from business process through to ICT system – is to be achieved. The work first begins with the specialist documentation of business processes. The monitoring and controlling of processes are inexorably linked to business process management. Among other things, process controlling should also be enabled through eGovernment und business process management. These controls are typically achieved through indicators of efficiency, effectiveness and outcome, which are typically also addressed in policy evaluations. Thereafter, changes in the organisational structure of the administration may also be required through the active implementation of business process management. The standardisations of BPM, BPMN, and the corresponding instruments and tools play a key role from the perspective of eGovernment in Switzerland. Only by engaging with the corresponding considerations can interoperable cooperation beyond the boundaries of administrative units be achieved, i.e. so that inter-organisational collaboration can be designed on the basis of process inputs and outputs. Through the modelling of business processes, local, federal, and subsidiary divisions of tasks can on the one hand be broken up and on the other be integrated into process chains or process networks across several organisational units. The collaboration between administrative units becomes transparent as a result, both at and between Federal Administration levels. However, as there are no institutional authorities active in the area between the administrative units, a critical role is played by the specification of service level agreements between the administrations involved in the administration process chain, with this also based on the organisational concept for eGovernment in Switzerland [18]. Here, the conditions governing the exchange of services (inter-organisational business process management) in the context of cross-organisational business projects are negotiated, set down, and documented in order to guarantee smooth interaction between the administrative units. It should be borne in mind here that not only should such services be differentiated towards an end client, but government-to-government (or G2G-specific) service catalogues should be drawn up from both a service recipient and service provider perspective[10]. Based on [18], this encompasses service level agreements between recently differentiated distribution and production units, as well as the specification of cooperation parameters. In certain circumstances, the corresponding service level agreements may also be negotiated across several organisational administrative units, e.g. at state or federal level and thereafter generalised in the context of ordinances or laws. Given the non-existence of any intermediaries between federal units (administrative units) that might play a role in the sense of process control as required by [18], BPM and BPMN standards have an even more significant role to play. These must be broad-based and accepted, however. Conceivable options in this interim area include differentiations with respect to public, private, and mixed public-private intermediaries between administrative units and administrative levels, via which intermediary tasks for inter-organisational processes and interoperability might be enabled or facilitated.

3   Deployment Context for BPM in Swiss Public Administration

As part of the implementation of the Swiss eGovernment strategy, a number of recurring problems for designing distribution and production structures and cross-administrative collaboration crop up in a number of prioritised plans[11] as well as in eGovernment projects of the Swiss Confederation, cantons, and communes ([18], p. 6 et seq.). To prevent these questions continually having to be tackled from scratch in an isolated manner, i.e. in the context of projects, an organisational concept for Swiss eGovernment was drawn up in the form of a collective reference framework, which among other things also defines a shared basis of understanding and discussion for local, regional and cross-area organisational structures against the background of business process management (organisational concept [18]). This facilitates the simplified communication of solution concepts and implementations already established in a number of places. In this respect, the organisational concept creates a federal framework. The modernisation objectives of the Swiss eGovernment strategy serve as a starting point here. On this basis, organisation-related structuring potential (or structuring

---

[10] Up until now, no attention has been paid on the issue of administrative service provisioning based on service catalogues and SLA's. But communicative service inventories for the end clients of the administration are also lacking. Each corresponding service of a G2G service catalogue must come with a corresponding service level agreement. As mentioned, the latter may also be concluded on an across-the-board basis, covering all institutions of the administration and the whole country.

[11] Cf. the following URL on the catalogue of prioritised plans for Swiss eGovernment: http://www.egovernment.ch/de/umsetzung/katalog_vorhaben.php (accessible as of 2010-05-09).

obstacles) of a federally structured and networked public administration are substantiated (or eliminated). The idea is for hidden, i.e. unvoiced and implicit "construction principles" that are effective in practice – and which strengthen and reposition client orientation and the client-oriented capability of the public administration – to be brought to light. Only awareness and explicit knowledge of what is done (and how) in public administration on a daily basis can enable the administration to cast a critical spotlight on existing structures and redesign these where appropriate. In the above-mentioned organisational concept, therefore, one of the questions tackled is how to break up administrative structures (often of a "backyard" nature) with fixed modes of organisation and responsibilities that lead to the establishment of closed and non-interoperable systems. In this context, the above-mentioned BPM and BPMN-based approach is the ultimate critical prerequisite. Without encroaching on the sovereign division of tasks or eliminating federal scope for action, the quality of processes, results and structures of public administration can be fundamentally improved in a networked administration. Based on the organisational concept for Swiss eGovernment, which is geared to a specialist audience, a document has emerged that forms the basis for all process-oriented aspects in eGovernment in Switzerland and the corresponding standardisations. The organisational concept provides responses to the following four interrelated questions of eGovernment organisational structure:

- How is a client-oriented stance for public administration achieved?
- How can business processes and services in cross-administrative networks be optimised?
- How can the resources, building blocks, and infrastructures required for the distribution and production of public services be jointly used?
- What culture of collaboration needs to be established? What organisational and specialist capabilities support the administration in the implementation of the new service and process orientation?

3.1 Idiosyncrasies of BPM in the Administrative Environment

In line with version 2.0 of the BPMN standard[12], which envisages the service documentation of cross-organisational cooperation interrelations [2], the following conceptual distinctions appear expedient ([18], p. 34 et seq.):

- In cross-administration procedures, services, processes, and authorities are involved in either a "leading" or "participatory" way. This participation is set down in law.
- A service sought by a client represents the "leading service" in the overarching procedure.

---

[12] Cf. Object Management Group, www.omg.org. Link to the Business Process Modelling Notation (BPMN) standard: http://www.omg.org/spec/BPMN. Version 2.0 of the BPMN standard has the advantage that organisation-related and cross-organisational process views can be illustrated in needs-oriented forms of notation.

- The authority responsible for (and hence "leading") the "leading service" in the process "consumes" the services from the "participating" yet independently executed processes of the other involved authorities.
- As a supplement to "local" service and process documentation, the "public" process describes the shared specialist perspective of the authorities with respect to the unfolding of the cooperative service production, in particular taking into account the aspect of cross-area process controlling, according to which the focus lies on the regulated exchange of mutually agreed services.

Viewed from the production perspective, public services arise through the procedural coupling of nationally assigned sub-services that are consequently to be managed locally to create an "overall product or service". The latter describes the service provided to the client.

3.2 BPM Deployment with Respect to Institutitional Administrative Parameters

The first step is to specify the institutional settings in the administration that are to be reconfigured with respect to the deployment of BPM in eGovernment:

- Internal institutional ("local") processes (cf. Fig. 1): These are processes or process modules which occur in an administrative unit and can be described from an external perspective as "black boxes". Necessarily viewed from outside, however, is the connectivity to intra-institutional ("public") processes in the sense of (G2G) service catalogues with respect to the input-output relations of black boxes.
- Intra-institutional ("public") processes (cf. Fig. 1): Couplings of "local" processes based on service levels or service level agreements. These cross-administrative processes can likewise be documented on the basis of BPMN.

Based on the institutional innovations described here, the aim is then to position BPM as a tool for highlighting the interrelationships in and between different institutional settings. On the one hand, BPM can be used to map internal institutional processes. On the other, BPM can also be used for the inter-organizational definition of collaboration such as in the form of so-called "swim lane" diagrams in which process steps that follow on from one another are assignable to different organisational units. For example, this may be necessary to facilitate the (potentially institutional) interplay between distribution and production, as well as between different units involved in the production process.

3.3 Specification of Standardisations in the BPM Environment in Switzerland

A stand-alone association has been set up for standardisation issues in eGovernment and eHealth in Switzerland: www.eCH.ch. This acts as home to a whole spectrum of predominantly approved standards and tools with direct or indirect reference to BPM and BPMN in the area of business process management:

- eCH-0070 – Inventory of public services in Switzerland: The public services
  provided by the Swiss authorities are registered and maintained in the eGov
  CH inventory of services. This is a component of the documentation on
  business process management for eGovernment in Switzerland (BPM documentation eGov CH). Document eCH-0070 is aimed at business managers,
  business process managers, subject specialists and eGovernment architects.
- eCH-0073 – Service and process descriptions standard for eGovernment in
  Switzerland: The standard sets out guidelines for the standardised specialist
  documentation of public services and processes, and is aimed at business
  managers, business process managers, subject specialists and eGovernment
  architects.
- eCH-0096 – BPM Starter Kit including BPM project guidelines, tool, and
  community platform for the exchange of BPM experiences and the exchange
  of process models: The tool provides practice-oriented support for BPM introduction projects in public administration and facilitates the creation of
  standard-compliant electronic BPM documentation (incl. free provision of a
  BPM application on an open-source basis). The BPM Starter Kit is equally
  appropriate for use by eGovernment implementers and by administration
  managers, process managers and process teams of the public administration, as well as by external service providers[13].

One of the aims of BPM deployment is process integration without media dis-
continuities. Worthy of mention here is the eGovernment project that has been
given priority as part of eGovernment implementation in Switzerland, namely
B1.03, "Standardised inventory and reference database of public services" (reference eGov)[14].

The existing BPM results and standards also need to be positioned in this
context. Project B1.03 also includes the work of the Swiss Federal Chancellery
in classifying BPM(N) standards in a larger BPM framework as a basis for Swiss
eGovernment as set out in Fig. 2. In this framework, differentiation is addressed
at different levels for Swiss eGovernment based on the organisation concept [18]:
eGovernment strategy Switzerland (in Fig. 2 right at the bottom), reference
model eGovernment (based on the organisational concept), eCH BPM guidelines,
eCH BPM tools, eCH BPM results, and BPM repositories. The organisational
concept and the BPM framework differentiate between organisational units for
distribution and those for production. This differentiation has been carried over
into the BPM framework of Swiss eGovernment. As a result, the positioning
of the described BPM-relevant eCH standards and tools as illustrated below
and the organisational concept itself can be undertaken. In addition to the eCH
standards briefly described above, Fig. 2 also refers to other eCH standards and
tools:

---

[13] See download option for the BPM Starter Kit (BPM project guidelines, BPM tool
and other aids) via the following URL: http://www.ech-bpm.ch/de.
[14] Cf. http://www.egovernment.ch/de/umsetzung/katalog_vorhaben.php (accessible
as of 2010-05-10) and http://www.egovernment.ch/dokumente/katalog/E-Gov-
CH_Katalog_2009-05-18_D.pdf (accessible as of 2010-05-07).

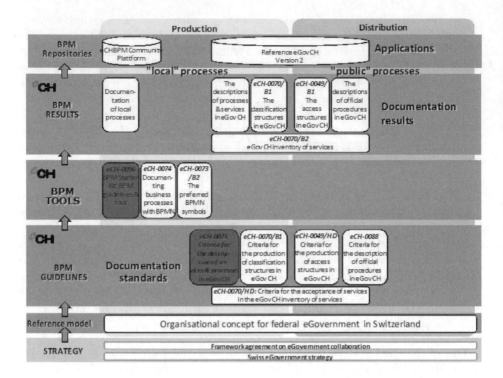

Fig. 2. BPM framework of Swiss eGovernment – BPM ecosystem

- eCH-0074 – Documenting business processes with BPMN: This aid is a component of the reference documentation for the enterprise architecture of Swiss eGovernment. It supports the implementation of the eCH-0073 standard, "Documentation of public services and processes" (documentation standard). It contains a practice-oriented overview and instructions for use of the open Business Process Modelling Notation (BPMN) standard for the graphic mapping of processes. Moreover, it also contains a recommendation on the documentation of business process management of an individual organisation (administrative unit). This aid is aimed at business managers, business process managers, subject experts, and business/ICT architects.
- eCH-0049 – Criteria for the creation of E-Gov CH access structures: The subject catalogues provide a client-friendly breakdown of public services in Swiss eGovernment portals. They simplify and standardise access to public services. The standard is aimed at business managers, business process managers, subject experts and eGovernment architects.
- eCH-0088 – Criteria for the description of official procedures. The client view of administration procedures is illustrated by this standard. The standard is currently undergoing development.

Fig. 2 allows for a positioning of the different BPM-related eCH-standards in the Swiss Government BPM ecosystem. In this ecosystem, interrelationships are mapped for business processes, such as between the Swiss eGovernment strategy and the repositories. In the repositories, business processes are maintained in a structured manner and are substantiated both as documents and illustrations. On the basis of these process illustrations, local and federal process interrelationships can be highlighted while future targeted supplements or enhancements to existing and new standards can be concretised. A concrete distinction can be made in Fig. 2 between documentation standards, tools, results and applications.

4 Summary and Outlook

This article sets out the potential of BPM and BPMN from the perspective of public administration and eGovernment as a best practice example. In addition, and using the Swiss example, it also illustrates what classifications the corresponding standards relevant to business process management in a BPM ecosystem or framework undergo, and what relationships the standards and tools have with one another with respect to federal eGovernment. This includes administration modernisation through the networking of local and public services and processes as well as the distribution and production structures. There is also peripheral exploration of the ramifications, applications, and benefits of the BPM approach in the context of enterprise architecture management, IT governance, and Business IT alignment. As regards an outlook for the future, further development possibilities of BPM implementation in the area of public administration are conceivable as follows: Definition of the output of BPM efforts as a central element of business architecture, linking of the application management area and application architecture to the business architecture on the basis of BPM initiatives, concretisation of interoperability models in and between administrations units, as well as between administrations and external parties including clients, suppliers, stakeholders, etc.

References

[1] Algermissen, L., Instinsky, M., vor der Pähler Holte, N.: Prozessmanagement im Zeichen von Dienstleistungen: Eine methodische Unterstützung zur Umsetzung der Dienst-leistungsrichtlinie. In: Wimmer, M.A., Brinkhoff, U., Kaiser, S., Lück-Schneider, D., Schweighofer, E., Wiebe, A. (eds.) Vernetzte IT für einen effektiven Staat Gemeinsame Fachtagung Verwaltungsinformatik (FTVI) und Fachtagung Rechtsinformatik (FTRI) 2010. LNI, pp. 65–76. GI, Koblenz (2010)
[2] Allweyer, R.: Kollaborationen, Choreographien und Konversationen in BPMN 2.0 Erweiterte Konzepte zur Modellierung übergreifender Geschäftsprozesse, Kaiserslautern (2009)
[3] Alpar, P., Olbrich, S.: Legal Requirements and Modelling of Processes in e-Government. Electronic Journal of e-Government 3(3), 107–116 (2005)
[4] Ami, T., Sommer, R.: Comparison and evaluation of business process modelling and management tools. International Journal of Services and Standards 3, 249–261 (2007)

[5] Becker, J., Algermissen, L., Falk, T.: Prozessorientierte Verwaltungsmodernisierung Prozessmanagement im Zeitalter von E-Government und New Public Management. Springer, Berlin (2009)

[6] Behjat, S.: Wertschöpfungsprozesse der öffentlichen Verwaltungen als Grundlage von e-Government (2003), http://deposit.d-nb.de/cgi-bin/dokserv? idn=970740263\&dok_var=d1\&dok_ext=pdf\&filename=970740-263.pdf (as of August 17, 2009; created 2003)

[7] Brüggemeier, M., Ecker, K.-P., Knopp, M., Schilling, P., Steffens, P., Tschichholz, M.: FRESKO die effiziente Prozessketten-Verbindung zwischen Unternehmen und Verwaltungen. In: Wimmer, M.A., Brinkhoff, U., Kaiscr, S., Lück-Schneider, D., Schweighofer, E., Wiebe, A. (eds.) Proceedings: Vernetzte IT für einen effektiven StaatGemeinsame Fachtagung Verwaltungsinformatik (FTVI) und Fachtagung Rechtsinformatik (FTRI) 2010. LNI, pp. 40–52. GI, Koblenz (2010)

[8] Brüggemeier, M., Schulz, S.: Datenpointernetzwerk: Informationsintegration für eine vernetz arbeitende, transparentere und weniger spürbare Verwaltung der Zukunft. In: Wimmer, M.A., Brinkhoff, U., Kaiser, S., Lück-Schneider, D., Schweighofer, E., Wiebe, A. (eds.) Proceedings: Vernetzte IT für einen effektiven Staat Gemeinsame Fachtagung Ver-waltungsinformatik (FTVI) und Fachtagung Rechtsinformatik (FTRI) 2010. LNI, pp. 17–28. GI, Koblenz (2010)

[9] Charalabidis, Y., Lampathaki, F., Psarras, J.: Combination of Interoperability Registries with Process and Data Management Tools for Governmental Services Transformation. In: Proceedings of the 42nd Hawaii International Conference on System Sciences 2009, pp. 1–10 (2009)

[10] Cherbakova, L., Galambos, G., Harishankar, R., Kalyana, S., Rackham, G.: Impact of service orientation at business level. IBM Systems Journal 44(4), 653–668 (2005)

[11] Corradini, F., Polini, A., Polzonetti, A., Re, B.: Formal Methods to Assess and Improve Public Administration Service Delivery Processes. In: Proceedings of 1st International Conference on Methodologies, Technologies and Tool enabling e-Government MeTTeG 2009, Vigo, Spain (September 2009)

[12] Corradini, F., Hinkelmann, K., Polini, A., Polzonetti, A., Re, B.: C2ST: A Quality Framework to Evaluate E-Government Service Delivery. In: Wimmer, M.A., Scholl, H.J., Janssen, M., Traunmüller, R. (eds.) EGOV 2009. LNCS, vol. 5693, Springer, Heidelberg (2009)

[13] Dahinden, M.: VEKTOR Wirkungsorientierte Ressourcensteuerung im Netz der diplomatischen und konsularischen Vertretungen der Schweiz (2007), http://www.egovernment.bfh.ch/fileadmin/wgs_upload/wirtschaft/ forschun-g_dienstleistungen/pdf/dahinden.pdf (as of September 20, 2009; created August 31, 2007)

[14] Guthier, T., Hünemohr, H.: eBundesrat: Referenzprozess für die elektronische Vorgangsbearbeitung in Bundesratsangelegenheiten. In: Wimmer, M.A., Brinkhoff, U., Kaiser, S., Lück-Schneider, D., Schweighofer, E., Wiebe, A. (eds.) Proceedings: Vernetzte IT für einen effektiven Staat Gemeinsame Fachtagung Verwaltungsinformatik (FTVI) und Fach-tagung Rechtsinformatik (FTRI) 2010. LNI, pp. 88–96. GI, Koblenz (2010)

[15] Hach, H.: Evaluation und Optimierung kommunaler E-Government-Prozee (2005), http://www.zhb-flensburg.de/diert/hach/diertation-hhach-veroeffentlichung. pdf (as of October 24, 2008; created 2006)

[16] Heer, I., Walser, K., Wälti, D., Gehrke, J.: Agrardatenbankenvernetzung in der Schweiz mittels SOA Das IT-Programm ASA2011 (2009), http://141.30.91.15/egov09/files/egovlectures/11/walser-heer.pdf (as of May 10, 2010 created November 23, 2009)

[17] Lenk, K.: Verwaltungsinformatik als Modernisierungschance Strategien, Modelle, Erfahrungen Aufsätze 1988-2003, edition sigma, Berlin (2004)

[18] Lenk, K., Schuppan, T., Schaffroth, M.: Organisationskonzept für das E-Government Schweiz, White Paper eCH and Federal Strategy Unit for IT (2010)

[19] Licker, J., Mayer, A., Kaiser, S.: Modulare Einführung für eine bedarfsorientierte Unterstützung der Vorgangsbearbeitung. In: Wimmer, M.A., Brinkhoff, U., Kaiser, S., Lück-Schneider, D., Schweighofer, E., Wiebe, A. (eds.) Proceedings: Vernetzte IT für einen effektiven Staat Gemeinsame Fachtagung Verwaltungsinformatik (FTVI) und Fachtagung Rechtsinformatik (FTRI) 2010. LNI, pp. 77–87. GI, Koblenz (2010)

[20] Müller, W., Schmid, B., Schroth, C., Janner, T.: Design Rules for Swiss eGovernment Version 1.0, St. Gallen (2009)

[21] Olbrich, S.: Modellierung von Geschäftsprozessen unter Berücksichtigung des Gesetztes Auf dem Weg zur prozessorientierten Gesetzgebung. In: Schweighofer, E., Geist, A., Heindl, G., Szücs, C. (eds.) Komplexitätsgrenzen der Rechtsinformatik, pp. 58–61 (2008), http://irisj.eu/inhalte/IRIS2008.pdf (as of May 9, 2010)

[22] Olbrich, S.: Modellierung gesetzlicher Rahmenbedingungen für E-Government-Prozesse mit Beispielen aus der Metropolregion Rhein-Neckar, Gabler, Wiesbaden (2008)

[23] Petraviciute, Z., Kulvietis, G., Ostasius, E.: SOA Approach for E-service. In: Proceedings of the 5th WSEAS International Conference on E-Activities, Venice, Italy, November 20-22, pp. 127–129 (2006)

[24] Pfister, M., Weber, B.: Geschäftsprozessmanagement im Bereich der konsularischen Aufgaben (2008), http://www.telematiktage.ch/bin/dokserv?idn=970740263x/referate2008/government_verwaltung/Sol._3_CSC.pdf (as of September 20, 2009; created 2008)

[25] Schaffroth, M.: Interoperabilität und Geschäftsprozessmanagement im E-Government. eGov Präsenz 2, 46–49 (2008)

[26] Schedler, K., Proeller, I.: New Public Management, Haupt/UTB, Bern et al (2006)

[27] Schuppan, T.: E-Government Competencies: Looking Beyond Technology. In: Shea, C.M., Garson, G.D. (eds.) Handbook of Public Information Systems, pp. 353–370. CRC Press/Taylor & Francis Group, London (2008)

[28] Schweighofer, E., Geist, A., Heindl, G., Szücs, C.: Komplexitätsgrenzen der Rechtsinformatik (2008), http://irisj.eu/inhalte/IRIS2008.pdf (as of May 9, 2010)

[29] Simon, C., Olbrich, S.: Integration Of Legal Constraints Into Business Process Models. In: Irani, Z. (ed.) Transforming Government: People, Process and Policy, Emerald, Bradford, vol. 2 (2007)

[30] Snellen, A., Zuurmond, I.: From Bureacracy to Infocracy: Management through information architecture. In: Tyler, Z., Snellen, A. (eds.) Beyond BPR in Public Administration Institutional Transformation in an Information Age, pp. 205–224. IOS Press, Amsterdam (1997)

[31] Walser, K., Riedl, R.: Skizzierung transorganisationaler modularer E-Government-Geschäftsarchitekturen (2009), http://www.wirtschaft.bfh.ch/uploads/tx_frppublikationen/Walser_Riedl_Ar-tikel.pdf (as of May 10, 2010)

120   K. Walser and M. Schaffroth

[32] Walser, K., Schaffroth, B.L.: Verwaltungsprozessmanagement unter Ver-wendung des eCH-0096 BPM Starter Kits. In: Wimmer, M.A., Brinkhoff, U., Kaiser, S., Lück-Schneider, D., Schweighofer, E., Wiebe, A. (eds.) Proceedings: Vernetzte IT für einen effektiven Staat Gemeinsame Fachtagung Verwaltungsinformatik (FTVI) und Fachtagung Rechtsinformatik (FTRI) 2010. LNI, pp. 52–64. GI, Koblenz (2010)

[33] Weerakkody, V., Baire, S., Choudrie, J.: E-Government: The Need for Effective Process Management in the Public Sector. In: Proceedings of the 39th Hawaii International Conference on System Sciences 2006, pp. 1–10 (2006)

[34] Wimmer, M., Traunmüller, R.: Geschäftsprozessmodellierung in E-Government: eine Zwischenbilanz, eGov days (2003), www.egov.ocg.at (as of February 6, 2004)

[35] Wolf, P., Jurisch, M., Krcmar, H.: Analyse und Design von Prozessketten. In: Wimmer, M.A., Brinkhoff, U., Kaiser, S., Lück-Schneider, D., Schweighofer, E., Wiebe, A. (eds.) Vernetzte IT für einen effektiven Staat Gemeinsame Fachtagung Verwaltungs-informatik (FTVI) und Fachtagung Rechtsinformatik (FTRI) 2010. LNI, pp. 29–39. GI, Koblenz (2010)

Establishing Conceptual and Functional Links between S-BPM and Business Rules

Alexander Sellner and Erwin Zinser

FH JOANNEUM – University of Applied Sciences
Alte Poststraße 149, 8020 Graz, Austria
{alexander.sellner,erwin.zinser}@fh-joanneum.at

Abstract. Traditional business process management (BPM) and the business rules approach present two different concepts for achieving enterprise agility. Integrating business rules into business processes can leverage business performance in organizational environments which are decision intensive and process driven. The concept of subjectoriented business process modeling (S-BPM) presents a design paradigm quite similar to the business rules concept, both being based on naturally spoken language and both being quite easy to understand. The research presented here aims at establishing conceptual and functional links between S-BPM modeling environments and business rule repositories and presents a prototype for enacting business rules in S-BPM processes.

Keywords: Subjectoriented business process modeling, S-BPM, business rules, natural language modeling.

1 Introduction

The two areas of business rules and business process management have evolved as quite separate fields over the last few years [1]. On the one hand, the concept of business rules is to define non-executable statements which are accessed by business systems following the primary goal of keeping them well separated from business processes [2] [4]. On the other hand, one of the main BPM principles is to establish a seamless business-IT alignment whereas business rules are often implicitly included and, as a result, cannot be separately managed and maintained. The establishment of BPM initiatives has led to standardized notations to model and describe business processes such as the Business Process Modeling Notation (BPMN) or Event Driven Process Chains (EPC) [5] [6]. A quite new approach in this field is subjectoriented Business Process Modeling (S-BPM).

This paper presents a first approach of linking the business rules concept and the S-BPM approach along with a close business-IT alignment. The main motivation for this was that both concepts aim at being understood by non-IT focused people by using the natural language as basis for creating models. The general approach was to technically integrate business rules into S-BPM by establishing a shared business vocabulary.

A. Fleischmann et al. (Eds.): S-BPM ONE 2010, CCIS 138, pp. 121–133, 2011.

A prototype was developed, using the jCOM1 BPM Suite[1] as S-BPM modeling tool and the Rules Composer component of Microsoft BizTalk Server[2] for modeling and integrating business rules. The development of this prototype led to conclusions regarding general requirements for the integration of business rules into business processes and provided insights into the automatic generation of executable code based on Extensible Markup Language (XML) documents.

The paper is structured as follows: Section 2 briefly explains the two concepts of business rules and S-BPM as well as the business process and rules integration. Section 3 describes the general requirements for technically integrating the two concepts. Section 4 describes the procedure for rule enactment within S-BPM. Section 5 presents use cases for the approach. Section 6 gives a brief outlook on future research topics and concludes the paper.

2   Background

2.1   S-BPM Approach

Subject-oriented business process modeling (S-BPM) brings together the two concepts of flow-based and object oriented process descriptions. The idea is to present an easy to learn and reusable approach where real-life processes can be immediately captured in an abstract form [6].

The basic principle of this modeling approach is to describe business processes starting from definitions in the natural language by using the generic elements of human communication, namely subject, predicate, and object. As this modeling language is very easy to understand by non-IT personnel, it can help a lot in order to close the gap between business-oriented and IT-focused departments.

As already revealed by the name, S-BPM focuses on all subjects being involved in a process. The subjects perform interactions which are equivalent to predicates. The use of predicates leads to the need for objects as elements being affected by subject interactions.

Following these principles, the basic grammatical constituents of the sentences "Customer (subject1) sends (predicate1) request (object1)" and "Vendor (subject2) creates (predicate2) offer (object2)" can be separately modeled within the S-BPM approach, before they are combined to a generic process.

Having a look at the jCOM1 BPM suite as the practical application of S-BPM, the basic elements are expressed in the following way:

- Subjects are directly expressed by a modeling shape
- Objects are comparable to message items. They can be represented as so called "business objects" making use of XML schemas for the representation of data structures

[1] jCOM1 S-BPM Suite - http://www.jcom1.com/
[2] Microsoft BizTalk Server - http://www.microsoft.com/biztalk/en/us/default.aspx

– Predicates are defined by the internal behavior of subjects, making use of three basic modeling shapes: send action, receive action, and internal function

Figure 1 displays a sample S-BPM process model and the basic shapes of a subject's internal behavior.

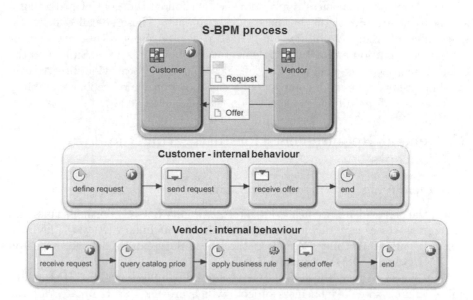

Fig. 1. Sample S-BPM process model

One of the major advantages of the jCOM1 suite is also that process models can be immediately validated meaning they can be executed on a web server. This enables direct workflow integration and facilitates modifications or changes to S-BPM processes.

2.2   Business Rules Approach

In general, business rules are instructions or restrictions triggered by business events. Hence, they represent derivatives from a company's strategy and aim at establishing unified descriptions of a company's business activities in order to achieve customer satisfaction and an effective use of resources [3] [7] [8].

To give an example, a business rule might be defined as follows: If the total amount of an order exceeds $5000, a rebate of 5% is granted. The example illustrates that, similar to the S-BPM approach described above, business rules are also defined using natural language. Again, the idea is to provide a fully

integrated approach for directly executing business directives within IT systems
defined by people with strong business background.

An important prerequisite for the integration of the business rules approach is
the definition of a business vocabulary. Only such an 'organizational dictionary'
can ensure, that common terms used throughout the whole company are used
consistently [9]. For instance the word "customer" might have a totally different
meaning in the marketing (potential client) and in the production department
(e.g. wholesale).

There are many business applications which follow the goal of providing a
seamless integration of the business rules approach. These so-called rules engines offer different possibilities for the setup of a business vocabulary and for
the actual definition and actual implementation of business rules. Similar to the
S-BPM approach, the common goal of rules engines is to provide directly executable business rules to a company's IT environment while keeping the ability
of updating and modifying these rules on the business side [2].

3   General Requirements for Integrating the Two Concepts

3.1   Identifying Intermediary Standards

One of the prerequisites for achieving interoperability between business rules and
business processes is to define a common business vocabulary [10] [11]. Having a
look at the BizTalk Rules Composer, this vocabulary can be defined, based on
the XML Schema (XSD) standard [12].

As a matter of fact, the jCOM1 BPM Suite also makes use of this standard
when defining so-called business objects which are used as templates for the
XSD documents created during the runtime of S-BPM processes. Consequently,
XSD files can be used for defining the business vocabulary and for transferring
it between the two software applications. It doesn't matter whether the XML
Schema is originally defined within the jCOM1 BPM Suite and then imported
into the BizTalk Rules Composer or vice versa.

In addition, an XML Schema created in one of the applications can also be
modified or expanded in the other application. In that case, it will of course be
vital to always make use of the most up-to-date version of the business vocabulary in both applications when performing such changes. A common routine for
keeping the business vocabulary synchronized between all involved applications
would be a further improvement in that context.

The code snippet of an XSD schema used within the prototypical implementation is provided in Figure 2. This sample XML definition is used for creating
forms within the S-BPM process and includes terms based on the organizational
dictionary.

For example, the elements "Amount" and "Article" are used for the request by
the customer and the elements "catalog_price" and "offer_price" are included in
the offer provided by the vendor, together with the previously submitted element
"Request".

```
<complexType name="Request">
  <sequence>
    <element name="Amount" type="int"></element>
    <element name="Article" type="tns:Article"></element>
  </sequence>
</complexType>
<complexType name="Offer">
  <sequence>
    <element name="catalog_price" type="double"/>
    <element name="offer_price" type="double" />
    <element name="Request" type="tns:Request"/>
  </sequence>
</complexType>
```

Fig. 2. Sample XSD code used within the prototype including shared business vocabulary

The element "catalog_price" particularly is a good example for shared business vocabulary as it is also included within a business rule statement. A closer look into such a business rule statement will be provided in Section 3.2.

After defining the business vocabulary, the logical next step is to define business rules in the BizTalk Rules Composer and to establish processes in the jCOM1 BPM Suite design tool jPASS, following the approach of Subject-Oriented business process modeling. The modeling of S-BPM processes and business rules can be followed simultaneously, and the actual link will be established afterwards. Such an independent simultaneous modeling is required because of the divergent conceptual backgrounds of S-BPM and business rules.

On the business rules side, models are established, following the top-down procedure of the Business Motivation Model, where a company's course of action, namely the strategy, is governed by directives in the form of business rules [13].

In contrast, the S-BPM approach can be seen as bottom-up approach, putting together the information of all subjects being involved in a process and connecting these pieces, until the entire process is captured. The output of these two modeling approaches leads to a business rules repository on the one hand and a repository containing subject-oriented business processes on the other hand. These two repositories can be linked as they are based on a common business vocabulary in the form of XML Schema definitions.

The goal of that combination is having business rules which are invoked by subject-oriented business processes during runtime. Assuming that S-BPM processes are executed in the form of applications or web-services, the implementation of business rules means transferring the semantic definitions in which they are expressed into machine-coded language [14]. This raises the question which constraints need to be set up for the definition of business rules, in order to allow such a conversion.

The originally developed and still common method for applying business rules is forward chaining [15] [16]. This method demands, that rules are defined with several conditions on a left hand side leading to actions to be taken that are defined on the right hand side. This approach is closely related to IF/THEN conditions in programming languages. As a result, the conversion from business rules into machine code seems easily feasible, following the method of forward chaining.

3.2   Capabilities of the BizTalk Rules Composer towards Process Integration

Several challenges arise during the implementation of business rules in process-oriented languages [17]. As a result, the following requirements need to be fulfilled by rules engines in order to enable the integration into business processes:

1. Split business rules into modular fragments (business vocabulary, values) and assign a unique identifier to each of these fragments
2. Preserve structure of rules (left hand side (LHS) and right hand side (RHS) according to forward chaining)
3. Represent semantic expressions of rules as mathematical operations

Having a look at the way rules are stored within the BizTalk Rules Composer, it shows that these requirements are only met in a very generic way. Rules are stored and exported in a Microsoft proprietary Business Rules Language (BRL) format (see Figure 2 for sample code). This standard fulfills the above-mentioned implications in the following way:

- Rules are directly stored as binary coded XML documents in the underlying database – therefore access to each individual rule fragment can only be achieved by parsing, modifying and reparsing the respective rule out of the database. This also creates a performance issue as elements cannot be queried on database level.
- BRL addresses each vocabulary element via a unique ID, which complies with the requirements mentioned above. On the other hand, the constant values contained in the XML document have no unique identifier which means a big loss of control when propagating modified versions of rules into organizations' IT environments.
- Having a look at the way how rules are stored in the document, it shows that the principles of the forward chaining are followed by the BRL format. There are <lhs> and <rhs> XML tags for expressing left/right hand side conditions and actions. Unfortunately these elements can also be cascaded into each other which means that, for instance, <rhs> tags can again contain <lhs> and <rhs> sub-structures. It is controversial whether this is an optimal implementation of the forward chaining method, as it again broadens the gap between rules definitions and execution in IT systems.
- A further aspect which can be criticized having a look at the BRL format is that there are also <if>/<then> tags which would represent the actual <lhs>/<rhs> representation. This is a redundant implementation of the forward chaining method.

– The third above-given requirement is also the one where the least regard can be found in BRL. To give an example, the mathematical operator "greater than" is used outside of the <lhs> or <rhs> tags of a rule (usually as child element of the <if> tag). When converting such a rule back to machine-readable code a certain rearrangement of the elements has to be conducted in order to retrieve a mathematical expression. In that specific case, a closer relationship to standards already expressing mathematical expressions – such as MathML - would be preferable [18].

```
<if>
<compare operator="greater than">
  <vocabularylink uri="3f0e9bcc" element="b276a0f4"/>
    <lhs>
    <function>
<xmldocumentmember xmldocumentref="xml_31" type="double"
sideeffects="false">
<field>
*[local-name()='catalog_price' and namespace-
uri()='http://www.example.org/order]
</field>
        <fieldalias>tns:catalog_price</fieldalias>
      </xmldocumentmember>
      </function>
      </lhs>
      <rhs>
        <constant>
          <double>5000</double>
        </constant>
      </rhs>
    </compare>
    </if>
```

Fig. 3. Sample BRL code for the LHS rule statement 'IF catalog_price > 5000'

Summing up, it can be said that the most important prerequisite for establishing a direct link between a rule that has been defined in a rule designer and machine-executable code is an intermediary language fulfilling the criteria of portability and interoperability.

4 Procedure for Rule Enactment within S-BPM

The final step towards the integration of the business rules repository and the jCOM1 suite was to develop an approach to invoke those rules during process runtime.

Initial technical attempts had shown that hard-coded rules could be executed during runtime by making use of so-called "refinements". A refinement can basically be seen as a Java code snippet which can be placed at a certain point of the internal behavior of subjects modeled in S-BPM. These first efforts of hard-coding business rules as IF-THEN statements also revealed the challenges towards an actual business rule implementation as well as further possibilities for such an enactment.

Hard-coded, static implementations of business rules are not applicable when defining flexible business processes along the goal of enterprise agility [4]. In order to reach this goal, the following technical action alternatives were discovered:

1. Providing the rules as web service and making calls for possible changes during runtime. Providing a service layer for communication between the rule repository and the S-BPM processes was identified as the most viable way for a thorough business rule enactment based on a BPM reference architecture [17] [19] . As it turned out that little support was provided by both technical environments – the BizTalk Business Rules Engine as well as the jCOM1 Suite, this approach could not be enacted within the prototype. Among many other challenges, the main problems identified were the mix of Java and .NET technology as well as the general design of the database where the rules were stored by the BizTalk Rules composer. Simple queries to this database were not possible due to the fact, that rules were stored in plain XML format, requiring a constant data conversion when being run as web service.

2. Pull approach with code snippets. Based on updates on the database where the business rules are stored, every time such a change is detected a dynamic generation of code snippets occurs having direct impact on the process at runtime. A sample for this approach can be identified having a look at Visual Rules toolkit[3]. The fact that refinements keep being instantiated as soon as an S-BPM process is being run on the web server turned out to be a dead end, regarding the prototypical implementation.

3. Semi-automatic approach of providing static constructs of rules, making queries for updated values during runtime. The most feasible approach regarding the rule enactment within the prototype was to create code snippets with a general structure of the rules, based on the BRL definition and to separate dynamic parts of the rules such as definition names and actual values from this structure, making it possible to have dynamic database queries for modifications to these parts.

After investigating these different technical implementation alternatives the semi-automatic approach for enacting rules was identified and carried out because of the very little support for web service calls and due to the technical

---

[3] http://www.visual-rules.com

restrictions for executing dynamically compiled code during runtime of S-BPM processes,.

This approach can be seen as a bit disadvantageous because being bound to static rule constructs is accompanied with a certain loss of flexibility regarding a seamless business rule enactment. On the other hand, assuming that changes to the generic structure of business rules occur rather infrequently after their initial definition, the chosen method still leads to the required applicability. A high extend of practicability is still provided as flexible changes to values of rules, such as price limits and sizes of discounts are still possible.

A great improvement in terms of usability within the prototype was made by using the concept of refinement templates provided by the jCOM1 BPM suite. These refinement templates automatically generate code based on certain templates. Another advantage is that a refinement template can provide a graphical user interface which means that users never actually come in touch with any program code. Regarding the prototype, refinement templates were used to generate dynamic code based on rule definitions within the business rule repository. A sample for the S-BPM integration of a business rule within a subject's internal behavior is shown in Figure 4.

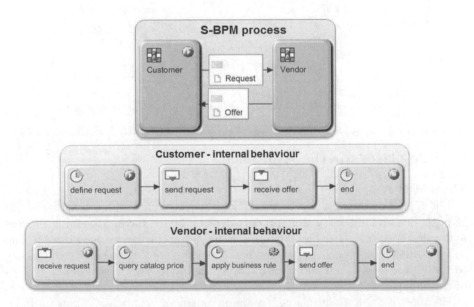

Fig. 4. Internal behavior of S-BPM process with integrated business rule

Summing up, the complete approach for enacting business rules within the jCOM1 suite is successfully applied according to the following steps (also see Figure 5):

1. Establish business vocabulary (XML schema) either in the Business rules composer or in jCOM1 suite.
2. Define business rules (2a) and S-BPM processes (2b) based on the common business vocabulary.
3. Export business rules as BRL XML file.
4. Place business rules at respective positions within the internal behavior of S-BPM processes using refinement templates for automatic code generation.
5. Upload S-BPM processes together with automatically compiled code of rules to web server for execution.
6. During process runtime queries to the rule database are made each time a new instance of an S-BPM process is created – as a result, any modification to business rules within the business rules composer is immediately reflected within running processes.

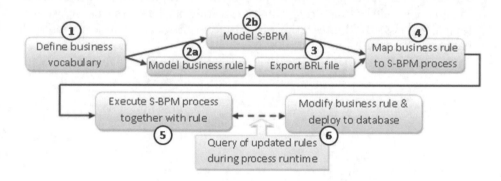

Fig. 5. Procedure for enacting business rules in S-BPM processes

5   Use Cases for the Approach

The practical applicability of the prototypical implementation described above can be expressed the best way by thinking of a company running a business which is both decision intensive and process driven, hence having business process and rule repositories [2] [20]. Being able to define processes according to the subjectoriented approach and adding business rules stored in a central repository to these processes would add a lot of transparency to the to the inner activities of this company.

Because of an initially defined common business vocabulary allowing independent modeling of business processes and rules, it would for instance become possible to have a team of business analysts establishing the rule repository and a team of business process subject matter experts creating S-BPM models. When thinking of the bottom-up approach of S-BPM, the processes modeling could also be performed collaboratively, by putting together individual definitions of each subject being involved in the process.

Regarding the need for initial training when introducing the two concepts, such efforts will be relatively low in comparison to other concepts of process modeling and decision support, as both the business rules approach as well as the subjectoriented business process modeling aim at being quickly understandable. The simple adoption of the concepts was proved in educational background, where modeling with the jCOM1 Suite could be explained to students within two lab exercises whereas the use of the BizTalk rule components was also easily delivered.

Another big advantage of the concepts is that although there is a direct connection between business and IT, there is still a clear separation of the layers from a technical point of view. This adds a lot of dynamic when looking at possible scenarios for implementation. Basically, it will be possible to clearly separate data, business logic and presentation layers, in accordance to the principles of Service Oriented Architectures (SOA) [4].

It will also be possible to either move the layers individually or the full scenario into a cloud computing environment in order to achieve very scalable workflows [21]. The full control of both processes and business rules will still be in the hand of the respective company as well as the decision to deploy changes to the whole business and transaction logic.

Having a look at the currently ongoing heavy debate in relation to data security within the cloud, it is event thinkable that the data provision is being performed by the organization's own IT infrastructure thus only making it possible not to expose critical business data but only to make polls to secured data resources during process runtime. This can be compared to running an enterprise service bus which is independent from the cloud [4].

6   Related Work

A lot of related work can be found within the area of business process and rule integration covering approaches such as the composition of Web services [17], a deployment of rules within SOA using Event Propagation Chains, Business Process Execution Language and the ARIS framework [11] and the use of reactive rules in Complex Event Processing [22].

Further related work investigates the relationships between business process and rule modeling languages [23], the limitations of business rule modeling [24] and shortcomings of BPM languages [25].

To the best of our knowledge, there is no approach so far focusing on independent modeling of business processes and rules based on the natural language. Within the area of business rule management, the Semantics of Business Vocabulary and Business Rules standard [26] uses controlled natural languages for establishing rules [27]. A similar approach can be identified within the BPM domain, having a look at Semantic Business Process Management which focuses on semantic descriptions of business processes from a management perspective [28].

7   Conclusion

The prototype described in this paper has proved the general feasibility of combining the S-BPM concept provided by the jCOM1 suite and the business rules approach using the Microsoft BizTalk Rules Composer. Future research will aim at achieving an even closer integration of the two components and to investigate possibilities of running the scenario within cloud computing environments.

That way, it will be possible to provide the best of both approaches - S-BPM and business rules - to different business environments with different options regarding the degree of system independence and scalability.

References

[1] Harmon, P.: Business Rules and Business Processes. Business Process Trends, http://www.bptrends.com/ (accessed 2009)
[2] von Halle, B., Goldberg, L.: The Business Rule Revolution. Happy About, Silicon Valley (2006)
[3] Rosen, M., Lublinsky, B., Smith, K., Balcer, M.: Applied SOA. John Wiley and Sons, New York (2008)
[4] (OMG), O. BPMN 1.2., http://www.omg.org/spec/BPMN/1.2/ (accessed 2009)
[5] Keller, N.: Scheer Semantische Prozemodellierung auf der Grundlage Ereignisgesteuerter Prozeketten (EPK) Verffentlichungen des Instituts fr Wirtschaftsinformatik(Hcft 89) (1992)
[6] Schmidt, W., Fleischmann, A., Gilbert, O.: Subjektorientiertes Geschftsprozessmanagement Praxis der Wirtschaftsinformatik (2009)
[7] Schacher, M., Grssle, P.: Agile Unternehmen durch Business Rules. Springer, Berlin (2006)
[8] Morgan, T.: Business Rules and Information Systems. Addison-Wesley, Indianapolis (2002)
[9] Ross, R.: Business Rule Concepts: Getting to the Point of Knowledge Business Rule Solutions (2009)
[10] Demey, J., Jarrar, M., Meersman, R.: A Markup Language for ORM Business Rules. In: Proceedings of the International Workshop on Rule Markup Languages for Business Rules on the Semantic Web Sardinia (2002)
[11] El Kharbili, M., Keil, T.: Bringing Agility to Business Process Management: Rules Deployment in SOA. Emerging Web Services Technology, III, 157–170 (2010)
[12] (W3C), W. XML Schema 1.1 Standard, http://www.w3.org/XML/Schema.html (accessed 2004)
[13] Business Rules Group The Business Motivation Model - Business Governance in a Volatile World (2007)
[14] Frankel, D.: Model driven architecture. Wiley, Chichester (2003)
[15] Hermans, L., van Stokkum, W.: How business rules should be modeled and implemented in OO. In: Demeyer, S., Dannenberg, R.B. (eds.) ECOOP 1998 Workshops. LNCS, vol. 1543, pp. 211–213. Springer, Heidelberg (1998)
[16] Linehan, M.H.: SBVR use cases. In: Bassiliades, N., Governatori, G., Paschke, A. (eds.) RuleML 2008. LNCS, vol. 5321, pp. 182–196. Springer, Heidelberg (2008)
[17] Charfi, A., Mezini, M.: Hybrid Web Service Composition: Business Processes Meet Business Rules. In: Proceedings of the 2nd International Conference on Service Oriented Computing, pp. 30–38 (2004)

[18] Boley, H., Tabet, S., Wagner, G.: Design Rationale of RuleML: A Markup Language for Semantic Web Rules. In: International Semantic Web Working Symposium (2001)

[19] Havey, M.: Essential Business Process Modeling. O'Reilly, Sebastopol (2005)

[20] zur Muehlen, M., Indulska, M., Kittel, K. Towards Integrated Modeling of Business Processes and Business Rules. In: 19th Australasian Conference on Information Systems (2008)

[21] Hoheisel, A., Dollmann, T., Fellmann, M.: EPK-Modellen in ausfhrbare Grid- und Cloud-Prozesse. 8. In: Workshop der Gesellschaft fr Informatik e.V (GI) und Treffen ihres Arbeitskreises Geschftsprozessmanagement mit Ereignisgesteuerten Prozessketten (2009)

[22] Luckham, D.: The Power of Events - An Introduction to Complex Event Processing in Distributed Enterprise Systems. Pearson Education, Boston (2002)

[23] zur Muehlen, M., Indulska, M.: Modeling languages for business processes and business rules: A representational analysis. Information Systems 35(4), 379–390 (2009)

[24] Green, P., Rosemann, M.: Perceived Ontological Weakness of Process Modelling Techniques: Further Evidence (2002)

[25] Rosemann, M., Recker, J., Indulska, M., Green, P.: A Study of the Evolution of the Representational Capabilities of Process Modeling Grammars (2006)

[26] (OMG), O. M. G. Semantics of Business Vocabulary and Business Rules, http://www.omg.org/spec/SBVR/1.0/ (accessed 2008)

[27] Spreeuwenberg, S., Healy, K.: SBVR's approach to controlled natural language (2010)

[28] Hepp, M., Leymann, F., Domingue, J., Wahler, A., Wahler, F.D.: Semantic Business Process Management: A Vision Towards Using Semantic Web Services for Business Process Management (2005)

Using Multi-subjects for Process Synchronization on Different Abstraction Levels

Jörg Rodenhagen[1] and Florian Strecker[2]

[1] Acando GmbH, Millerntorplatz 1, 20359 Hamburg, Germany
[2] Metasonic AG, Münchner Str. 29 - Hettenshausen, 85276 Pfaffenhofen, Germany
joerg.rodenhagen@acando.de,
florian.strecker@metasonic.de

Abstract. For business process design, analysis, and optimizing purposes, a couple of modeling techniques is available. To construct process models that provide a behavior congruent to corresponding complex real world processes, a comprehensive set of control flow constructs and a strong semantics are required. Especially in the logistics context there are numerous examples where process modeling and synchronization on different abstraction levels with multiple object relations and as consequence multiple process instance handling are required. Typical situations are sketched and challenges for process modeling are specified. While the first generation of imperative process modeling techniques (as the EPC) is mostly used to sketch a process with simple constructs, modern process modeling techniques provide more expressiveness to specify real process behavior. In this article we show how the innovative Subjectoriented BPM (S-BPM) and its Multi-Subjects as advanced modeling concept are used to handle such situations. Additionally, some recommendations for implementation using the S-BPM Suite are given.

Keywords: S-BPM, Modeling Techniques, Control Flow, Multiple Instances.

1 Introduction

For business process design, analysis, and optimizing purposes, various methods, modeling techniques, and tools are available[1]. Traditionally, imperative modeling techniques as the "Event-driven Process Chain" (EPC) from Scheer et al. [6], [7] or the "Business Process Modeling Notation" (BPMN) [8], [9] are used, following the interpretation of a process as a predefined sequence of tasks. Additionally the Unified Modeling Language (UML) [23] is established as modeling technique for an Object Oriented approach, although the Activity Diagram for process flow specification follow the imperative paradigm, either. An innovative approach defines the Subjectoriented BPM (S-BPM), where business processes

---

[1] See e.g. [1], [2], [3], [4], [5] as BPM standard literature, www.bptrends.com, www.bpminstitute.org, www.bpmenterprise.com as leading BPM communities (in English), or www.BPM-Netzwerk.de (in German).

A. Fleischmann et al. (Eds.): S-BPM ONE 2010, CCIS 138, pp. 134–162, 2011.
© Springer-Verlag Berlin Heidelberg 2011

are interpreted as either the communication between a defined number of actors (Subjects) or as the internal behavior of these actors.

In practice, business processes – especially the core processes of a company – regularly describe the end-to-end-view of the business "from the customer to the customer". Such a process starts with a customer triggered event, as e.g. the notification of an incident or the placement of a customer order. It usually ends with the required result for the customer, e.g. with the resolved incident or the delivered goods. Thus, in numerous situations a business process can be interpreted as the description of the lifecycle of a central object within the defined scope, from the entrance of the object into the considered scope to its completion [10], p. 98 ff. In the IT Service Management context, the Incident Management process describes the lifecycle of the central object Incident, starting with its notification in the call center by the customer, its identification, logging, categorization, prioritization and so on until its resolution and recovery and its closure [11], Figure 4.2 Incident Management process flow. The typical order process is similar; it defines the lifecycle of the central object Customer Order within the considered scope and starts with the reception of the order, followed by its registration, the availability check of the ordered goods, its consignment, and ends with the delivery of the ordered goods to the customer (Figure 1).

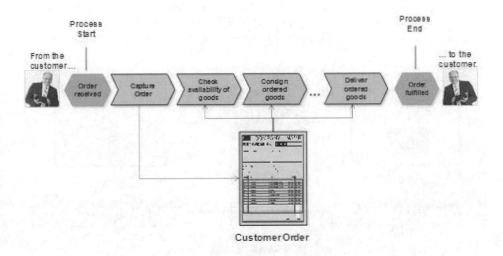

Fig. 1. Order Process

In a detailed consideration such objects are more complex than they appear on the top level; frequently they are composed by or are in complex relationships with other objects. For example, an Order is composed of an Order Header and a set of Order Positions (Figure 2), with complex relations to the surrounding objects product, consignment, or shipment. An incident refers to a couple of IT components that might be dropped out. However, in the corresponding data

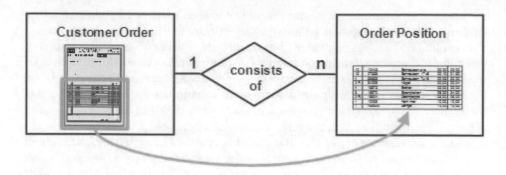

Fig. 2. 1:n-Relationship between Customer Order and Order Position

model (or class diagram, respectively) regularly we find 1:n-object compositions and 1:n-/n:m-relationships with other objects.

Following the interpretation of a business process as a specification of an object's lifecycle, in such situations not just the lifecycle of the central object is to be considered, but the lifecycle of the sub-objects or referenced objects, either. In our example, there is one process that describes the lifecycle of the Order and another process that defines the Order Position lifecycle. According to the 1:n-relationship of the objects in the data model or class diagram there is an analogous 1:n-relationship between the corresponding processes (Figure 3).

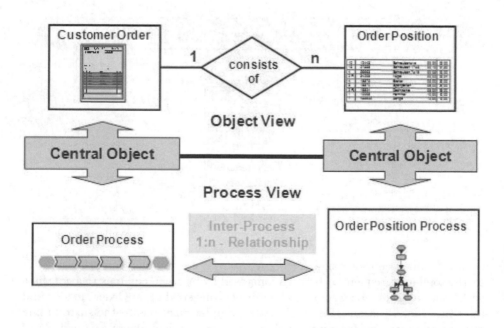

Fig. 3. 1:n-Relationships on Object and Process Level (see [10], p. 99)

In our Order Process the availability of the ordered goods will be checked as soon as the incoming order is captured. If the goods are available, the order can be fulfilled immediately. If not, the missing goods are to be purchased or produced. In the Order Process the order will be split into the Order Header and the n Order Positions. Each Order Position will be handed over to the Order Position Process. In consequence, n instances of this process are running concurrently. When all n process instances finished their execution – that means, to each order position a statement is given if the ordered goods are available or not – the process control will be returned to the Order Process. The Order Process continues at the Order object level and gives a feedback to the customer (Figure 4).

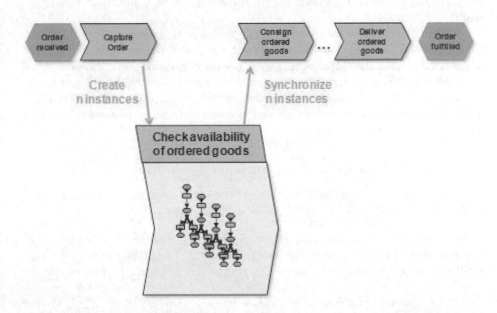

Fig. 4. Generation and synchronization of multiple process instances

For such situations, a formal construct is required to express the synchronization of processes on different abstraction levels with an 1:n-relationship. This kind of synchronization of one master process with n instances of a dependent process is known as "multi-instancing".

The situation sketched in this example is applicable for a couple of similar situations, especially in the logistics context. Maybe there is a container with n euro pallets, each containing m cardboard boxes, and each one containing p articles. Another example is the split-up of several customer orders and their consignment to shipments. However, in all sketched situations the challenge is to express 1:n-process synchronizations on different abstraction levels by adequate control flow patterns correctly and consistently, supported by an BPM

Suite implementation (e.g. modeling environment, execution environment, and business rule composer).

2 Requirements for the Business Process Model Design

To be able to express multi-instancing in process models, some additional control concepts beyond the traditional basic concepts (Sequence, Parallel Split, Synchronization, Exclusive Choice, and Simple Merge, see [12]) are required. In detail, special control concepts are necessary for the generation of multi process instances on the one hand and for the synchronization of a number of concurrently running process instances on the other hand. Both the process modeling technique and the process design and runtime environment must sup-port these additional concepts.

To identify adequate control flow concepts for such multi instance handling, we refer to the Control Flow Patterns of van der Aalst and his team in [13], [20]. They defined a number of patterns for expressive control flow specifications with well-defined semantics. On their Website [12] for each Control Flow Pattern the authors offer a textual description, implementation examples, evaluation criteria, a product evaluation, an executable flash model to visualize the behavior of that pattern, and more.

2.1 Control Patterns for Multi-instance Generation

For the generation of the multiple Order Position Process instances within the Order Process execution, we make some assumptions:

A1. Variable number n of Order Positions. The number of Order Positions (marked as n) can vary from order to order. Thus, the number of Order Position Process instances to be generated is not known at the process design time.

A2. A priori runtime knowledge about the number n of Order Positions. As soon as the Order Process execution started (i.e. a new order was placed by the customer) the number n of Order Positions is known. Thus, the number of Order Position Process instances to be generated is known at the process runtime before decomposing the order into its positions.

A3. Order change on the fly during order processing. An Order Position can be added during the execution of the Order Process, i.e. the customer wants to change his order after the order processing has been started. In this case, instances of the Order Position Process might be added while other instances are already running.

For these assumptions the following Control Flow Patterns are matching:

Pattern 12 "Multiple Instances without Synchronization" as in [15]. "Within a given process instance, multiple instances of a task can be created. These instances are independent of each other and run concurrently. There is no requirement to synchronize them upon completion. Each of the instances of the multiple instance task that are created must execute within the context of the process instance from which they were started (i.e. they must share the same case identifier and have access to the same data elements) and each of them must execute independently from and without reference to the task that started them."

Pattern 14 "Multiple Instances with a priori Run-Time Knowledge" as in [16]. "Within a given process instance, multiple instances of a task can be created. The required number of instances may depend on a number of runtime factors, including state data, resource availability and inter-process communications, but is known before the task instances must be created. Once initiated, these in-stances are independent of each other and run concurrently. It is necessary to synchronize the instances at completion before any subsequent tasks can be triggered."

Pattern 15: "Multiple Instances without a priori Run-Time Knowledge" as in [17]. "Within a given process instance, multiple instances of a task can be created. The required number of instances may depend on a number of runtime factors, including state data, resource availability and inter-process communications and is not known until the final instance has completed. Once initiated, these in-stances are independent of each other and run concurrently. At any time, whilst instances are running, it is possible for additional instances to be initiated. It is necessary to synchronize the instances at completion before any subsequent tasks can be triggered."

Patterns 14 and 15 support the assumptions A1 and A2. They expect a synchronization (here: termination) of all generated n process instances at a later time. In our example, all instances of the Order Position Process must be terminated before the superior Order Process can terminate, either. We have to confirm the availability status for all order positions before we can give the customer a commitment to the entire order acceptance. If assumption A3 holds additionally, only pattern 15 is the matching control flow construct.

In other contexts, a synchronization of the n process instances at a later time is not required. Maybe the process specification does not contain a previous availability check for each order position. In this case all available goods can be assigned directly to shipments. Therefore, Pattern 12 is applicable, implementing a process dispatcher that just distributes all ordered goods to shipments. On the other hand it is usual to initiate the bill process after shipping all goods requested in the customer order. In this case multiple instance synchronization is required at a later time after order fulfillment but before billing. We see, it depends on the de-fined scope which pattern is applicable in concrete situations.

Generally, there are two options for the process instance generation (see detail specification of e.g. [15]):

Sequential generation. The Order Position Process instance generation task runs within a loop, thus the n process instances are created sequentially.

Concurrent generation. All n Order Position Process instances are generated simultaneously.

2.2   Control Patterns for Multi-instance Synchronization

In contrast to the introducing example we assume now that not only the availability check will be performed on the Order Position level. Also the consignment
and shipment should be possible for each order position individually. If partial
shipping is useful depends on the order. When the ordered good is a multi-part
product where the parts cannot be used separately (as an IKEA cupboard construction kit), partial shipment of single positions does not make sense. In the
case that the order positions are usable separately (as an order of some books
that can be read in an arbitrary order), partial shipping can be offered as special customer service to deliver the first book as soon as it is available, see e.g.
www.amazon.com. Without partial shipment, the shipping process has to wait
until the last position has been consigned. Figure 5 illustrates the advantage of
a partial shipment in two terms where the first term contains five of the ordered
nine goods and is delivered at the half of the overall delivery time.

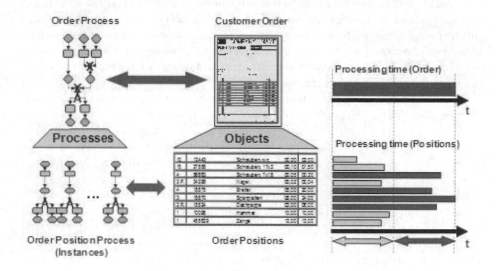

Fig. 5. Full versus partial order shipping

For the synchronization of the Order Position processes some variants are
imaginable:

V1. Only complete shipment. All order positions must be consigned before
the order will be shipped as an inseparable unit. Therefore, all running instances
of the subordinated Order Position Process must be terminated and synchronized
before.

V2. Partial shipment "n of m". Partial shipment is possible when a sufficient number n of all m Order Positions terminated, so partial shipment makes
sense from the logistic and the economic point of view.

V3. Partial shipment with time trigger. Another alternative is the shipment of all order positions that are ready at a defined timestamp. All remaining order positions that need more time for their consignment will be delivered with the next shipment. This timestamp can be either fixed (e.g. always two weeks after order entrance) or set dy-namically by the user.

Variant V1 is covered by Pattern 14 "Multiple Instances with a priori Run-Time Knowledge", either (description see above). Variants V2 and V3 are supported by Pattern 36 "Dynamic Partial Join for Multiple Instances" as in [18]: "Within a given process instance, multiple concurrent instances of a task can be created. The required number of instances may depend on a number of runtime factors, including state data, resource availability and inter-process communications and is not known until the final instance has completed. At any time, whilst instances are running, it is possible for additional instances to be initiated providing the ability to do so had not been disabled. A completion condition is specified which is evaluated each time an instance of the task completes. Once the completion condition evaluates to true, the next task in the process is triggered. Subsequent completions of the remaining task instances are inconsequential and no new instances can be created."

We interpret the completion condition as configurable as "n of m" or with a time trigger.

3   Support of the Requirements by Process Modeling Techniques

In this section we first have a look if the most popular process modeling techniques support the required control flow patterns. In [13], [20] van der Aalst et al. evaluated the EPC, BPMN Version 1.0, and the UML 2.0 Activity Diagrams. In later works they evaluated UML 2.0 Activity Diagrams ([19], [20], and [21]) in detail. Table 1 gives an overview over the result.

To be able to appraise the expressiveness of the evaluated process modeling technique we have to consider the historical background, the target groups, and the modeling purposes.

In the first wave, from the beginning up to the end of the 1990ies, most process models (better: process pictures) were used to document simple "Process Chains", i.e. static sequences of activities to be performed "step-by-step". The first enhancements, as in the early EPC definition and implementations in the mid 1990ies, encompass concepts for splitting and synchronizing processes into (sub-) processes on different process path (AND-Split, AND-Join), to continue a process on exactly one / one or more process path (XOR-Split and OR-Split), and to merge several processes to a common process path again (XOR-Join and

---

[2] In [10] a loop is defined that sequentially generates multiple instances of the subprocess. This construct follows the EPC syntax rules but violates the statement of Scheer et al that at each time on each process path no more than one process map (or process instance, respectively) can be executed. It is an indicator that there is no multi instancing concept supported by the EPC.

Table 1. Control flow pattern support by selected process modeling techniques (see [13], [20], [19], [20], [21])

CF Pattern	EPC (as implemented in ARIS Toolset V6.2)	BPMN 1.0	UML 2.0 (Activity Diagram)
Pattern 12: Multiple Instances without Synchronization	Not supported. There is no explicit notion of instances and there is no notation for interprocess connections. [2]	Supported via multiple instance task with MI Flow Condition attribute set to none.	Supported by spawning off new activity instances in a loop.
Pattern 14: Multiple Instances with a priori Run-Time Knowledge	Not supported	Supported via multiple instance task with MI Condition attribute set at run-time to the actual number of instances required.	Supported through the use of the Expansion Region construct.
Pattern 15: Multiple Instances without a priori Run-Time Knowledge	Not supported	Not supported. There is no means of adding further instances to a multiple instance task once started.	Not supported. No means of adding additional activity instances after commencement.
Pattern 36: Dynamic Partial Join for Multiple Instances	Not supported	There is no ability to dynamically add instances to an multiple instance activity.	Not supported. A MI activity can only complete when all N instances specified in the Expansion Region have completed.

OR-Join). The main purpose of such process models was to get more transparency in a hidden world and to ensure a common understanding how the collaborative work should be done. There-fore the processes just needed to be sketched, sometimes enriched with verbal explanations or textual comments; a formal specification was not required. For this purposes semi-formal process modeling techniques with operational semantics – as the EPC – seemed to be sufficient.

In the next wave, beginning at the start of the 21th century, the same process models were (re-)used for process analysis to identify and localize process performance problems. The analysis results served as decision base for process optimizing projects. For such purposes the requirements dedicated to the process modelers and the modeling technique are much higher. On the one hand, the process models must be realistic specifications, e.g. the process model behavior must be congruent to the behavior of the corresponding real world processes. On the other hand we need methods and process modeling techniques that provide the required expressiveness including concepts, syntactical constructs, and a well-defined semantics. For the process model validation (i.e. the comparison between model and reality) a couple of techniques as simulation or process walkthrough are available. In contrast, the model verification (i.e. the check of syntax violation) results are reliable with restrictions. Here multi instancing constructs are required to express the concurrently running process instances correctly. But missing concepts and control structures will not be detected by the syntax checker.

In practice, we regularly find one of the following situations:

1. Either the process modelers do not have the required formal background. They are more process painters than process modelers. Thus, they are not able to differentiate between single and multi instancing, between the split and synchronization of different processes (AND-split and AND-Join) in comparison with the synchronization of concurrently running instances of the same process. In this case the modeler continues painting process pictures as usual.

2. The process modeler has the formal background. He knows about the advanced requirements, but is forced to continue modeling with the given environment. In numerous situations companies invested a lot in the first generation of process modeling techniques and tools (as EPC) and are not eager to invest again with all effort of remodeling or model transformation. In this case the modeler tries to express the reality as good as possible with the available means. If there is no control construct to express the simultaneous generation of process instances, he alternatively uses a loop that generates the process instances sequentially [10].

3. The process modeler replaces the existing modeling environment with a better one that provides the required expressiveness. We are convinced that option 3 is the most suitable and suggest the S-BPM as method and modeling technique.

4   Design and Execution of Multiple Process Instances with the S-BPM Method

Apart from the well-known methods in business process modeling (see section 3), there is the S-BPM concept. S-BPM is a subject-oriented approach, using only 5 different symbols. S-BPM is an application of the PASS-concept ([22]) on business process modeling.

4.1   A Short Method Overview

The basic concept behind S-BPM[3] is to split a process model into two layers or views: The communication view depicts all participants of a process and shows

---

[3] Resp. its description scheme "PASS" (parallel activities specification scheme).

the different communication-channels between them. Each participant is represented as a "subject". Therefore, the process basically consists of the structured communication between its participants. This structured communication neither includes a time-frame (it is not required to send messages in a predefined order), nor a condition regarding the number of messages to send (it is possible to send a message if a communication-channel has been defined; this message can be sent once or multiple times, or not at all in an instance of the process). See Figure 6 for a simple example.

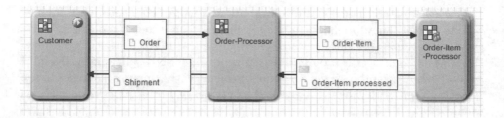

Fig. 6. Communication View of an Order-Process. Legend: The shadowed boxes represent subjects, the arrows in connection with the un-shadowed boxes contain the names of the messages which can be exchanged between the subjects. The box on the right represents a so-called "multi-subject" – this is an array of subjects, each with identical behaviour.

The second part of an S-BPM process definition is the internal behavior of each participant. The internal behavior defines what the subject can do at a certain point, when the subject can send a message to another subject or when it has to wait until a message from another communication partner is received. For creation of internal behaviors, S-BPM provides three different "states":

SEND. sending to a communication-partner.

RECEIVE. waiting, until a message from a communication-partner is received.

FUNCTION. "doing something" without communicating at this point.

See Figure 7 for a simple example of the internal behavior of a customer.

The subjects are pair wise independent, i.e. their internal behavior can be performed pair wise concurrently. The synchronization will be performed by simple communication. A subject is working according to its internal behavior specification until it gets into the RECEIVE state, i.e. waiting for a message from another subject.

Additionally, S-BPM comprises a concept for multiple process instance enabling. For this purpose, "multi-subjects" are available as modeling concept[4]. A subject which has been marked as multi-subject within the communication view can be instantiated multiple times at process execution time. If a subject is instantiated multiple times, "multiple" internal behaviors are also instantiated.

---

[4] See Figure 6 as example.

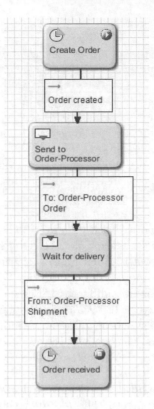

Fig. 7. Simple internal behaviour. Legend: The grey boxes represent the different states within a subjects behaviour. The "clock"-symbol marks a FUNCTION state, whereas an "outgoing envelope" represents SEND and an "incoming envelope" a RECEIVE.

All these behaviors rely to the same model, but run independently like "simple" subjects. This concept is the formal base to implement the workflow control patterns ([15], [16], [17], [18]) in a simple and understandable way.

If combined with so called "external subjects"[5], it is possible to connect multiple processes with each other. The arisen construct creates a conglomerate of "multi processes". In real world processes, these connectors are needed to structure the underlying business cases in smaller entities. Later on, we are going to apply this concept to the order process sketched in section 1.

4.2 Implementation of Multi Instance Patterns in S-BPM

There is a common communication view specification for all multi instance patterns we examine here (Figure 8), comprising only two subjects: A "Task Creator" who is responsible for the generation (and synchronization if needed) of

---

[5] A standard S-BPM concept, enabling us to use an external subject as interface to another S-BPM process model.

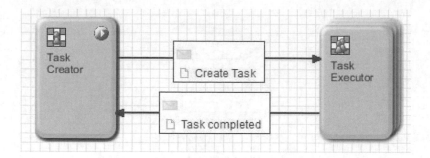

Fig. 8. Communication view for multi instance patterns (with synchronization)

single and multiple tasks and a "Task Executor" who simply executes a created task. The Task Creator initiates each new task by sending a message "Create Task" to a (new) Task Executor. Each Task Executor returns a message "Task completed" to the creator upon task completion. With this concept, the Task Creator is able to synchronize the different tasks.

The only exception is pattern 12 because of the lack of synchronization. With exception of pattern 12 (no synchronization) the internal behaviour of the Task Executor is always the same, as shown in Figure 9.

The following sections depict the differences between the pattern implementations.

Multiple Instances without synchronization [15]. The "unsynchronized" multi instance generation pattern, offers a more simple communication view (Figure 10) and internal behaviours of both the Task Creator and the Task Executor than the other patterns. The message "Task completed" is not applicable, therefore the Task Executor does not reply any message to the Task Creator after task completion. The Task Creator decides how many tasks are to be executed and sends a corresponding number of messages to the Task Executor as Multi-Subject (Figure 11). In consequence, multiple instances of the Task Executor are running concurrently without further synchronization (Figure 12).

Multiple Instances with a Priori Run-Time Knowledge [16]. The key factor in pattern 14 is that – in contrast to pattern 12 – tasks are synchronized (here: all initiated tasks are completed) before the superior process continues processing. In S-BPM such a behaviour is implemented within the Task Creator that remains in a RECEIVE-state after initiating the multiple tasks. It cannot leave this state until the Task Executor has received the message "Task completed" for all tasks (Figure 13).

Multiple Instances without a Priori Run-Time Knowledge [17]. Pattern 15 extends pattern 14 by the option to instantiate new tasks during the process execution time, i.e. some tasks might have been created before. This behaviour can be implemented in S-BPM with a small change (an additional loop) within the Task Creator (Figure 14).

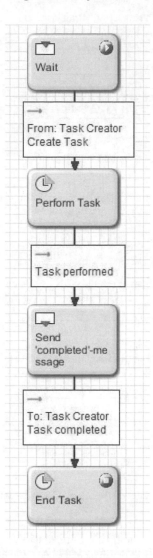

Fig. 9. Internal Behavior of Task Executor (with synchronization)

Dynamic Partial Join for Multiple Instances [18]. Pattern 36 can again be seen as an extension; this time of pattern 15. There are two additional requirements in the current pattern:

Synchronization now means that after each task execution the Task Creator must check a completion condition. If the condition evaluates to true, the superior process continues processing without waiting for further tasks completions.

The creation of additional tasks can be enabled or disabled. This requirement can be met by implementing a second RECEIVE-state into the internal behaviour of the Task Creator, including two transitions to switch between the two "wait" states (Figure 15).

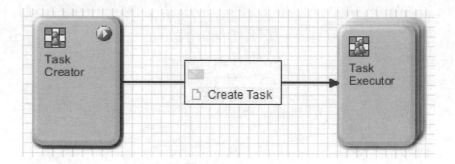

Fig. 10. Communication view without synchronization

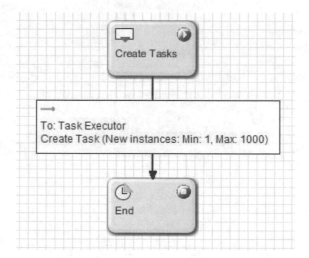

Fig. 11. Internal behavior of the Task Creator without synchronization

The control flow patterns identified in section 2 are needed to design the real-world order-process sketched in section 1. We have seen that S-BPM process models are able to implement these patterns easily. In the next section we demonstrate how to implement the order process with the S-BPM approach.

4.3 Application of the Workflow Control Patterns to an Order Process Using S-BPM

S-BPM provides all features to model an "Order Process" (including the subsequent Order Position Process) based on the assumptions A1-A3 made in section 2.

A1. Variable number n of Order Positions
A2. A priori runtime knowledge about the number n of Order Positions
A3. Order change on the fly during order processing

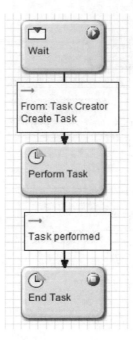

Fig. 12. Internal behavior of the Task Executor without synchronization

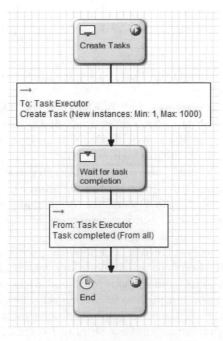

Fig. 13. Internal behavior of Task Creator in pattern 14

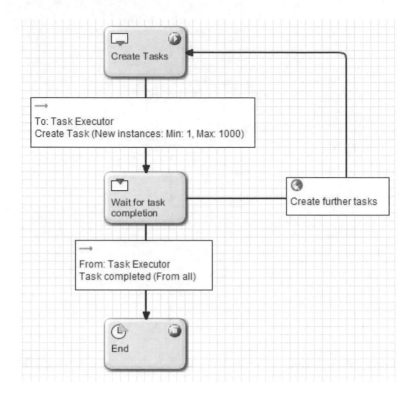

Fig. 14. Internal behavior of Task Creator in pattern 15

First of all, we model an Order Position Process. The communication view is sketched in Figure 16.

This process basically consists of only one subject, the "Order-Item-Processor". This subject is based on the "Task Executor" of the implementations of the workflow control patterns: It receives an Order-Item from the Order-Processor, executes it and sends the result back (Figure 17).

A real-world process could involve some more steps or even other subjects. Therefore, we split this Order-Item-Processing from the surrounding Order-Process. The connection to the Order-Process is made by implementing the "Order-Processor" as external subject, enabling it to connect to another process.

The Order-Item-Process is entirely independent from the variants V1-V3 (of section 2). Thus, S-BPM enables us to divide our real-world problem in such a way, that single parts of the solution can be reused without change.

The Order-Process as main process varies slightly depending on the variant used in the implementation. Again, an important outcome of the S-BPM concept is the fact, that the communication view (Figure 18) remains the same for each variant: Customers can send orders to the order-processor, who distributes the different order-items to the appropriate processors (in subordinate instances). He

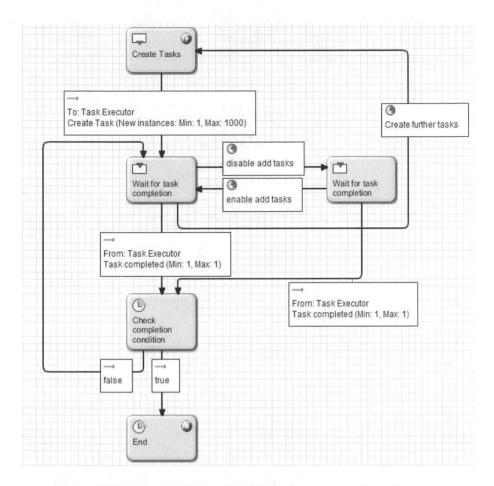

Fig. 15. Internal behavior of Task Creator in pattern 36

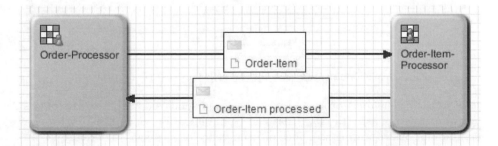

Fig. 16. Communication view of Order Position Process

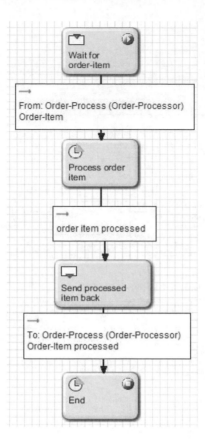

Fig. 17. Internal behavior of the Order-Item-Processor

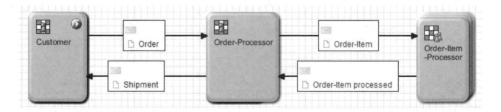

Fig. 18. Communication view of the order-process (main process)

collects the order-items-processed messages, and sends shipments to customers. We want to emphasize the fact that the communication view in S-BPM makes no assumptions regarding sequence or occurrence of messages. Therefore we are enabled to model each of our variants using the same communication view.

The differences, like sketched in the example implementations of our 4 used workflow control patterns, can be found within the internal behaviours of the order-processor and the customer.

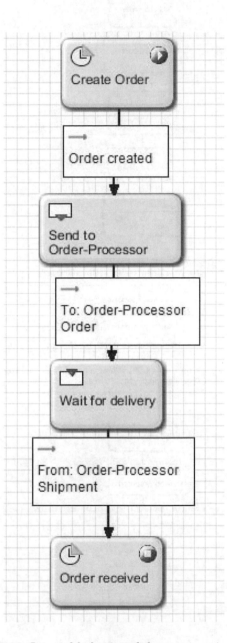

Fig. 19. Internal behavior of the customer in V1

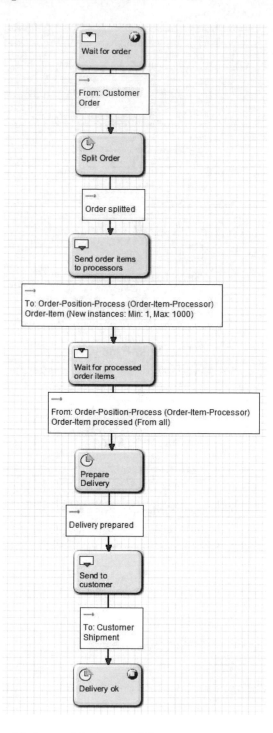

Fig. 20. Internal behavior of the order-processor in V1

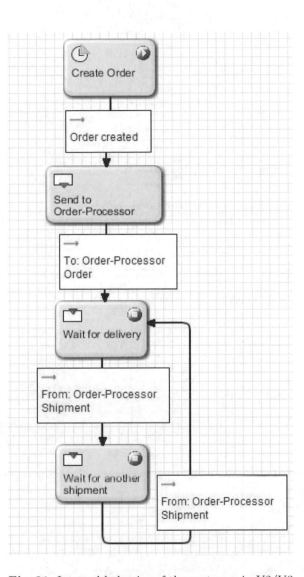

Fig. 21. Internal behavior of the customer in V2/V3

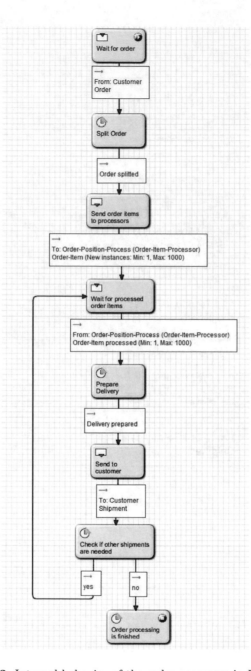

Fig. 22. Internal behavior of the order-processor in V2/V3

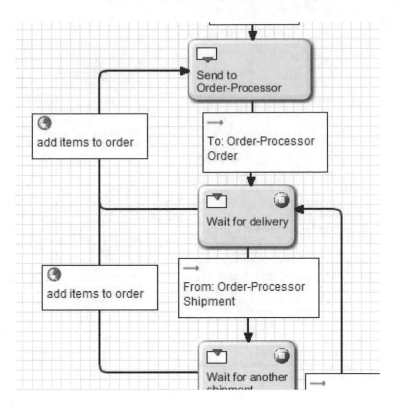

Fig. 23. Customer implementing A2. Figure shows only the essential part of the behaviour.

In V1, only a complete shipment is required. Therefore, the behaviours of the customer and the order-processor are very simple: The customer creates his order and sends it to the order-processor. He waits for the delivery until he has finally received the single shipment (Figure 19). The order-processor receives an order, splits it up into its order-items, distributes the items by creating multiple-instances of the order-position-process, waits until all of these instances are finished and finally sends the shipment to the customer (Figure 20).

The variants V2 & V3 use both the same pattern (CP36). The reason for this is, that the basic extension of V1 is the possibility to send more than one shipment. This does not affect the relation between the order-processor and the order-item-processors, it affects only the decision within the order-processor (when to do a shipment). This decision is always based on runtime-data (data contained in the initial order-form, the mentioned time-triggers, ...) and is therefore out-of-scope of this process-model[6]. Thus, there is no difference in the behaviours of the subjects between these two variants.

---

[6] Data information like forms etc. do not need to be modeled into the basic behaviours.

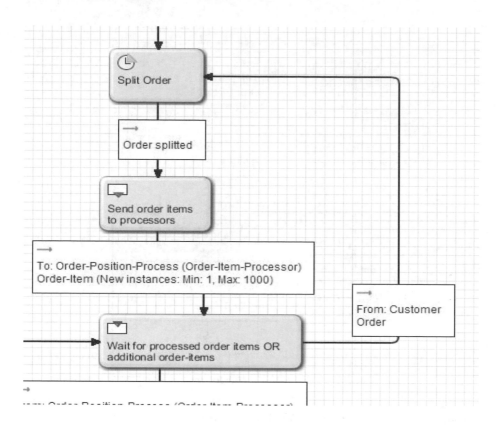

Fig. 24. Order-processor implementing A2. Figure shows only the essential part of the behaviour.

First, we enable the customer to receive more than one delivery. This is simply done by adding a second receive-state and a loop between both resulting receives (Figure 21). Both mentioned stated have to be potential end-states because the customer "doesn't know" how many shipments will be sent (at least not at modelling time).

The order-processor can be enabled to create multiple shipments in a similar way. The difference is that the loop has to get back to the receiving of the order-items. Therefore, the order-processor can receive some of the created order-items, deliver a shipment (of these items) to the customer and afterwards get back to receive more order-items, or leave the loop and ending his own behaviour.

For reasons of clarity, we left out the loops of additional order-items sent by the customer while a process is already running in the above variants. To model such a behaviour (see A2 in section 2), the customer has to be enabled to send additional order-items while he is waiting for, or already got a shipment. This is simply done by adding exit-transitions to the receive-states which lead to the sending of a new order (Figure 23).

In case of the order-processor, the receive-state "Wait for processed..." has to be extended by a second transition enabling the subject to receive new order-items from the customer (alternatively to processing "old" order-items). This new transition leads again to the splitting-task, which results in dispatching the new order-items to order-items-processors (Figure 24).

With the internal behaviours shown above it is possible to model all of our assumptions and variants regarding real-world order- or logistics-processes.

5   Conclusion

The "order processing" problem sketched in this article is a regular pattern, which arises particularly in complex processes. Typical applications of this problem can be found especially in the logistics context, where complex objects regularly are decomposed in an early stage and remerged (as in our example) or composed into new objects[7] at a later time. All these sketched scenarios result in a common challenge: a high level process modeling technique with expressiveness and a strong semantics is required that supports the concurrent creation and processing of multi-instance processes on the one hand, and their synchronization on different abstraction levels on the other hand.

Because of the lack of modeling techniques with expressive control flow constructs, process modelers tried to bridge the gap in the past with alternative constructs. Instead of generating process instances concurrently they did it sequentially with a loop construct or other means supported by informal process notations. In a high level consideration the process structure appears similar, but the process behavior is completely different. For illustration purposes we take the overall processing time as main KPI. Having full concurrent execution of the process instances, the overall processing time is the maximum of all instance processing times (the slowest process instance determines the overall processing time). Having an artificial serialization of the instance generation (caused by a loop construct in the process specification), the overall processing time is the sum of all instance processing times (see Figure 5).

The overall processing time reduction caused by utilizing full concurrency has an economical impact and result in measurable competitive advantages. Here it does not matter if we talk about manual processes (e.g. cleaning all articles in a cardboard box[8]) or fully automated processes running in an ERP system (as the availability check for all Order Positions[9]). The ability to offer flexible partial shipment emphasizes such advantages once more.

These processes, multi-instantiation and synchronization schemes have to be specified with adequate expressive modeling techniques. S-BPM satisfies these

---

[7] E.g. order positions of different orders but with the same shipment address and delivery date, can be composed to common "shipments".

[8] To be able to use full concurrency in manual processes, the required number of resources must be available. Otherwise we talk about "interleaving", i.e. concurrent processes can only be performed serially caused by the lack of resources.

[9] Supported by multi-threaded architectures or interleaving- and timeslice-procedures.

Table 2. Control flow pattern support by selected process modeling techniques (see [13], [20], [19], [20], [21]) in comparisons to S-BPM

CF Pattern	EPC (as implemented in ARIS Toolset V6.2)	BPMN 1.0	UML 2.0 (Activity Diagram)	S-BPM
Pattern 12: Multiple Instances without Synchronization	Not supported. There is no explicit notion of instances and there is no notation for interprocess connections. [10]	Supported via multiple instance task with MI Flow Condition attribute set to none.	Supported by spawning off new activity instances in a loop.	Supported by using a simple multi-subject
Pattern 14: Multiple Instances with a priori Run-Time Knowledge	Not supported	Supported via multiple instance task with MI Condition attribute set at runtime to the actual number of instances required.	Supported through the use of the Expansion Region construct.	Supported by using a simple multi-subject
Pattern 15: Multiple Instances without a priori Run-Time Knowledge	Not supported	Not supported. There is no means of adding further instances to a multiple instance task once started.	Not supported. No means of adding additional activity instances after commencement.	Supported by using a simple multi-subject and adding a suitable loop to the behaviour of a simple subject.
Pattern 36: Dynamic Partial Join for Multiple Instances	Not supported	There is no ability to dynamically add instances to an multiple instance activity.	Not supported. A MI activity can only complete when all N instances specified in the Expansion Region have completed.	Supported by using a simple multi-suject and adding suitable loops to the behaviour of a simple subject.

---

[10] In [10] a loop is defined that sequentially generates multiple instances of the sub-process. This construct follows the EPC syntax rules but violates the statement of Scheer et al that at each time on each process path no more than one process map (or process instance, respectively) can be executed. It is an indicator that there is no multi instancing concept supported by the EPC.

challenging requirements, the corresponding S-BPM process control patterns are specified with all variants in chapter 4 of this article. Therefore we can enhance Table 1 by adding a column for the outcome of using S-BPM on the mentioned patterns, see Table 2.

A great advantage of S-BPM is the ability for process execution during the design time. This allows an ad hoc model validation by all involved actors. The entire process (model) behavior is visible at design time. Logistics specialists are enabled to check the models behavior and to assess the congruence and discrepancies to the real processes. Process designers and IT-analysts support them with their methodological expertise. Thus, S-BPM is an important factor for business-IT-alignment and cooperation between these two "worlds".

Future work could focus on the implementation of further workflow patterns by the S-BPM concepts. Especially control patterns that are created by BPM research teams (as van der Aalst et al) and that are not supported by popular BPM modeling techniques (as UML or BPMN) yet, a unique selling proposition can be realized. We think about patterns supporting the flexible withdraw at runtime of Orders or Order Positions. Another interesting subject is the automated execution of conditions and rules regarding the data integration within automated multi-instance workflows. This leads to possibilities of intelligent process-control via monitoring the integrated data of real-time mapping of the according KPI to these data.

New versions of the BPMN or UML are not considered in this paper. Future work could integrate new constructs defined by BPMN 2.0 or UML 2.3 in the conceptual consideration and in the comparison with the S-BPM.

References

[1] Hepp, M., Leymann, F., Domingue, J., Wahler, A., Wahler, F.D.: Semantic Business Process Management: A Vision Towards Using Semantic Web Services for Business Process Management (2005)

[2] van Brocke, J., Rosemann, M.: Handbook on Business Process Management 1: Introduction, Methods, and Information Systems. Springer, Berlin (2010)

[3] van Brocke, J., Rosemann, M. (eds.): Handbook on Business Process Management 2: Strategic Alignment, Governance, People and Culture. Springer, Berlin (2010)

[4] Harmon, P.: Business Process Change: A Guide for Business Managers and BPM and Six Sigma Professionals, 2nd edn. Morgan Kaufmann, San Francisco (2007)

[5] Jeston, J., Nelis, J.: Business Process Management: Practical Guidelines to Successful Implementations, 2nd edn. Butterworth Heinemann, Butterworths (2008)

[6] Scheer, A.-W.: Architektur integrierter Informationssysteme: Grundlagen der Unternehmensmodellierung, 2nd edn. Springer, Heidelberg (1997)

[7] Scheer, A.-W.: ARIS: Vom Geschäftsprozess zum Anwendungssystem, 4th edn. Springer, Berlin (2006)

[8] Object Management Group (OMG): Business Process Modeling Notation (BPMN): Version 1.2 (2009), http://www.omg.org/spec/BPMN/1.2/pdf

[9] Object Management Group (OMG): Business Process Model and Notation (BPMN): Version FTF Beta 1 for Version 2.0 (2009), http://www.omg.org/spec/BPMN/2.0

[10] Rodenhagen, J.: Ereignisgesteuerte Prozessketten (EPK): Multiinstanzi-ierungsfähigkeit und referentielle Persistenz. In: Nüttgens, M., Rump, F. (eds.) EPK 2002: Geschäftsprozessmanagement mit Ereignisgesteuerten Prozessketten, Workshop der Gesellschaft für Informatik e.V (GI) und Treffen ihres Arbeitskreises "Geschäftsprozessmanagement mit Ereignisgesteuerten Prozessketten (WI-EPK), Trier, pp. 95–107 (2002)

[11] Office of Government Commerce (OGC): ITIL V3: Service Operation. TSO (The Stationery Office), United Kingdom (2007)

[12] van der Aalst, W.M.P.: http://www.workflowpatterns.com/patterns/control/

[13] van der Aalst, W.M.P., ter Hofstede, A.H.M., Kiepuszewski, B., Barros, A.P.: Workflow Patterns. Distributed and Parallel Databases 14(3), 5–51 (2003)

[14] Russell, N., ter Hofstede, A.H.M., van der Aalst, W.M.P., Mulyar, N.: Workflow Control-Flow Patterns: A Revised View. BPM Center Report BPM, 6–22 (2006)

[15] van der Aalst, W.M.P.: http://www.workflowpatterns.com/patterns/control/multiple_instancewcp12.php

[16] van der Aalst, W.M.P.: http://www.workflowpatterns.com/patterns/control/multiple_instancewcp14.php

[17] van der Aalst, W.M.P.: http://www.workflowpatterns.com/patterns/control/multiple_instancewcp15.php

[18] van der Aalst, W.M.P.: http://www.workflowpatterns.com/patterns/control/new/wcp36.php

[19] Dumas, M., ter Hofstede, A.H.M.: UML activity diagrams as a workflow specification language. In: Gogolla, M., Kobryn, C. (eds.) UML 2001. LNCS, vol. 2185, p. 76. Springer, Heidelberg (2001)

[20] Russell, N., van der Aalst, W.M.P., ter Hofstede, A.H.M., Wohed, P.: On the Suitability of UML 2.0 Activity Diagrams for Business Process Modelling. In: Stumptner, M., Hartmann, S., Kiyoki, Y. (eds.) Proceedings of the Third Asia-Pacific Conference on Conceptual Modelling (APCCM 2006), vol. 53, pp. 95–104. CRPIT, Hobart (2006)

[21] Wohed, P., van der Aalst, W.M.P., Dumas, M., ter Hofstede, A.H.M., Russell, N.: Pattern-based analysis of the control-flow perspective of UML activity diagrams. In: Delcambre, L.M.L., Kop, C., Mayr, H.C., Mylopoulos, J., Pastor, Ó. (eds.) ER 2005. LNCS, vol. 3716, pp. 63–78. Springer, Heidelberg (2005)

[22] Fleischmann, A.: Distributed Systems: Software design and Implementation. Springer, Berlin (1994)

[23] Object Management Group (OMG): UML Version 2.3 (2010), http://www.omg.org/spec/UML/2.3/

Exporting Natural Language: Generating NL Sentences Out of S-BPM Process Models

Stephan H. Sneed

Metasonic AG, Münchner Str. 29 - Hettenshausen, 85276 Pfaffenhofen, Germany
stephan.sneed@metasonic.de

Abstract. Assuming that a formal theory such as S-BPM is serving as a source for generation, it is possible to map certain model constructs on to a subset of the natural language and to formulate sentences with them. Hence natural language is a possible output of the S-BPM method. Due to the close relation between the syntax of the S-BPM method and the syntax of a natural language, this mapping can also be rather simple. This paper identifies at least four potential users within a business process and their requirements: Human actors who are assigned a role in the business process, people responsible for negotiating the service level agreements, requirement analysts and test analysts. Then the basic S-BPM elements are introduced as well as some modeling guide lines that ensure proper semantics of the S-BPM model and for the exported natural language. The required functionality and the definition of NL sentences and their elements are shown as well as the mapping and the algorithms needed to generate NL output.

Keywords: S-BPM, Natural Language, Human Actor Behavior Descriptions, Service Level Agreements, Requirement Specification, Test Plan.

1   Motivation for This Work

Since generation of natural language (NL) is a common issue of many tools today and NL approaches are being developed for the main competing BPM methods and tools, the necessity of such study is obvious. As stated above there are at least four potential recipients of natural language texts exported from the current business process models: These are:

- human actors who derive their behavior from their role in a business process,
- people who are responsible for service level agreements derived from the process,
- requirement analysts who are to specify internal or external it services and
- test planers who derive test cases for these services. Since the natural language texts exported here are written into some kind of document, there can

A. Fleischmann et al. (Eds.): S-BPM ONE 2010, CCIS 138, pp. 163–179, 2011.

be no single standard for the description of human behavior in process roles, but for the other recipients, there are well defined documents. It has to be clearly stated that these documents are not generated as a whole but as text segments that can be further edited using copy and paste techniques. The system requirements derived from a process model can be easily inserted into the requirement document of that system. The test cases derived from the process model can be included in the test specification. The required behavior of an external service can be built into a service level agreement. So we have four target documents that are relevant for to our natural language generation:

- behavior descriptions for human actors
- service level agreements
- requirement specifications for software systems
- test specifications for system testing.

2   The Source of Generation: S-BPM Models

Before the mapping of a business process model to natural language can be discussed, both the generation source and targets must be defined. The source of the natural language exports introduced here is any S-BPM process model. There are two dimensions of any language, whether it be a natural or a formal language. These are syntax and semantics, i.e. structure and content. The syntax of the generation source language is the S-BPM process model definition. The semantics, on the other hand, is the meaning expressed by such a model. In other words, the semantics of a business process model is what the model and its parts are representing in the real world. The basic elements of a S-BPM process model are subjects, objects, messages, actions like send and receive, states like waiting and running, state transitions and sub-processes. It is up to the analyst to assign an existing software system to a SUBJECT[1], to an action of this SUBJECT or to a process. Hence the question of semantics is a question of architecture. Therefore syntax and semantics are explained here via the modeling method and modeling architecture.

The central element of the S-BPM method is, of course the SUBJECT. Within S-BPM, there are two levels of modeling. The communication view shows the interaction of different SUBJECTS that form a process, while the behavior view shows the internal behavior of all SUBJECTS. Although the knowledge of S-BPM syntax (methodology) is crucial for this paper, it is not the purpose here to explain it in detail. It is explained in the work of Albert Fleischmann on the S-BPM method [1].

---

[1] There are many meanings of the term 'subject' as listed by Fleischmann [1]. In this paper only two meanings are used: The term is uppercase like 'SUBJECT' when it refers to a S-BPM model element. When it appears in lower case, the subject of a natural language sentence is meant.

2.1   Semantics of Actions and Interface SUBJECTS: Architectural Proposal

The problem with any modeling method is the fact, that it could be used in different ways. One of the most problematic issues when it comes to modeling is the question of granularity or the infinite nesting of systems or functionality.[2] What should be defined as a process and what should be defined as an action within a process, or what should be defined as an object and what should be defined as an attribute of an object? Such definitions are context dependent. What seems to be a process from a low level perspective may be only an action step from the perspective of a higher level. Thus, it is impossible to model anything without first establishing from which perspective the model is being constructed. It is not within the scope of this paper to define all the modeling rules necessary to ensure the proper semantics for an entire business (business ontology), since this would require a perspective for almost every role in the business, but at least some aspects regarding service SUBJECTS[3] should be mentioned here, which will serve well as example here explaining the possibilities of an NL generator.

2.2   Example: Semantic Definition of a Service SUBJECT

Any service can be modeled as a process, as a SUBJECT or as an internal action. The decision as to which semantic level to choose will not only affect the resulting model but also the output of the natural language export. A service can be provided within one's own business or by an external partner. If it is provided by an external partner, it might be necessary to change the interface between the own business and the external partner from time to time. An interface to an external partner could either be defined technically, e.g. as a web service, or informally as a human interface. In both cases, a service level agreement (SLA) is necessary to ensure a proper partnership. If an external service happens to be integrated in a business process, it should always be modeled as an interface of the type SUBJECT within a service process, because then (and only then) can the SLA be automatically derived from the business model. The other criteria for defining interface SUBJECTS is the modularity criteria. A service within service oriented architectures (SOA) is a modular piece of functionality that can be accessed by many clients via a specified WSDL interface. But this interface can change. In order to minimize the impact domain of such a change on the process side, there should be only one interface specification, i.e. one WSDL schema, within the executable S-BPM process. If there is more than one position within the process architecture of the business, which was actually the motivation for SOA in the first place) the service should be modeled as an interface SUBJECT

---

[2] The problem is this: The atomic entities in software development are instructions. Any composition of more than one instruction can be called "system". Systems consist of instructions or other systems. Hence systems can be endlessly nested.

[3] Service SUBJECTS are explained as well within the SBPM method paper of Fleischmann [1].

within the service process. Otherwise a change of the interface on the server side will have a greater impact on the client, in this case the using process. An interface SUBJECT within a service process is modeled when

- the service is provided by an external partner
- the service is accessed from multiple positions within the business process architecture.

2.3   Semantic Definition of an Action

As already mentioned, one of the big questions when it comes to modeling is the question of granularity. On the one hand, one could define one SUBJECT representing ones business and containing one action: create value. On the other hand, one could model each and every logical instruction required to perform a task as a separate S-BPM action. This would lead to many details and a non-comprehensible model. An action is always representing some functionality consisting of 1 to n logical instructions. This functionality can be represented by a name like "Get_Weather_Data". The moment we assign a name to something within a context that is to be semantically interpreted like it is the case here, we are referring to the purpose of that something and hence defining it. But let us assume that there are different ways to get weather data. It could be requested by country, region or by city, thereby leading to differing results. It depends on the implementation of the provided service, whether the input message structure varies or if the input message structure remains constant. If the message structure varies or if it contains different business objects for returning weather data by city than by region, then the action is no longer the same and should be split up into one action for each different message type, e.g. "Get Weather Data by Region" and "Get Weather Data by City". This is necessary because the inputs and the outputs have to be handled differently, or, in business process modeling terms, within another branch of the process. Actually no one action should ever be describable with "or" and "and" clauses. Each action should be an elementary entity of the process in the sense that it produces one result type from one argument type, $x = f(y)$. This way it can be separately called using the semantic modeling entities of the process. According to this, a function should be represented as a separate action in the following cases:

- when the function can be distinguished by its name
- when the function can be distinguished by its input (differing pre conditions)
- when the function can be distinguished by its output (differing post conditions)

The granularity of the S-BPM communication structure, i.e. its messages, requests and responses is determined by the granularity of the actions. No two messages should ever be processed by one action.

3   Example: An Interface SUBJECT for Weather Forecasts

With these rules of semantics in mind we can now model the before mentioned example of a weather forecast service. Let us assume a travel agency is using an external weather forecast web service in order to provide their customers this extra information along with their last minute offers. The web service can process a request for either a city or a region but never for both. Another service can search for all regions that are currently fulfilling some weather criteria like temperature and precipitation. Yet another service performs the same for the cities. There is a service for every different object type. If the input data is not valid for some reason, an error code is returned. Since the online last minute booking process could also be processed without any weather data, as is the case when the customer has to rely on his luck regarding the weather, there have to be additional services to handle the exception conditions since otherwise the whole process would crash. Since the service is external, we model the weather forecast as an interface SUBJECT using a service process. All the functions of the web services are receiving and returning different message types and hence are modeled as separate actions. The internal behavior of the service SUBJECT "WeatherForeCast" (WFC) would then look like shown in figure 1.

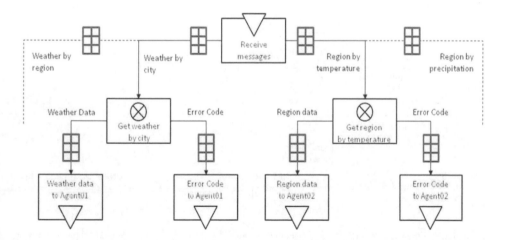

Fig. 1. Internal behavior of an interface SUBJECT "WFC" within a service process

4   Basic Linguistic Concepts

Any natural language description is an structured set of NL sentences. Every sentence consists of atomic elements, parts of a sentence or conjunctive, nested sentences. The possibility of formulating sentences is more or less infinite. In generating natural language one must reduce the number of possible sentence types to a set of well- defined reproducible ones. With respect to a natural language export, every exported sentence needs to be formally defined. It would be beyond the scope of the paper here to define all the sentence types that appear in the requirement definition in section 5.4. The purpose of this paper is just to show the general way of exporting NL from S-BPM models and how the export could then be extended. Figure 2 shows the syntactic structure [2] of a sentence represented as tree where the sentence is the root and the atomic elements are the leaves. The typical sentence in many languages (English, German, French and many others) has the structure of [subject – (predicate – object(s))] which is very close to the S-BPM method [1]. This applies as well to the sentence needed for the communication view export of our interface Subject "Weather-ForeCast". Figuree 2 will be referred to frequently from the rest of the paper and explained step by step. It is intended to depict the structure of a NL sentence. A sentence is composed of syntactical structures like nominal phrases (NP), verbal phrases (VP), prepositional phrases (PP) and others [2]. However, there is no strict definition of these structures and it depends on the requirements which structure definition serves best for the purpose. In general it can be said that linguistics is a wide and complex issue. Natural languages have many exceptions and each language differs more or less from others. The solution presented here is motivated by the need to fulfill a certain task. However, before going into the solution, some basis linguistic concepts should be shortly introduced.

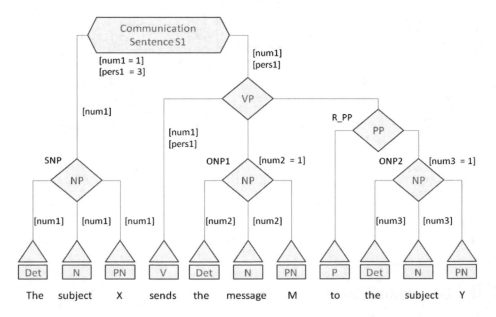

Fig. 2. Syntactical structure of a NL sentence describing the S-BPM communication view

4.1   The Concept of Governance

Within a NL sentence there is a structure of governance. For example, the linguistic cases in languages like German are given by the sentence structure and then inherited by the atomic elements from the syntactical structures. While some cases are defined by the sentence, others are defined by lower level elements, propagated to the sentence structure and then inherited again from other structures [3].

4.2   Morphing Nominal and Verbal Phrases

Within most sentences, verbs do not occur by their linguistic lemma (canonical form). The form "sends" is part of a lexeme with the lemma "send". The verb within a sentence has to be adjusted (flexion, verbal agreement) according to the linguistic categories such as person, number, gender, tense and so forth and appears as a morphed lexeme of the lemma. The same applies to nouns and other syntactical structures. For the NL export it is easy to morph verbs, adjectives, and nouns according to their occurrence, since all sentences are using the third person and tense. Other aspects are not relevant. Prepositions will be inserted directly into the sentence and not morphed as well as proper names.

5   Implementation of NL Sentences

The programming language of choice for computer linguistics is the logical programming language PROLOG or LISP. Due to its ability to unify expressions, it fits much better to this task than any functional or object-oriented language. But since the standard for programming business applications is Java, this paper will introduce a java implementation of the English NL export.

5.1   Definition of the Morphing Atomic Elements

As already stated, we have to morph certain structures in order to get the proper form of a given lemma. Therefore we need a lexicon that contains all the forms needed. Given the lemma and the number, it should return the proper finite form. Since prepositions and proper names will be inserted directly and without any morphs, we will only make use of the English determiner "the". Only lexemes for nouns and verbs are to be defined.

Nouns: Nouns are atomic elements regarding the structure of a sentence. All the nouns in the NL sub set are accessed by one static class. This class has access to all the finite forms that exists to a noun. They could be stored in a property file or a data base. In any case, there is a method that returns the proper lexeme when given the lemma of a noun along with the demanded number.

```
public static string getFiniteForm(lemma, num){};
```

For the input parameters ("subject", "plu") the method would return the string "subjects". For the basic NL sub set introduced here the required nouns are:

- subject
- message
- business objects

Verbs: Verbs are atomic elements as well. Also all verbs in the NL sub set are accessed by one static class. This class has access to all the finite forms that exists to a verb like the class representing the nouns. There is a method that returns the proper lexeme when given the lemma of a verb with the demanded number.

```
public static string getFiniteForm(lemma, num){};
```

An example would be the following input parameter structure: ("execute", "sing"). The method would then return the string "executes". For the basic NL sub set, the required verbs are:

- execute
- send
- receive

5.2   Definition of the Composed Elements

As already said, there is not one single way to do something in computer linguistics but always more options. What might fit well for one language or purpose might turn out to be a disadvantage for the other. Within S-BPM, a SUBJECT has (ingoing and outgoing) messages and a message contains a business object, a sender and a receiver. This fits well to the traditional way of nesting structures like in figure 2: A sentence contains a subject and a predicate, while the predicate contains its objects. The parameters are assigned to the highest level structure, the sentence and then passed to the composed ones and finally to the atomic ones as shown in figure 2.

Nominal phrases: A nominal phrase in general contains all elements that are related to a noun. A nominal phase contains the number of all its elements according to the principle of government or information inheritance). As already said, there are many ways to define composed elements. For our purpose we need a NP that consists of a determiner, a noun and a proper name. The definition according to the notation used by Fanselow [3] would be the following: The element in front of the arrow consists of elements after it:

$$NP \rightarrow Det, N, PN.$$

Again, all NPs that we can define are represented by one java class. This time, the class is not static. It provides a constructor that is representing the

NP definition as shown above. Besides it declares a string for the determiner and assigns it the value "the". Each variant of an NP would be represented by a constructor. This fits well to Java, because they will all differ in their parameter structure. If the constructor is called, it passes noun and number to the static noun class in order to get the required lexeme.

```
public NP(noun, properName, num) {};
```

The NP class also has a method like the classes representing atomic elements to return the current sentence as a string representation composed by the specific constructor from its atomic elements, the fixed determiner, the finite form of the noun and the proper name.

```
public string getNP(){};
```

For example, if we were to call this NP constructor with the parameter structure ("subject", "Travel Agency", "sing") and then call the getNP() method on the object instantiated, we would get the string "the subject 'Travel Agency'".

Prepositional Phrases: A prepositional phrase can be defined by giving a preposition P and an NP. This definition serves well for our purpose with respect to our sample in figure 2. Of course, this is not a standard case. If necessary this can be changed or enhanced as needed by defining new PPs, NPs and sentences.

$$PP \rightarrow P, NP \text{ (Det, N, PN)}.$$

The PP is as well represented by a non static java class. There is one constructor that returns the PP java object with the following structure:

```
public PP(preposition, noun, properName, num) {};
```

The PP class has also a method like the classes representing atomic elements in order to return the PP as a string representation composed by the specific constructor from its subordinate elements.

```
public string getPP(){};
```

When the PP constructor is called, not only the static class representing the prepositions is called. Also the NP constructor is called. If in return the getPP() method is called, it calls the getNP() method of the NP object instantiated within the PP constructor, which returns a concatenation of two strings. For example, if we would call the PP constructor with the parameter structure ("from", "subject", "'Travel Agency'", "sing") and then call the getPP() method on the object instantiated, we would get the string "from the subject 'Travel Agency'".

Verbal phrases: A verbal phrase contains all elements that are related to a verb. The basic sentence consists of a NP and a predicate (verb) like "A student reads". This predicate can be extended by further objects, like "A student reads a book" or "A student reads a book on Aristotle". So, the verbal phrase consist of the whole rest of the sentence and hence of a verb, possibly containing some further NPs and prepositions. So, there are many VPs to define but we are initially satisfied with one definition:

$$VP \rightarrow V, NP (Det, N, NP), PP (P, NP (Det, N, PN)).$$

The VP is well represented by a non static java class. There is one constructor that calls the subordinate ones and returns the VP java object. It has the following structure:

```
public VP(verb, num, NP, PP) {};
```

The VP class has also a method like the classes representing atomic elements in order to return the VP as a string representation composed by the corresponding constructor from its atomic elements:

```
public string getVP(){};
```

For example, if we would call the VP constructor with the parameter structure ("receive", "sing", NP("message" "M", PP("from", NP("subject", "Y")) and then call the getVP() method on the object instantiated, we would get the string "receives message 'A' from subject 'Y'".

5.3   Definition of Sentences

Having defined all the atomic and composed elements, it is now possible to define NL sentences on top of those elements. Of course, the possibilities here are limited. But with the proposed architecture, it is very easy to expand the basic elements to gain the ability of defining more sentences than are really needed. All sentences should be represented by a class. But then the problem of limited constructors appears. Hence it is better to create a class per sentence type by extending a sentence super class. If a type of sentence is to be expanded (like: "Subject A sends message M to Subject C" should be extended to: "Subject A sends message M to subject C along with business object B") more parameters are needed and this can be solved by adding new constructors. The sentence in the sample of figure 2 would have the following definition:

$$S1 \rightarrow NP (Det, N, PN), VP (V, NP (Det, N, PP), PP (P, NP (N, PN))).$$

The round brackets here are used to define the exact type of the composed elements, since there are more NPs for example, like it is proposed by Fanselow [3]. This sentence would then have the following constructor:

```
public S1(noun1, properName1, num1, verb,
          noun2, properName2, num2, preposition,
          noun3, properName3, num3){};
```

This constructor is now instantiating all subordinate elements with corresponding parameters. However, there is yet another open issue that comes along with languages like German: The specification of the cases. They are defined within the constructor by setting the appropriate cases when instantiating the subordinated structures. The sentence also determines the pending determiners (le, la, les, der, die das, etc.) for languages like German and French by calling the getGender(noun) method of the static noun class and forwarding it to the NP or PP constructor. Of course, each sentence also has a method to return the concatenated string representing the sentence:

```
public string getS1(){};
```

For example, if we would call the S1 constructor with the parameter structure ("subject", "Weather Forecast", "sing", "receives", "message", "get Weather by City", "sing", "from", "subject", "Travel Agency", "sing") and then call the getS1() method on the object instantiated, we would get the string "The subject 'Weather Forecast' receives the message 'get Weather by City" from subject 'Travel Agency'". Hence the free variables for the sentence S1 are the following:

- noun1
- properName1
- num1
- verb
- noun2
- properName2
- num2
- preposition
- noun3
- properName3
- num3

6   Mapping Rules and Implementation

The Mapping rules are defining what elements of the S-BPM model are mapped to the fee variables of the NL sentences. Of course, there has to be a defined mapping for each sentence. S1 (communication sentence 1) is a sentence designated to describe the S-BPM communication view, so the communication view provides all information needed, except for the language variable. This variable is allocated by the language code setting of the modeling environment. S1 is able to describe the complete set of communication attributes of a subject. Since the proposition can either be "from" or "to", it can be used for describing all outgoing and ingoing messages of a SUBJECT. In both cases, the sentence subject is the SUBJECT that we are currently focused on. The verb is either "send" or "receive" in accordance with the preposition. The NPs of the VP are representing the message and the destination SUBJECT.

First, we want to focus on the outgoing messages. Therefore, the verb "send" and the preposition "to" are selected and assigned. The subject of the sentence, the first NP, is the SUBJECT we want to describe. Currently this is the SUB-JECT "applicant". Since it is a SUBJECT, the noun1 is set to "subject" and the properName1 to its name. The verb is defined. The noun2 is the message, because we have defined CS1 in order to describe SUBJECT-message-SUBJECT relations, so noun2 is set to "message" while properName2 is set to its name. The third NP is the receiver (in the "send" case) and hence again the noun3 is set to "subject" while the properName3 is set to its name.

Outgoing messages: noun1 → subject, properName1 → travel agency, verb → send, noun2 → message, properName2 → request (city), preposition → to, noun3 → subject, properName3 → WFC, num1 = num2 = num3 → sing.

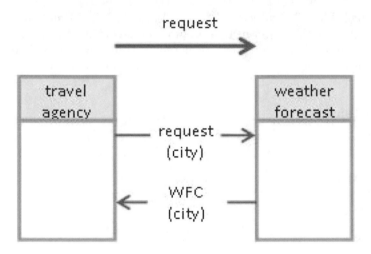

Fig. 3. Variable setting of the outgoing messages

The ingoing messages would be described in the same way, except for the verb and the preposition. The verb would be "receives" and the preposition would be "from". Now we have everything we need for an algorithm that maps the essential communication elements to our NL sentence S1. Let us assume that all SUBJECTS of a S-BPM process model are stored in a vector or something similar, and that all ingoing and outgoing messages are accessible as well form the SUBJECT. Also assume that messages are containing their recipient SUBJECT. The following code example is a Java like syntax but not full Java that could be implemented, because the details would deviate from the essentials:

```
for (all subjects) {
 currentSubject.getOutgoingMessages;
  for (all outgoingMessages) {
   noun1 = "subject";
```

```
    properName1 = currentSubject.getName();
    verb = "sends";
    noun2 = "message";
    properName2 = currentMessage.getName();
    preposition = "to";
    noun3 = noun1;
    properName3 = currentMessage().getRecipient().
    getName();
    CS1 = new CS1(noun1, properName1, verb, noun2,
    properName2, preposition, noun3, properName3,
    language);
    CS1.print();
}

for (all incomingMessages) {
    noun1 = "subject";
    properName1 = currentSubject.getName();
    verb = "receives";
    noun2 = "message";
    properName2 = currentMessage.getName();
    preposition = "from";
    noun3 = noun1;
    properName3 = currentMessage().getRecipient().
    getName();
    CS1 = new CS1(noun1, properName1, verb, noun2,
    properName2, preposition, noun3, properName3,
    language);
    CS1.print();
    }
}
```

Setting the first character of the complete string to uppercase and adding a point to the end of it, the result for the given example would be the following:

The subject 'travel agency' sends the message 'request(city)' to the subject 'WFC'.

The subject 'travel agency' receives the message 'temp>20' from the subject 'WFC'.

The subject 'travel agency' receives the message 'temp<20' from the subject 'WFC'.

This is a complete description of the communication aspects of the SUBJECT applicant in natural language. Of course, the solution can be enhanced. For example, one could think of constructing a sentence that is a conjunction of proper names like "the messages accepted and rejected" or an expandable list like "the messages A, B and C". Therefore we would need a new sentence definition, assigning a "plur" parameter to the num1 variable which is the passed to the atomic noun class which would return "messages" on the noun1 parameter "message" as lexeme or finite form. One could also think of a more structured presentation, for example generating a listing with dots like:

The subject 'travel agency' would receive the following messages:

- message 'temp>20' from the subject 'weather forecast (WFC)'
- message 'temp<20' from the subject 'weather forecast (WFC)'

However, this paper is restricted to demonstrating the principle of exporting natural language sentences out of S-BPM models. What has yet to be explained is the way to describe the internal behavior of the SUBJECTs since for that a more sophisticated algorithm is needed which deals with directed graphs.

7   Generating NL for the Internal Behavior

As stated in the requirement definition in section 5, the internal behavior of a SUBJECT is relevant to deriving a complete description of target documents. The internal behavior of a SUBJECT within S-BPM is a directed graph with multi labeled edges and the three types of states as nodes. The ingoing edge can be seen as precondition for each state. It would go beyond the scope of this paper to explain all possible combination of states and edges. Here is just one case presented since otherwise there would be many distinctions of cases in the code example making it very complex. The case chosen here is the one from the S-BPM definition in section 3.1.3. There is a receive state that is followed by two actions, depending on the message that is received. A natural language representation of such a construct would look like this:

If the subject X receives the message M from the subject Y // The subject X executes the action A.

Therefore some new sentences are needed. At first, we need a simpler version of S1 for the second part of the if-clause: "the subject X executes the action A." The verbal phrase in this sentence has only one object. Therefore we must define a new verbal phrase without the preposition phrase from above. In this section only the linguistic definition is noted since the implementation is always the same: The class for verbal phrases gets a new constructor.

$$\text{VP} \rightarrow \text{V, NP (Det, N, NP)}.$$

With this new verbal phrase it is possible to extend the sentence structure. Since the verbal phrase parameter structure is also represented by the parameter structure of the new sentence, we can also define a new sentence S2.

$$\text{S2} \rightarrow \text{NP (Det, N, PN), VP (V, NP (Det, N, PN)}.$$

The first part of the if-clause has also to be defined. But first we need the if-part of the sentence.

$$\text{S3} \rightarrow \text{C, NP (Det, N, PN), VP (V, NP (Det, N, PN),}$$
$$\text{PP (P, NP (Det, N, PN)))}.$$

Now the complete sentence can be defined. It is also possible with Java to have recursive instantiation in the sense of instantiating a sentence with another sentence. The composed sentence S3 would look like this:

S3 →

C, NP (Det, N, PN), VP (V, NP (Det, N, PN), PP (P, NP (Det, N, PN))),

NP (Det, N, PN), VP (V, NP (Det, N, PN).

C is here a condition parameter defined directly within the sentence constructor where it is allocated with the string "if", similar to the preposition parameter. Having all the necessary linguistic components set, the mapping rules have to be extended for the internal behavior view of the S-BPM method. The sentence subject NP1 is always the subject currently under inspection. The second NP2 is the message and its name, the third the sender SUBJECT and its name, NP4 is equal to NP1 and NP5 consist of the type of the state, here an action and its name.

Action state after receive (SUBJECT travel agency): noun1 → subject, properName1 → travel agency, verb1 → receive, noun2 → message, properName2 → temp>20, preposition → from, noun3 → subject, properName3 → WFC, verb2 → executes, noun4 → action, properName4 → list city as destination, num1 = num2 = num3 = num4 → sing.

Here too the algorithm has to iterate through all subjects as it was the case with the first one.

```
for (all subjects){
 currentSubject.getStartNode;
 recFunc(startNode)
}
```

Fig. 4. Variable setting of the outgoing messages

In order to produce a complete description of an S-BPM SUBJECT behavior, the complete directed graph representing its internal behavior has to be scanned. This is done by a recursive function that gets a SUBJECT and its start node as parameters. The outgoing edges of the start state are pushed onto a stack. As long as the stack has more than zero elements the loop processes one edge after another. Each edge is popped from the stack and then processed. The information about the sentence subject is taken from the current SUBJECT under inspection. The message information is taken from the current edge. The information about the sender subject is gained by the message definition, containing its sender. Then the next node is determined by the destination of the current edge, which, as assumed, is an object of type SUBJECT. With this node, the function is called again.

```
public void recFunc (node, currentSubject) {
stack = node.getOutgoingEdges();
 for (stack{\textgreater}0) {
   edge = stack.pop();
   noun1 = "subject";
   properName1 = currentSubject.getName();
   verb1 = "receive";
   noun2 = "message";
   properName2 = edge.getMessage().getName();
   preposition = "from";
   noun3 = subject;
   properName3 = edge.getMessage().getSender().
   getName();
   nextNode = edge.getDestination();
   noun4 = nextNode.getType()
   properName4 = nextNode.getName();
   recFunc (nextNode, currentSubject);
 }
}
```

This will proceed until an end state is reached that has no outgoing edges, causing the for-condition to fail. The algorithm will now backtrack until a node is reached where there are still edges on the stack. This works fine as long as there are no loops in the graph. A loop would prevent this algorithm from terminating: If the branch of a directed graph loops back to an existing element, this element is treated like a "new" element, causing the same fork, branch and loop to be processed endlessly. It is the general halting problem, which has been the center of attention of many programming debates. There is, of course, a solution to this termination problem caused by overlapping loops in directed graphs, but explaining this would go beyond the scope of this paper. Setting the first character of the complete string to uppercase and adding a point to the end of it, the result for the given example would be the following:

If the subject 'travel agency' receives the message 'temp>20' from the subject 'WFC', the subject 'travel agency' executes the action "list city as destination".

If the subject 'travel agency' receives the message 'temp<20' from the subject 'WFC', the subject 'travel agency' executes the action "skip city".

This is the way a receive message is constructed by the two follow up actions depending on the composition of the incoming message. However, to generate NL output for the complete S-BPM internal behavior, there are still some open issues like sequences forks, business objects and other languages. However, the prototype has shown that they are feasible.

8   Conclusion

The practical approach to natural language generation presented here serves well to generate a NL output for different purposes. It was explained how the generator is to be implemented and how it could be extended. It is notable, that the S-BPM method makes a natural language export easier due to its close relation to the natural language. The S-BPM method consists of the same key elements: Subject, predicate and object [1]. Hence the mapping of S-BPM elements to natural language sentences is quite straight forward. The subject is always the SUBJECT under inspection. The predicates are either send, receive or execute. The sentence's objects are representing other communication partners (SUB-JECTS), messages, business objects and so on. Furthermore, descriptions can easily be generated per SUBJECT, representing either a human actor (or process with human interface) or a system (or process with automated interface). A S-BPM model contains many aspects that are necessary for system design, development and test phases. Requirements and test cases are nothing else then structured documents consisting of a subset of natural language as proposed by Christine Rupp [4] or H. M. Sneed [5]. Fundamental parts of these artifacts are therefore easy to generate out of S-BPM models using the presented solution. Also service level agreements can be generated for external (service) SUBJECTS. Therefore, the S-BPM method together with the natural language export presented here promises to be a useful approach to closing the gap between the IT and the business worlds.

References

[1] Fleischmann, A.: What is S-BPM? In: Buchwald, H., Fleischmann, A., Seese, S., Stary, C. (eds.) S-BPM, CICS Band 85, pp. 85–106. Springer, Heidelberg (2010)
[2] Pollard, C., Sag, I.: Information based syntax and semantics, CSLI Lecture Notes Number 13, Stanford (1987)
[3] Fanselow, G., Felix, S.: Sprachtheorie 2. Die Rektions- und Bindungstheorie. Wilhelm Fink Verlag, München (1987)
[4] Rupp, C.: Reuirements Engineering und Management. Carl Hanser Verlag, München (2007)
[5] Sneed, H.: Der Systemtest .Carl Hanser Verlag, München (2009)

Business Objects as a Mediator between Processes and Data

Peter Kesch

Metasonic AG, Münchner Str. 29 - Hettenshausen, 85276 Pfaffenhofen, Germany
peter.kesch@metasonic.de

Abstract. Business processes are forming a dynamic unit. They describe a context sensitive view on a sequence of process steps. In order to fulfil those tasks it is necessary to work with data. Data structures are historically driven defined and managed statically.

Using the new Business Objects from Metasonic's S-BPM Suite it is now possible to overcome the disadvantages of these static definitions and to model data and their usage dynamically according to processes.

Keywords: Business Objects, S-BPM.

1 Introduction

1.1 Existing Solutions for Handling Data in Applications

Dealing with highly dynamic data is one of the most complex tasks in IT during developing business solutions. After the introduction of databases in the 1970s and the success of relational database solutions in the 1980s it became a common solution to handle data not only in the program code but in an external application which is specialized in data handling [1]. The introduction of Object-oriented programming went a step further and encapsulated the data logic and the data handling in objects [2]. The object is the owner of the data, provides methods to manipulate this data and to store information. The only way to retrieve information of object related data is to call the pre-defined object methods.

Consequently, both techniques were combined to create object-oriented databases in the 1990s [4]. This approach contains the integration of object-oriented patterns within the tables of a relational database. This design aims primarily the outsourcing of business logic to the database system.

We will focus on using relational databases, hence, having all data stored in a database the business logic is providing methods to manage the data and the database engines provide the basic methods to create, read, update and delete data in the database storage. Furthermore the database engine is taking care of the consistency of the data and the permissions, which are necessary to do those modifications. These basic concepts are still state of the art today and almost all applications follow these concepts.

A. Fleischmann et al. (Eds.): S-BPM ONE 2010, CCIS 138, pp. 180–191, 2011.

1.2   Advantages and Disadvantages of the Existing Solutions

Using constraints in the definition of data in databases is one of the most powerful concepts of relational databases. Constraints define how the data, which is stored in the database engine, has to be managed and how different datasets are related to each other [1]. In order to understand these principles we need to have a closer look at those data structures. All data in a database is stored in tables as data records. Each table has a very clear definition about the data elements in such a data record. Every element has a specific data type such as Integer, String, Decimal, Boolean and the table even defines what kinds of elements are mandatory. Now, a new record can only be stored or changed in the database if all the constraints that are defined in the table structure are met. Only by those constraints it is possible to build reliable business applications.

Let's have a look at material management in companies. Almost all companies need physical material for their business. Typically those materials' data is handled in an Enterprise Resource Planning (ERP) application that stores its data in a database [3] (in the following called "Material Master"). A material record can have several fields such as material name, material number, price, description and so on. Some of these fields are mandatory; others do not need to be filled. In order to manage all material in a company the material manager needs reliable information about the material types. This information is only useful for the material manager if it is complete and consistent. The database makes sure that the integrity of the data is kept as it allows only storing new material records when all constraints which are defined in the table structure are met.

In addition to the integrity of the data in a database table constraints can also describe how different tables are linked to each other. Data is very complex and it is not possible to store all company related information only in one table. A database typically contains hundreds of tables. In our material management example we have material table in the database. If we also want to store material orders we need a new table. Let's call it "Material Order". A material order record will have a link to the materials that are ordered and the amount per material. In a relational database this information is normalized and stored in additional tables. In our case we would need two more tables:

One table to store the individual orders: "Material Order" and one table to store the positions of the order which can be more than one material: "Order Positions".

In an Entity Relationship (ER) diagram the table structure would look similar to Figure 1.

The relations between the different tables, in our case "Material Master", "Material Order" and "Order Positions" are described as constraints or relations between those tables. This is called a foreign key constraint in a relational database model. These constraints describe that a Material Order can have multiple positions and each of those positions is exactly linked to one Material Master. Furthermore it says that one Material Master can be referenced in more than one Order Position. Also here the database is taking care about the

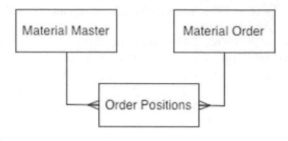

Fig. 1. ER Diagram

consistency of the data. An Order Position can only be saved in a Material Order if it has a valid reference to an existing Material Master.

So far we have seen now two huge advantages of common solutions using databases as carrier of data:

- The consistency of a database record is managed by the database engine
- The consistency of more complex data is managed via relations between database tables

In addition to these two main advantages the security aspect has to be mentioned here, too. Each of those database tables has its own permissions describing which role or user (who) is allowed to do certain operations like create, read, update or delete. In conclusion a database manages to keep a secure, consistent storage for all data records.

However, the advantages that have been mentioned so far are also a pain if we think about change management and dynamic business solutions. Today, if the database needs to be changed this implicates also a change of the database structure including the methods how the data is retrieved or managed. The implications are huge and the more tables and relations between those tables are defined the more complex is the change process. This also implicates that all reports that are based on the data definitions have to be reworked. The changes go through from the data definition all the way to the end user interface of the business applications. Based on our experience in customer projects the complexity of changes are the main obstacle and most of companies are afraid in those changes. One additional aspect here is the demand for more flexible business solutions that are not data driven but process driven. Flexibility can only be achieved if the solutions can be changed fast and the changes do not have too many dependencies to the underlying data structure. On the one side business needs reliable data but on the other side the demand for flexibility and fast new solution development requires new ways how to work with data.

1.3   Requirements for More Dynamic Data Handling

Most of the requirements for more dynamic data handling derive from the way how business applications are compiled using a process oriented way. Process oriented here means that the business logic is described in a business process and each process describes the necessary steps that have to be done in order to fulfil a task. Business processes are focused on the business logic and not on the data. Business processes are focused on the sequence of steps and on "who is doing what" in a process. Based on the way how business solutions are defined from a process point of view we can define some basic key requirements:

1. It should be possible to change the business logic or to shift one task from one business user to another without changing the data structure or the permissions.
2. Changes in data structures that are necessary for one specific business process should not impact other business processes but keep the data integrity.
3. Data collection processes should be able to be implemented in an easy way.

2   The Business Objects from Metasonic

2.1   Current Business Objects from Metasonic

In order to enable the business process designer to describe the way how the business user should work with data according to the defined process Metasonic introduced the Metasonic Business Objects in 2006. Business Objects can be seen as a mediator between the data storage and the process. They describe the data structure that will be used to store the data in a database and they also contain a "state" concept for dynamic data handling. The data structure was based on XML Schema Definition (XSD) as shown in Figure 2.

Each Business Object can have different states. A state defines a subset of the Business Object data. In a specific process step the modeller can describe e.g. that the valid data of an order is necessary to go to the next state. Furthermore he is able to indicate what specific state of the Business Object form should be

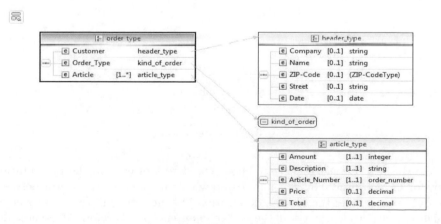

Fig. 2. XSD Editor

used to show/create those orders. The Business Object can be seen as a kind of a structured attachment in a workflow. The workflow system is routing the tasks from one user to another and provides the user with all the information or forms that have been necessary for her/him to fulfil the task.

The following layout of those forms was created automatically by the system:

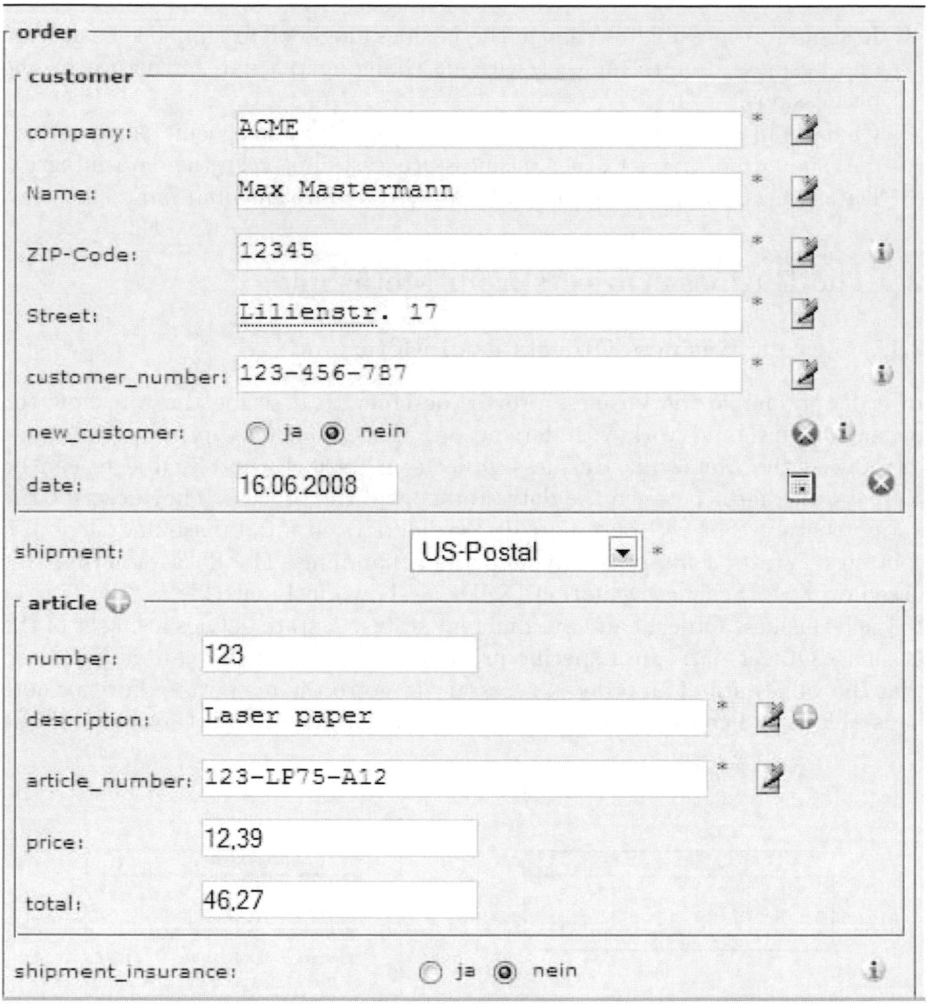

Fig. 3. The order Form

The Business Object takes care about the data storage and the presentation view for the end-user. This was a first step which introduced a mediator between the data storage and the process description but did not fulfil the requirements which have been mentioned at the end of chapter 1.3. Therefore Metasonic decided to implement a completely new version of the Business Objects.

2.2   The New Business Objects from Metasonic

The new Business Objects follow a completely new concept in managing data for business processes.

The main structure of the Business Objects is shown in Figure 4.

Fig. 4. The new Business Object Structure of Metasonic

The principles for the new Business Objects are the following:

Business Objects: Each Business Object describes the data or the content of the object. The data is described in a hierarchical structure. Business Objects can be nested. Each Business Object can have a different connector and therefore be stored in different storage engines. This means, that all necessary descriptions that are needed to save the data in a database are part of the Business Object description. The description indicates the storage location which could be a database or any external system such as an anonymous web service. Furthermore it contains the information which is needed to save a consistent record such as mandatory fields, allowed values for fields and others. As mentioned above one of the important points here is that we have introduced the possibility to nest Business Objects. A Business Object like our Material Order can contain other Business Objects such as the Material Master. This linkage information is kept in the Business Object. It is not necessarily part of a relationship description in databases.

The Business Object acts here as a mediator, which is a kind of a meta structure such as a shelf around the data; encapsulating and protecting it. Therefore it is possible to use Business Objects from one source (for example a database) and link it together with a different source via the nested Business Object logic. This is possible without, and this is the important point here, the necessity to implement constraints between those objects. Of course this is not only the case if the Business Objects have different sources. The object itself will be stored in the database engine and the Business Objects within the Metasonic Suite takes care about their relations. This means that the relations are not stored as foreign key constraints but managed in so called Relationship Tables from the Metasonic Suite.

To sum up the Business Object is the description of the data that is necessary to store it and to keep the integrity of the data records. The views are representing a linkage to the process steps.

Views: Each Business Object can have multiple, different views. A view represents the subset of a Business Object's data that will be presented to the

Fig. 5. The Business Object Editor

end-user in a form. But besides the description of this subset, the view also is able to change the Business Object definition in some parts. For example it is possible to define completely different mandatory fields per view for one and the same Business Object. This is necessary if you have a data collection process as mentioned in 1.3. In a business process you usually collect all necessary data for a Business Object from different users. It is recommended to have different forms for each user where you are able to show only a part of the Business Object data and define individual mandatory fields. In addition you may want to have some fields included in the view that should not be shown. This is for example reasonable for computed values that should not be shown to the user. Views provide all the necessary techniques that are needed for a flexible process design. Another important aspect of the view concept is the permission handling. Each view comes with its own permissions for create, read, update or delete. This means that the permission concept is no longer part of the database definition, but part of the view. The view is the element that will be used to handle data and therefore it is also the element, which will be linked to a process step. In a process step the process designer indicates what the end-user should do. He for example indicates that he should create a new Material Oder using a specific view. This means that the view in a specific process state defines the permission for the end-user. This concept allows much more flexibility for process designs. It is now possible to design situation related permissions. A business user might be allowed in a specific process step to create or update an order but not be allowed to update it in the very next step.

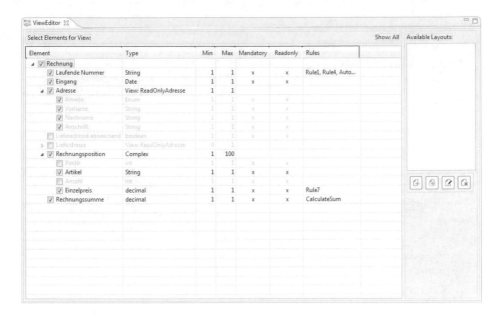

Fig. 6. The View Editor

Template: Based on the views of a Business Object there is a so called Templating Engine implemented. This Templating Engine itself consists of two parts: one coding part and one template part. The coding part is responsible for making various calculations that take the end-user device in account, the resolution and the language and automatically generates a best-fit layout for the end-user. This coding part can be enhanced from the customer and each company can build their best solution for generating automated layouts. Nevertheless some standard layout logics will be delivered with the product. Each of these coding parts in addition has a template part which can be customized. Based on this customization the implemented logic of the coding part can be adapted. The main idea here is based on experience from many projects. The customer must be able to make adaptions to the logic how layouts are generated. It will never be possible to fulfil all type of customer requirements out of the box with a standard solution. The demands here are various from simple colour changes to complete changes towards the logic how fields will be arranged. The target is to get a template that will fulfil 80% of all form layout requirements. The rest can be done, if necessary using the layout designer.

Layout: The layout is generated automatically. The only thing the designer has to specify is if the layout should have one, two or more columns. The automatic layout uses a best guess to place the elements in the form. Nevertheless it is useful to keep the layout changeable. Therefore the new Business Objects come with a new well-arranged Layout Designer. The Layout Designer (Figure 9) can load the

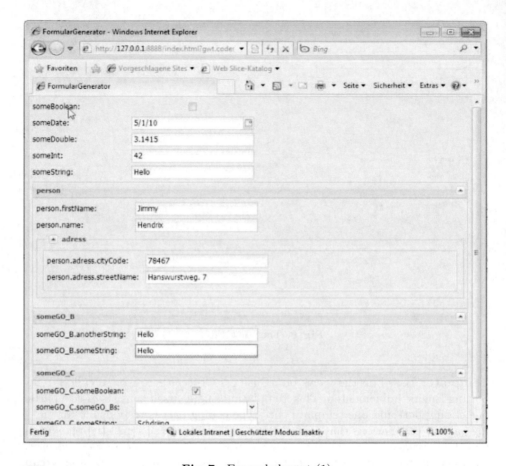

Fig. 7. Example layout (1)

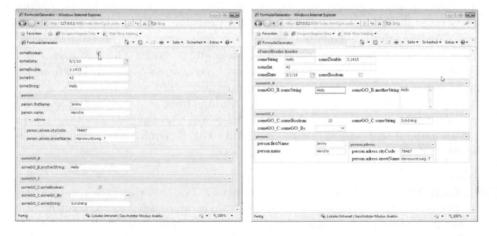

Fig. 8. Example layout (2)

automatically generated layouts and provide the designer with functionalities to re-arrange the layout (Figure 8).

It is possible to move fields, labels or containers, fix them to rulers and move everything that is fixed to a ruler. It also allows the designer to add custom html elements in the form design.

This means that even though the layouts will be generated automatically (remember the target on page 8 that we would like to have 80% of the requirements fulfilled) the designer will have full flexibility to change "almost" everything.

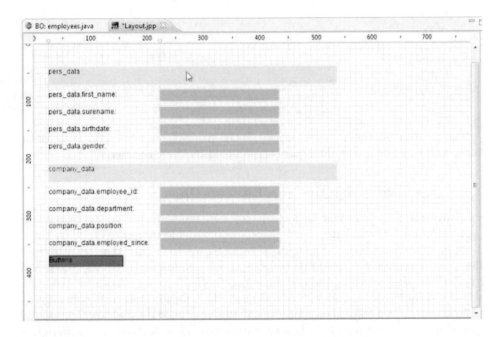

Fig. 9. The layout designer

In addition to the described design capabilities of the new Business Objects they come with a fully integrated rules engine which allows dynamic form development. The rules are implemented on the client as well as on the server side. On the client side the rules can be triggered based on two main events:

- on change
- on render

These triggers can be linked to any field element of the form. Based on the triggers various actions are available to manipulate the form; everything implemented on the client side without any server interaction.

These actions can be:

- set value of a field
- make field mandatory

- hide field / section
- calculate sum
- .....

On the server side there are triggers and actions too:
Triggers:

- pre save
- post save
- pre save draft
- post save draft
- pre create
- post create
- pre delete
- post delete
- ...

The actions on the server side can be in principle any method call. Both actions, server and client side, can be enhanced by the customer.

2.3 Advantages Using the New Business Objects

Basically the new Business Objects have been implemented to overcome the backdrafts from the old Business Objects and provide more flexible data handling in a business process. The main advantages are the separation of authorizations and data objects, the ability to have view based mandatory fields and other restrictions. One additional major advantage is the fact that the data structure and the definition of the views are dislinked. This means that in bigger organizations, where typically the ownership of the system, data and applications is spread over different people, it is now possible to define someone to prepare the data structure, another one to prepare the form layouts and the form logic and a third one to design the processes and link the forms to the right states in the process.

3   Conclusion and Future Steps

The new Business Objects created by Metasonic provide an approach to manage data and to link it to processes. They enable the data designer to build their consistent set of data and the process designer to build forms that represent the demands from the process point of view and not the data point of view. Based on the new Business Objects Metasonic will continue to build even more inventive functionality in close future which will allow the process designer not only to link data views to a state of the process but also to enrich the process model with a complete data management description. This means that the process will carry the complete description which is necessary not only to create workflows but complete business applications.

References

[1] Kudraß, T.: Taschenbuch Datenbanken. Carl Hanser Verlag, München (2007)
[2] Dogac, A., Özsu, M., Biliris, A., Sellis, T.: Advances in Object-Oriented Database Systems. Springer, Heidelberg (1994)
[3] Leon, A.: ERP Demystified. Tata McGraw-Hill, New Delhi (2008)
[4] Atkinson, M., Bancilhon, F., DeWitt, D., Dittrich, K., Maier, D., Zdonik, S.: The Object-Oriented Database System Manifesto. In: Proceedings of the First International Conference on Deductive and Object-Oriented Databases, Kyoto, Japan, pp. 223–240 (December 1989)

A Study of the Subject-Oriented Approach for Automation and Process Modeling of a Service Company

Yuliya Stavenko and Alexander Gromoff

National Research University Higher School of Economic,
Myasnitskaya str. 20, 101978 Moscow, Russia
yuliastavenko@mail.ru,
alexanderg@convera.ru

Abstract. Nowadays business requirements can be met through a subject oriented approach to modeling and process automation of enterprise services. As a consequence of the wide-ranging implementation of IT infrastructure, the time needed for an employee to adapt to a new environment is continually increasing. The subject-oriented approach can reduce this time substantially and as a result significantly improve enterprise relationship culture as well as increase the availability of the service approach for the organization's activities, for example, introduction of the ITIL v3 standard for IT departments or companies offering IT services. In this study the following issues are resolved:

- the analysis of the evolution of the service approach for managing the organization and IT, as well as standards for such management;
- the review of ITIL v3 and its proposed methods for achieving integration between business and IT;
- the practical application of the subject-oriented approach for modeling, validation and execution of business processes using Metasonic Suite.

Keywords: subject-oriented approach, entropy, bottom-up modeling, self-regulating system, ITIL.

1 Introduction

In the 20th century organizations were mainly functionally oriented. Strict vertical hierarchy of management and rigid division of labor grouped in accordance with specific tasks were prime common features of these organizations. The structure of these organizations is reluctant to change and has a vertical topology constructed in accordance with the functions performed and the principle of strict hierarchical subordination. This structure is characterized by the high level of overheads in communications and unnecessary coordination between functional units. For functionally-oriented organizations it was extremely expensive and difficult to implement any changes due to the isolation of each division (20% of

A. Fleischmann et al. (Eds.): S-BPM ONE 2010, CCIS 138, pp. 192–206, 2011.

time was wasted for operational performance, 80% for transmission of the results). This situation was sustainable until the market started requiring certain reflections from business in the area of quality management and enhancement within stable or even decreasing prices.

Business realized that it was unable to adapt quickly enough in response to market changes in the frame of a functional-oriented approach since this lacked a degree of flexibility and innovativeness. In the early 80s the applications of business process management (BPM) theory started to be widely used. An interest to these solutions was significantly activated by the wide-spread adoption of Deming's ideas of total quality management (TQM) and holistic system consideration.

The process approach does not primarily focus on the organizational structure, but rather solely on the business processes. In this approach, a company is considered as a business system with certain goals, targets and tasks which are achieved by a set of related business processes with a management system focused on the integration between existing resources and requirements from business processes; and finally, a company's quality&risk systems are focused on the assurance of accomplishing the process. Although this works better in theory than in practice discounting numerous consulting bureaus and courses in MBA schools.

De facto modern organization constitutes a set of specialized functional departments which can be interrelated and penetrated by executive processes, with separate parts of these processes working in each department [1]. Recently it was clarified that - regardless of the process approach introduction - many companies lose in a global market economy due to both the inability to react to market volatility and the implementation of high speed technological innovation.

It is necessary to support contingency and the interrelations among all the structural units for provision of operational flexibility, so that any innovation can be rapidly spread to all parts of the organization. Companies need to achieve agility when integrating the solution which can satisfy business requirements into the processes, in other words, we can see clearly the necessity of SOA implementation relating to business globally. This can be achieved if realization of a service-oriented architecture is provided on the principles of service platform independence and its variability. However we also have to consider self-organized management systems.

Currently an idea of self-organized and systematic system management is realized in process management either voluntary, when top management doesn't involve itself to a great degree and everything works fine, or within the development of management theory sometimes reflected in practice. Organization and disorganization could be considered as patterns of structural transformation of an adaptation system.

Therefore the main task in searching for excellence in business practice is to improve collaboration between people and agents of support. So every human activity can be obtained from an organizational point of view in a sequence of informational transformations. It is one of the main ideas of presented study which can be implemented on a particular platform with predictable benefits.

2 Business Service Orientation

The major challenge for system survival in all environments is the ability to adapt to changing environmental conditions in terms of both time and accuracy. A successful application of new technologies and IT solutions depends entirely on the ability to adapt to changing business requirements. The extremely high level of complexity of modern ERP systems is a key issue for developers and users of IT services. The ultimate goal of innovation is to build a flexible architecture of a corporate enterprise. This can ensure comprehensive functionality in order to support real-time business processes, providing a fast reaction to ongoing environmental changes by selecting an appropriate business process optimization. Such an enterprise architecture should include description and allocation of the personnel roles, a description of the processes (functions and behavior), as well as an introduction of the required technology used throughout the life cycle of an enterprise, thereby providing business agility. In this regard, many IT professionals understand the necessity of developing new approaches to designing and implementing IT systems. One can believe that the next generation being based on advanced architectural principles and advanced technological solutions will be really able to improve the quality of social life.

Progressive companies are choosing organization through business services (SOA), and thus virtualizing the organization in order to implement business agility and continue normal operation in a complex, constantly changing and competitive environment. As a result they ensure efficiency and productivity of the business.

The advantages of business service orientation are as follows:

– Constant responsibility for results among the suppliers of services.
– Accurately formulated SLA (time, cost and quality). Service has a value for the consumer. That value of service has two main components: functional and warranty. The functional component is the direct service given as a result of common efforts of people, processes and technologies. The warranty component constitutes a guarantee that the functional component corresponds to the expected level of quality. Here we exclude consideration of other values inherent in service, such as emotional, prestige or impulsive, etc.
– Proactive event management.
– Cumulative service: increasing value of the result by successive additions of the portioned services.
– Changing principles of work of people: what they think about IT, how they work and use IT in routines, whether they can adopt new technologies and management trends.
– Active compliance management.

Attitude to the IT department is evolving and IT is no longer considered just as a supporting department. With the increasing maturity of business processes comes an increase in the level of interaction between business and IT, thereby resulting in more service orientation as opposed to the previous "technological" approach. The IT department does not simply supply equipment, communication or software installation, but also increasingly provides services for end users, in other words "customer service". Worldwide recognition of the prospects of using the service model for management in the IT sector is the emergence of ITIL version 3, which is solely focused on managing IT services [2].

3   Active Compliance Management

The organizational system has two aspects: the formal (a system of the roles assigned to people) and the informal (the actual performance of roles). Activities of a company which has implanted such principles of compliance management are built in accordance with a system of norms, rules, activities, relationships, regulations, etc., to ensure standards and controls. Another component is the control subsystem, which coordinates the activities of its members and administrates these. Thus, a continuous monitoring of standards and requirements such as information systems and risks assessment, connected with discrepancy of business, allows priority determination of business processes and information systems modernization. For example, the use of ITIL 3 in any organization ensures that the requirements of ISO 9000 [3], CobiT [4], SOX (Sarbanes–Oxley Act) [5], and COSO [6] are all met.

Active compliance management is the most appropriate tool for this task and is designed specifically to improve organizational effectiveness. Hidden interprocess communications often represent a problem in relation to information systems, as well as to the processes themselves which are not flexible enough to be easily rebuilt. As a result, the employee of the organization engaged in the process has to do extra work to verify the results due to numerous requirements.

The key issue of active compliance is the ability for self-modification of processes being inherent in the processes themselves. This approach allows you to modify the process in such a way that it complies with established requirements after each modification. But to achieve this result it is necessary to know everything about the process, including the way it is implemented by specific performers, or its 'natural behavior'. Building such a model using standard modeling thereby led to an increase of the decomposition and is often too difficult and impracticable.

4   New Role of Employees

Employees in most mature organizations realize a new role in organizational structure according to these new requirements.

Employees should understand the basic goals of the business and participate in achieving them, keeping a balance between business requirements and their capabilities.

Employees have to understand the responsibility and the consequences of mistakes in the work for business, including the deterioration of customer loyalty which directly impacts the company's competitiveness.

Management of division should be predictable and transparent due to unification of its processes, activity based costing and responsibility delegation among specialists.

It is necessary to measure the efficiency and reduce operating costs through reporting and measurement of qualitative and quantitative performance indicators in the process, thus creating a KPI culture.

It is necessary to modernize regularly the IT infrastructure in conformity with changing business requirements .

It is necessary to justify and optimize IT costs.

To meet some of these requirements, management of IT services has been allocated to a separate management process that was described in ITIL and legally enshrined in the Standard Systems IT Service Management ISO 20000.

5   ITSM and ITIL Version 3

The active compliance management in many IT service companies and departments must include adherence to the ITSM (Information Technology Service Management), which is the methodology of information technology management based on a process approach. This is currently believed to be the most effective means for management of IT infrastructure and the IT department of the organization.

The main provisions of an advanced experience in IT infrastructure are set out in the ITSM Library ITIL (Information Technology Infrastructure Library), which is globally recognized as the de facto standard. It is used in organizations to ensure that all of the above listed requirements will be met. At present the most relevant is the third version of ITIL, the ideological part of this version includes five books [2].

Service Strategy provides guidance on the design, development and implementation of Service Management, and puts the IT organization in a position to achieve operational effectiveness and to offer distinctive services to its customers. Its ultimate goal is to make the IT organization think and act in a strategic manner.

Service Design describes ways to design and develop IT services. Its scope includes the design of new services, as well as changes and improvements of existing ones. Increased profits can no longer be reached only by optimizing processes; they are obtained through fast reaction to changes in a modern competitive environment, live processes, policies and strategies and through active compliance management.

Service Transition is dedicated to the description of the delivery of all necessary services required by the business side. Basically the Service Transition is responsible for the implementation of all aspects of the service.

Service Operation offers the methodology for delivery of the services at agreed levels. Another purpose is to help with maintenance of the technology, infrastructure and applications implemented in an organization in order to meet customer needs.

Continual Service Improvement binds improvement efforts and outcomes with Service Strategy, Design, Transition and Operations. Successful implementation of Continual Service Improvement best practices enables IT departments to create and maintain value for customers through better design, introduction and operation of services.

6   Subject-Oriented Approach

Innovation in IT leads to innovation in the workplace. The catalyst for such innovations are the new methods of management. Processes within these systems have been standardized and automated, but for the sake of the lack of adaptability and flexibility. Automation systems have spread to nearly all areas of business, and some areas are really impossible to manage without automation systems.

Then there were the decisions focused on an employee, various workstations and portals, but this interaction was not yet flexible and again the price of change was too high.

The service-oriented approach has brought flexibility, but in a number of instances it was too expensive and the claims seeking the necessary changes were questioned.

The subject-oriented approach is a new paradigm of business process modeling. This method allows the business to illuminate and incorporate the true participants of the business activity while modeling the processes, and to adopt their understanding of their roles and responsibilities to the real productive system. So process flow involves the effective interaction of staff in accordance with their actual roles, which are defined by their duties. This approach allows the "inclusion" of activity of the employees participating in debugging and introduction of business processes, the use of reflexivity for changes and the introduction of models by the same people who carry out these business processes later. Thus, employees are motivated by their individual contribution to the company. Subject-oriented modeling supports service-oriented business and allows trial participants to determine the best process for achieving individual goals and key performance indicators.

7   Synergy between Natural and Artificial Environment

Business modeling activity (describing some areas of the organization with a clear formal approach such as the methodology, supported by specialized tools) represents the organization as an artificial environment. The business model is always a formalized description of a particular aspect or organization activity area (e.g.: tree of goals, business process model, organizational design, etc.), which is detailed to the required level, the corresponding target model [1].

Generations of analysts have tried to solve the problem of how to model the activity so it would reflect a desired level of abstraction and at the same time be as close to reality as possible. There can only be one answer here; we have clearly seen the gap between a model and a reality and always need to take this into account in our considerations and assumptions. From the management point of view it is a challenge to find a synergy in combining an artificial system as a model and a natural system as a reality being controlled. In order to achieve a synergistic effect, modeling of business processes must be considered in terms of describing natural-artificial systems. There are two approaches of modeling processes: modeling "top-down" and "bottom-up".

Modeling "top-down" is the formation (forming/shaping) of business process models from integrated to detailed decomposition. Modeling of the system "top-down" on each level gives us the requirements for the next level of detailization in terms of business performance as an artificial system.

Modeling "bottom-up" is the formation of the integrated business processes by aggregating detailed processes or procedures. When modeling a system from the "bottom", we create a "natural" model of transmission processes which are usually based on the principle of minimizing the amount of resources required to perform the individual processes.

At present, many companies find themselves in a stalemate because they describe processes only from an artificial point of view by modeling "top-down". They should, on the one hand, automate and standardize processes to reduce costs, improve efficiency and increase quality, but, on the other hand, be flexible to move forward respectively, considering the fast changing needs of consumers, markets and laws through the introduction of changes in corporate strategy at the operational level.

Thus, the research urgency is caused by the problem of effective management of constantly developing and increasingly complex systems and those people involved in their operation and development, in terms of synergy between artificial and natural components.

The main idea of the subject-oriented approach is to consider the subjects of an organization as the main participants in its description. The subject-oriented approach implies that employees can quickly and inexpensively integrate their methods of performing the process into the overall scheme of a process, thus achieving self-organization and adaptation of the system to the external environment.

8   Methodological Base of Research

In the early 90's (and thereafter) it became clear that the flow-oriented description of the process has a limited range of usage and does not correspond to actual operational needs, as well as the requirements for synchronization in distributed applications. UML activity diagrams have been developed for solving this problem.

Subject-oriented description of the processes combines the advantages of flow-based and object-oriented approaches. All participants are subjects in the models, whose behavior can be understood, supplemented or modified using simple and intuitive methods. Interaction between subjects (participants of a process) can be visualized.

The subject-oriented approach was implemented in the product Metasonic Suite which consists of three modules: Metasonic Build allows you to model the processes of the organization, Metasonic Proof was designed to validate the modeled processes and Metasonic Flow allows you to execute the processes directly. All of these activities in Metasonic Suite are integrated and interrelated. The business process as the consistent flow of functions and events is transformed into the interaction between subjects who exchange messages with each other, as well as carry out their "internal" functions [7].

The product line Metasonic Suite provides a continuous cost-effectiveness and safety throughout the process life cycle; it starts from the beginning of the idea of the process and ends with the performed working process. Processes can be described, tested and implemented by only a description of the process. The flow is controlled by code which is generated automatically based on the graphic model of the process. Since employees are included in the development process at an early stage, business processes can be immediately tested and their logic reaches a high level of decision-making to implement necessary modifications and process changes. All of this is accomplished before any investment in the IT sector is necessary.

Orientation on the service and independence of a platform shows huge potential for improvement of business processes.

Metasonic Suite runs on the following principles [7]:

- Processes are described by structured communication of participants.
- The process model is performed. Processes can be tested in reality after their creation, and then immediately optimized with regard to their participants.
- There are no collisions and discrepancies between functional and technical design.
- Each participant knows how to act in accordance with rules in each process.

The urgency of research is related to real companies' demand on the successful and rapid adaptation of changes of processes with a convenient and effective tool for modeling and process automation - Metasonic Suite.

Thus, description of business processes reaches a new level. All participants can review and evaluate the description of the process together. The person responsible for the process can develop the unique concept of business roles, as well as determine what interaction with public communication should be implemented.

Models of subject-oriented process descriptions are based on certain syntax. Interaction and technical properties of subjects can be done in detail and precisely described. Described business processes can be immediately tested live, the process identifies errors early and corrects these during the description of the process.

The subject-oriented description of the process supports both static and dynamic aspects. Firstly, the descriptive level (the interaction of subjects) is defined by subjects involved in the process. This includes the introduction of subjects related to the static structure of communications and public relations types of messages that will be used in the process of interaction. At the second level of description (the behavior of subjects) the internal structure of the flow of subjects is described, which enables data exchange and interaction as a result of one-time business operations. At the third level, interactions between the subjects are detailed so that the process can be performed. Thus, the validation process can be performed at an early stage of implementation.

Subject-oriented modeling is currently supported by tools that allow a seamless transition from the description of the process to developed applications, all the way from modeling to implementation.

8.1 Metasonic Build

Metasonic Build forms the basis of Metasonic Suite. This is the first tool for modeling business processes in which the process is described in terms of a specific participant in this process (the subject).

The structured description of the interaction between the subjects with the sequence of actions of each subject gives a complete picture of the process.

Employees are usually focused on the part of the process which is in their area of responsibility, as well as on interaction with other subjects of the process (employees or computer systems). Each party involved in the process, whether human or technical component (application system or other item of IT infrastructure), is included in the description of the process.

Using Metasonic Build gives the following results [7]:

- Each participant in the process is actively involved in the process modeling. Thus, identification and the cooperation of all employees involved in the process are achieved.
- The process is divided into individual packets of action correlated with specific subjects. The binding action of these packages is through the exchange of messages between them.
- An intuitive method of describing the processes allows a common process understanding among staff members of the IT department, which mostly facilitates the adaptation and training of new staff.
- Opportunities for optimizing processes are understood well, because the processes are easily adapted. The developed code is executed immediately.

8.2 Metasonic Proof

Validation of business processes is used to check the flow of the real-world environment. With regards to process models, validation checks to ensure the coordination of those models is correct and the automation works properly.

Already at this point all participants of a process are free to be involved in work on changes of this model and to "fit" the model for real needs. Thus, all simulated communications between subjects will be verified.

Using Metasonic Proof gives the following results [7]:

- Development of the logic of a process occurs with the help of support roles.
- Information flows and data flows with the associated process can be integrated in the validation.
- Validation of forms, input screens and dialogues at the appropriate stages of the process flow can be enabled.
- Testing can be done remotely.
- Training of new employees is simplified by the fact that processes can be "tested" in a nonproduction environment.
- Due to previous validations of process logic and information flow, time and costs, as well as performance risks , can be significantly reduced.
- Metasonic Proof begins after the process models created using Metasonic Build are uploaded to the server. All participants can then immediately test the process on the basis of their roles.

8.3   Metasonic Flow

In the case of processes that are built automatically, the models of the processes, which are described in Metasonic Build and validated in Metasonic Proof, can immediately be experienced live using Metasonic Flow, without conventional requirements for implementation. The subjects are grouped by roles and then assigned to departments and groups of employees within the organization.

In this case, employees receive full support from the IT through use of a system of workflows for process accomplishment. This system can be implemented with the help of a corporate portal, which shows the implementation of processes and customer interaction. Metasonic Flow provides the basic functions for management of processes by ensuring that each employee himself sees the tasks on each process which he is responsible for.

9   Degree of a Readiness of the Problem

During research quite a wide range of sources can be divided into two blocks: the literature on efficient control and the service approach to the organization and tools of its introduction on an example of the introduction of principles of the ITIL library in the third version, and the literature about Metasonic Suite, representing white papers and presentations of the founders of the subject-oriented methodology and the associated Metasonic Suite.

The resolution of innovative tasks demands from IT divisions a serious increase in the level of maturity in IT management, so the IT department needs to be considered as the division directly forming a surplus value, by providing (selling) services to other business entities (customers). Such an approach has been consolidated in the library of ITIL (IT Infrastructure Library), which contains the best practices in the form of a set of methods and tools that can be used by organizations to implement the management processes of IT services.

ITIL is a set of recommendations and implementations of some processes tailored to each individual company. Concrete implementation of IT processes is highly dependent on the architecture of IT, the level of delegation of authority to the employees and the maturity of the processes of corporate culture. Therefore, for each specific organization practical ITIL should be unique. The literature on ITIL v3 reflects the importance of the theoretical part of ITSM, which lies in the fact that IT departments should be seen as a business unit within an organization that both provides and manages services. But unfortunately, in the practice it needs further development.

In the literature about Metasonic Suite some principles of Metasonic Suite are discussed, such as the communication process between participants and the implementation and validation of the immediate optimization of processes in terms of their members [7].

In 2004 the company Metasonic AG announced the new subject-oriented approach to modeling and automated business processes. Its effective use in relation to the modeling of ITIL processes can be explained by the fact that the services described and characterized in terms of business processes define the roles, procedures and incoming and outgoing information. Activity on processes assumes the effective role interaction directed on goal achievement irrespective of the location of participants in the organizational structure of the IT Department.

However, technical organization of the process itself identifies, but does not eliminate, the problems. Implementing ITIL involves an understanding by all employees of their role in the provision of IT services. The subject-oriented approach in the chapter places emphasis on the importance of employees (subjects), without which the system will not work.

The literature does not show the practical application of Metasonic Suite to automate ITIL version 3.

10   Task

Research objectives: automation and process modeling by using a subject-oriented approach within Metasonic Suite. The goal is to create a process model based on "bottom-up" modeling, in which contractors agree about the method of direct implementation of processes. A specialized tool for modeling, Metasonic Suite, which is based on the S-BPM (Subject-oriented Business Process Management) methodology and notation, is used for modeling "bottom-up" and could then be interfaced with a modeling tool "top-down" and with additional expandable software products and tools.

11   Assumptions and Research Restrictions

Research is based on the fact that automation and process modeling using Metasonic Suite requires an understanding by all employees of their role in value creation. Without this improvement it is doomed to failure, even if all processes are organized according to their principles. We must bear in mind that the process itself does not eliminate the issues contained within the technical organization. The system will not work without the participation of people in solving this problem.

The company, on which the activity of a support service has been modeled and automated in its research, is a mature company, a system capable of self-organization (in terms of maturity, note that according to Gartner companies must be either Level 4 or 5: in relation to the Managing of the value chain). The methodology associated with Metasonic Suite is based largely on changing the culture of working relations, therefore understanding that the conduct of employees involved in the process is vital in understanding and being aware of its performance.

12   Example of Modeling and Automation of Processes of Library ITIL v3 by Means of Toolkit Metasonic Suite

Practical implementation of ITSM in any organization consists of enhancement of business procedure relating to its IT infrastructure. The essence of this reengineering is to select and implement only those recommendations from ITIL which will ensure benefits, including increased levels of process maturity. During the implementation, chosen methods "adjustment" to the organization's business processes should be carried out.

Implementing ITIL can start with any process of the IT services model. However, there are several typical implementation options, helping organizations to quickly cope with their problems and benefit from the changes.

There are three standard options for starting an implementation of ITSM, starting with one of the following processes: incident management; service level management; or change management (usually in conjunction with the configuration management process).

Implementing ITIL includes not only the formalization of the processes and regulations of the department of employees by identifying areas of responsibility and authority of the employee and the criteria for the quality of its work, but also the creation of a flexible service delivery model through additional support from IT. For this purpose employees should be motivated and understand the real possibilities of IT infrastructure and to articulate clear procedures to ensure continuity and service delivery, as well as their suitability for use in real emergencies. Metasonic Suite will improve the adaptability, flexibility and interoperability of services provided within the IT department, as well as reducing the time necessary to implement changes and increase the probability of successful implementations.

Let's consider the simulation of the incident management in Metasonic Suite. All subjects involved in the process (user, operator, engineer, manager of configuration changes) must be identified as process roles and their interaction defined by the messages they exchange (Fig. 1 shows an example).

It is necessary to improve the subjects by describing their behavior as a clearly and strictly sequential series of actions and interactions with states and

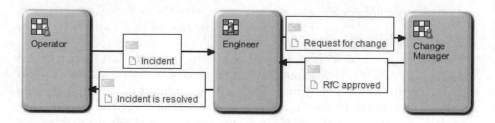

Fig. 1. Diagram of interaction of subjects in an incident management process

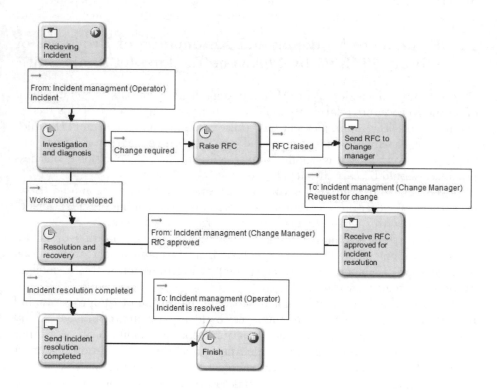

Fig. 2. Engineer behavior in an incident management process

transitions (Fig. 2 shows an example). In describing the actions of the subject there are probably three conditions: receipt of messages, sending messages, and execution of the functions (actions).

The subject-oriented process can be interactively tested and validated from the actual subject's point of view, i.e. employees who are the members of the service.

Then the model can be automatically converted into an executable program with the subjects that can simulate process logic and the exchange of information.

13   Results and Scientific Novelty of Research

The practical importance of the research is to develop recommendations for the formalization of the processes, for regulations of personnel and monitoring processes carried out on the basis of the model and for the formation of procedures to further improve ITSM processes by automating IT service delivery. Thus, firstly, it is necessary to consider IT as a source of increasing value-added products due to better management of operational processes, reducing production costs below the cost of competitors. Secondly, the process approach to managing IT activities helps to ensure the quality of customer services and to organize the work of IT services. The main advantage of the third version of ITIL is that it allows companies to maximize their return on IT investments. It gives them the chance to increase the level of innovation and business value through the use of the full potential inherent in the technology and expertise of IT professionals. Through active interaction with the IT structures the company's management can implement new business processes that increase the competitiveness and innovative business development. Through innovation, they can occupy niches in the market. The introduction of the offered model and its methods in the practice allows us to have clear procedures to ensure the provision of services, to adapt and adjust granting of services and to improve interaction in the company. All this can also reduce the time necessary to implement change, and will ensure a high probability of successful implementations.

Just a theoretical importance of research consists of using the subject-oriented approach to allow the use of latest trends in management and enable a reflexive self-organizing structure.

The scientific novelty of research consists of disclosing the principle of subject-oriented approach and its practical application to automate IT service delivery. With Metasonic Suite business processes can be immediately tested in the real world – a necessity before any investment in the IT sector takes place. The process model in Metasonic Build can be directly executed by Metasonic Flow without the conventional requirement for large scale implementations.

14   Issues for Further Research

The service approach is evolving. A modern organization can't be presented purely as a service provider, since today's customer is no longer interested in a set of fixed services, as he requires agility and durability of his investments. Today's customer is not buying just a license for the particular software use; he expects to foster certain relations with a supplier company for specific reasons, and these relations include expectations of professional consultancy in many business aspects. Solving problems of the customer, such as enhancing of the business process performance or reducing of the restriction impact, could be considered as a real value of assistance. In this respect, further research is required for widening of the boundaries in subject orientation amplification for the process modeling and automation to provide real value chains for the end-user.

In this case it is reasonable to consider the application of Metasonic Suite to such studies of the business process optimization, whose aim is the efficient flow of value creation, for example in well recommended practices:

- Six Sigma (The goal is to establish sustainable and predictable process flow for the successful business development. Certain key performance indicators (KPIs), which characterize the flow of manufacturing processes and business processes should be measured, monitored and used for improvements and changes in the processes. To achieve continuous quality improvement, the involvement of personnel at all levels of the organization is required, particularly at the senior management level).
- Lean (Lean Manufacturing is a tool to achieve a real reduction in production costs without sacrificing quality. The approach is directed to reduce the losses and everything that does not add value to the consumer. Lean manufacturing works on the same principles on which the modeling and automation of processes in Metasonic Suite are based, for example, Just-In-Time (Just in time) is the performance of the current operation determined by requirement of the former (information from the previous production stage that is necessary to start work), as well as quality control of products (services) which is directly involved in their manufacturing process (provision).)
- TOC (Theory of Constraints offers the concentration of organizational resources on elimination of conflicts (bottlenecks) that interfere with the company to fully realize its potential. In this particular case a process study reflected in Metasonic models could provide a quick and accurate analysis of the process faults, conflicts and restrictions.)

References

[1] Gromoff, A.I., Chebotarev, V.G.: Evolution of the approaches to business process management. Business Informatics 1, Higher School of Economics, Moscow (2010)
[2] OGC - Office of Government Commerce, Adams, S. ITIL V3 foundation handbook
[3] Dalfonso, M.: ISO 9000: achieving compliance and certification. Wiley, New York (1995)
[4] Roussey, R.: Management Guidelines for COBIT. ISACA Journal Volume 6 (2000)
[5] Autonomy Interwoven Achieving Compliance and Governance in IT Operations - Sarbanes-Oxley Regulations (ITIL, COSO, CobiT) Executive White Paper (2006)
[6] Chebotarev, V.G., Borodina, E., Grigoryev, D.M.: Features of the subject-oriented Business Process Modeling. Business Informatics, 2, Higher School of Economics, Moscow (2010)
[7] Fleischmann, A., Lippe, S., Meyer, N., Stary, C.: Coherent Task Modeling and Execution Based on Subject-Oriented Representations. In: England, D., Palanque, P., Vanderdonckt, J., Wild, P.J. (eds.) TAMODIA 2009. LNCS, vol. 5963, pp. 78–91. Springer, Heidelberg (2010)

Part III

Discussion

Why We Need to Re-think Current BPM Research Issues

Thomas J. Olbrich

taraneon Consulting Group GbR,
An den Bergen 29 D, 60437 Frankfurt am Main, Germany
thomas.olbrich@taraneon.com

Abstract. In this paper we argue that BPM research is lacking in making meaningful contributions to the development and application of organizational and technical aspects of BPM to businesses. In this respect, the academic community is as much to blame for the failure of BPM - measured against its potential – as the vendor of BPM systems, who continue to reduce the task of managing business processes to a purely technological and automation-oriented level.

1   I Apologize

It may seem unusual to end what by all accounts has been a highly successful conference with a very critical presentation on where research has failed the BPM community. Not to mention the risk involved when you're facing a gathering of leading researchers and telling them that they are working on the wrong issues. But then again, BPM has always been a challenging subject and why should conferences be any different? Thankfully, the first slide of my presentation has the words 'I apologize' written on them ...

Let me be as undiplomatic as I possibly can be without being offensive: BPM research has – for a number of reasons – failed to make any meaningful contributions over the past several years. This is not to say that research isn't being conducted and that results aren't being published and discussed. But what results and to what end?

2   The Past through Tomorrow

Let me draw a comparison to the situation we had twenty years ago when we saw the emergence of Workflow Management Systems (WFMS), a class of systems still very much at the core of what BPM systems of today do. At that time, the major relevant research activities were spread across fields like Human-Computer-Interaction (HCI), Computer-Supported-Cooperative-Work (CSCW), automation theory, organizational theory and others. The vision of WFM was to provide solutions that - to a certain degree - took care of the routing of processes across an organization. This quickly developed into systems that not only routed the processes but took over some of the process content processing tasks from

A. Fleischmann et al. (Eds.): S-BPM ONE 2010, CCIS 138, pp. 209–215, 2011.
© Springer-Verlag Berlin Heidelberg 2011

employees and paved the way for the vision of the automated enterprise and the – let's remind ourselves with a little smile on our faces – the paperless office.

This should ring a bell with anyone involved with BPM today as the way we employ BPMS in practice is very similar if not identical. The difference to those early days lies in what the WFMS and BPMS were then and are now actually able to accomplish. Looking back, most of us will probably admit that the WFMS available at that time were early prototypes of the BPMS of today, with limited functionality, messy system architectures and very expensive to run and administer. Small wonder that WFMS never did make the impact that everyone was hoping for. Full marks for vision and innovation, probably zero for ability to deliver.

By contrast, the BPMS of today work. And it should be worth mentioning this, because they didn't work all that long ago. Technically we can now do all the things we wanted our WFMS to be able to do twenty years ago and much more. So, while branding has changed from WFMS to BPMS, technical capabilities have increased and reached levels of stability and quality that make BPMS suited to demands from users and industry, while we've made dashboards and graphical representations of processes compulsory components of BPMS and integrated SOA and all the rest and can now even provide all the BPMS features in the cloud – we have made absolutely no progress in learning to handle these capabilities from a personal (e.g. process worker) and organizational point of view. And for this I blame research.

3   Technical Progress vs. Deficient Process Orientation

Allow me to make use of my nearly twenty year log involvement in the field of process management. I've been lucky enough to have worked in research, industry and in consulting. And while it's been an interesting journey with lots of surprises along the way, there are two issues I would have to call downright boring because they've been with me from day one and seem uninclined to leave me anytime soon:

– The 'Business - IT Gap'
– The 'Because We Can' approach to things

The business-IT discussion is of course not limited to the area of processes. Indeed it is only a specialized form of a more general communication problem: How do I transfer my understanding of an issue in the context in which I experience the issue in such a way that the person on the receiving end has an identical understanding and will base his conclusions (and his work) on that same understanding?

BPMS vendors have over the past few years suggested to their customers that standards like BPMN can solve the business-IT gap. Their argument being that a common understanding of a limited number of shapes or templates will lead to an identical understanding of the issue at hand and thus to the creation of IT-based process solutions that directly correspond to the business requirements.

The BPM industry has gone so far as to make BPMN one of the prime selling arguments for BPM. Visit any of the major industry exhibitions today and you will come away with the impression that BPMN will solve any business-IT problems you may have had in the past (and also provide a cure for the common cough, the middle-east crises and the disappearance of endangered species). The requirement and ability to 'process' has retreated to an extent comparable only to mobile phone providers whose main sales argument is the quality of the camera lens.

Unfortunately, much of the visible BPM research is currently focused on BPMN. In that, research provides the perfect alibi for vendors and users alike to remain as process-unaware as they've always been. My impression is that even if BPMN were to be the one and only 'language' available, we would still be stuck with the major problems we've been facing for years. Raise your hands if you have heard any of the following statements:

 − We went bankrupt because we didn't have unified semantics
 − Roundtrip integration has made me a happy man
 − Automation is the basis for agility
 − Thank God for BPEL, now I can finally manage my process

You may laugh or smile or shake your head, but these are the arguments we are currently putting forward for BPM and research has nothing better to do than to dive even deeper into these issues. New version of BPMN? Holistic integration? Process pattern recognition? Cloud integration?

Let me draw you attention to a paper written by Michael Rosemann and Michael zur Mühlen which addressed the problem of designing organizational structures in WFMS [1]. In this paper, the authors develop a method to couple processes with organizational structures. Many of you will know that this issue continues to pose problems for enterprises in that rigid structures seem to provide barriers to the advantages of dynamic processes. How do we solve this problem? We don't. The vendors don't (and can't), the consultants won't, and research . . . well it's not BPMN. Now, when Rosemann and zur Mühlen wrote their paper in 1997 you could be forgiven for regarding so-called soft issues like organizational and psychological aspects of processes as second rate problems as compared to WFMS that didn't perform under real-life conditions.

But fourteen years on we have solved a lot of the hard-core technical problems with the result that BPMS really do work. And what does the research community do? It seems to want to put the icing on the technological cake by continuing to work on issues that may be interesting for their own sake but have a far lesser impact on managing business processes than 10 years ago.

Sticking to the cake image, it has become multilayered and as impressive to look at as a giant wedding cake. And this is what we serve our customers. What a pity that we've forgotten to provide detailed instructions on how cut the cake into slices so that we may eat it instead of only marveling at the look and design of it. And even worse, we've ignored the fact that our digestive tract is in most case unable to handle the cake and survive without requiring major surgery afterwards.

4   Where the Real Issues Lie

Let me start with some basic statements and assumptions:

- BPM has until now failed to deliver.
- BPM is regarded as either
  - process automation
  - a management discipline
  - a combination of the two
  - something else altogether
- Users love the idea of BPM and hate the approach and the implications
- BPM has yet to define targets and objectives which can be translated into the business world

In addition, let me add some insights from the taraneon Process TestLab [2]:

- More than 90% of business process designs tested at the Process TestLab contained grave logical errors (IT would not have been able to implement the process)
- On average, testing found more than 70 warnings and errors per business process
- Nearly half of all processes put through the user validation test (is this what we meant to process to be?) required changes

What all this leads up to is a possible explanation of why BPM seldom produces real success stories:

All this indicates to me that – now that the hard-core technical challenges have been solved – we urgently need to refocus on the basics of BPM, starting with the question of what BPM actually is or could be.

It seems a pity that a lot of current research fails to provide a basic definition of what underlying understanding of 'process' and 'BPM' it bases its work on. Not that I'm advocating the 'one-size-fits-all' approach, but at least explain your understanding of processes before researching solutions.

5   Research Areas in Search of Researchers

One aspect of processes that I feel has been totally ignored by the research community is the aspect of dynamics and interaction, which I find quite bizzare, as processes by their very nature and the environment in which they are meant to perform are dynamic by themselves and constantly influenced by outside forces.

As our own analysis at the Process TestLab shows, enterprises have still to learn how to manage processes outside of isolated design environments. This touches on questions of process architectures, on (let's use the dirty word) employee empowerment, on management and leadership capability, on flexible organizational structures and a host of other issues.

So instead of headlining our research with BPM 2.0 and putting the next BPMN generation on the research table, how about doing some research into

We know that things don't work as they should

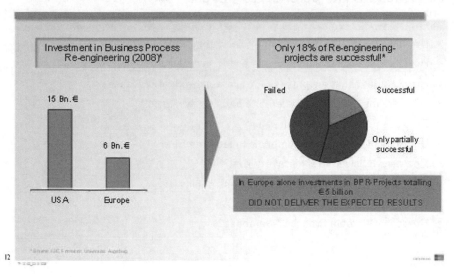

the reasons why processes still seem to fail when the technology works. And if you could come up with some solutions at the same time, I am sure BPM users would be most grateful. If I had a list of 10 research projects I could initiate, it would probably look something like this:

Most of these topics are of an interdisciplinary nature, which is hardly surprising as processes are multi-facetted. But to my mind, this is what needs to be worked on to make BPM accessible instead of making it even more indigestiable than it already is.

Industry has learned over the years that management theory, organizational theory, change management and many other disciplines contribute to BPM. But while industry may have learned the lesson – often the hard way – they have so far been unable to come up with the solutions. This is where research could finally again play a leading role, instead of simply following the trends and fads that vendors use to sell their products to frustrated customers.

6   Apology Revisited

Re-reading this small article has made me realize that some background information is probably in order for you to understand how this rant came about and to avoid any possible misunderstanding of my appreciation of the hard work being done on BPM.

I was originally invited to provide a critical (and if possible slightly amusing) close-of- conference keynote presentation. "Wake them up, be undiplomatic,

10 issues I'd like science to adress

- Develop common understanding of BPM in science and research
- How do you synchronize business and IT processes?
- How you do manage a process? ... and a network of processes?
- What are the factors that determine process dynamics?
- Do processes have a proven value?
- Do we need organisational models to facilitate BPM?
- How can we lower 40% discovery cost?
- How can we define and improve process quality?
- What makes a process successful?
- How can we create Process Awareness?

17

provoke them" was the brief I was given. So I put together some process anecdotes from the past 15 years and mapped them against the then-current research topics I was aware of or even involved with.

As I listened to the conference presentations on the day, I started to wonder how the various solutions, approaches etc. would contribute to solving the problems our clients were facing. While I was trying to work this out, the presentations turned into background noise and I found myself becoming more and more annoyed. Self inspection finally allowed me to identify the root cause: it was the term BPMN. Every time BPMN was mentioned in the presentations, my train of thought was rudely interrupted. Why? Because it was the one issue that seemed to be on everyone's agenda and every time it was mentioned I found myself saying 'no, doesn't help'. Do it once, it's ok. Do it every 20 minutes for a whole day and you'll be hard put to keep your blood pressure at an acceptable level.

So, half an hour before I was due on stage for the grand finale, I did a complete rewrite of my presentation and put all my anger and frustration into it. It was indeed as undiplomatic and provocative as requested, but luckily I was blessed with an audience of well-meaning researchers who even seemed to enjoy all the "where you got it wrong" examples I threw in their direction.

Rather than trying to hide (and ideally forget) what I said at the conference, the organizers and publishers have requested that I stick as much to the original intent as I possibly can. In that sense, this paper offers a compromise between what I said at the conference and what I had originally intended to say in my shelved presentation.

"BPM is an intellectual and not a technological challenge" was the title of a keynote I gave some years ago. If research is able to refocus to a certain extent, I am sure that we will be able to put the intellectual challenge to rest as well.

References

[1] Rosemann, M., Zur Muehlen, M.: Modellierung der Aufbauorganisation in Workflow-Management-Systemen: Kritische Bestandsaufnahme und Gestaltungsvorschlaege (Organizational Modeling in Workflow Management Systems – State-of-the-Art and Design Options). In: Jablonski, S. (ed.) Proceedings of the EMISA-Fachgruppentreffen 1997, Darmstadt , pp. 100-118 (1997); also published in: EMISA-Forum 1, pp. 78–84 (1998) (in German)
[2] http://ptl.taraneon.com

Do We Need to Re-think Current BPM Research Issues?

Albert Fleischmann

Metasonic AG, Münchner Str. 29 - Hettenshausen,
85276 Pfaffenhofen, Germany
albert.fleischmann@metasonic.de

1   Introduction

In Olbrich2010 Thomas Olbrich made some statements about research issues in
BPM. He identified 10 research areas in search for researchers (see Olbrich10
contained in that volume). After his presentation at the S-BPM ONE 2010 an
emotional discussion came up. Because of the time restrictions this discussion
could not be continued to a common agreement or understanding. Therefore the
program committee decided to add the Thomas' statements to the conference
proceedings with some contributions to that controversy.

In my personal opinion, Thomas is right. I do not agree with all the details
of his arguments but I think in research business process management is not
given enough holistic consideration. In research the focus is mainly on technical
and technological aspects. In the following remarks I want to describe some
indications which support Thomas' thesis.

2   Business Processes are Socio-technical Systems

Thomas claims that the technical problems are more or less solved. I think that
is not true, a lot of problems are still open e.g. specification and implementation
of cross company processes (see Meyer2010 in this volume). There are also some
serious technical problems in combining existing applications with the IT supported execution of business processes. His focus is on the research gap in soft
aspects of business process management (Sure he is a business consultant) like
governance, culture, people etc.

I have compared the research gaps he cites with publications of other authors
about their view on business process management. The publications I considered
are chosen more or less randomly (just available in my bookshelf).

Thomas' 10 topics he would like science to addrcss arc also identified as relevant for BPM in other publications e.g. [1] or in several contributions for the
Handbook on Business Process Management Volume 1 and Volume 2 [6].

In PEMM developed by Hammer (Process and Enterprise Maturity Modell,
see page 290 in [1]) following aspects are considered as essential for processes
and for the whole enterprise:

A. Fleischmann et al. (Eds.): S-BPM ONE 2010, CCIS 138, pp. 216–219, 2011.
© Springer-Verlag Berlin Heidelberg 2011

- Process
  - Design
  - Performers
  - Owner
  - Infrastructure
  - Metrics
- Enterprise
  - Leadership
  - Culture
  - Expertise
  - Governance

For the process design Hammer identified seven principles (see page 34 in [1]):

- Whether they should performed and under what circumstances
- How precisely they are performed
- What tasks are performed
- Who performs them
- When they are performed
- Where they are performed
- What information they employ

In Rosemann2010 (contained in [6] page 107) six core elements of business process management are identified.

- Strategic alignment
- Governance
- Methods
- Information Technology
- People
- Culture

These core elements are derived from various maturity models like PEMM. In Rosemann2010 many articles are mentioned from which these six core elements are derived. In [1] there is no literature mentioned. But nevertheless it shows that there is awareness that BPM has a wide range of aspects which must be considered. These few examples show that Thomas is right. There are well known authors which have a similar broad view on BPM.

He is right when he says that business processes are socio technical systems, which means sociological systems like organizations are combined with technical systems like information and communication technology. For a holistic view on business process management we have to consider all aspects. If we have a look at BPM papers published on international conferences, their focus is on theoretical/technical aspects. I have looked into the proceedings of the BPM 2009 [2], BPM 2010 (Hull et.al. 2010) and Business Process Management Workshop [4]. All these proceedings contain more or less only technical papers. This is also the case with this S-BPM 2010 conference. Here only technical contributions are presented. Even worse, most papers at all these conferences focus on very detailed problems. I could not find one contribution about complex cross company process networks which become very important in a work sharing global economy, sorry with one exception: In [2] there is an article about hierarchical service level agreements in business value networks [5]. In all these conferences the aspects design, methods and information technology are considered. If we consider the details of design proposed by Hammer, it seems that it's mainly the questions of what actions are executed when that are considered.

The structure of the Handbook on Business Process Management follows the six core elements of BPM. In that Handbook 579 pages deal with the aspects strategic alignment, governance, people and culture, approximately 125 pages for each aspect. The aspects methods and IT are handled in 450 pages which mean around 225 pages for each aspect.

All these examples above do not prove that Thomas is right but I think these are indicators that currently BPM research is focusing on the aspects methods and IT. Additionally I didn't find a single article about the relationship between the various aspects of BPM. For example I could not find an article which tries to explain in which extend e.g. BPMN supports strategic alignment, governance, people or culture. BPMN books cover more or less only the method aspect (e.g. see [8], [7]).

I want to round off this literature analysis with my personal experience. Our (Metasonic) product suite allows the specification of processes in a subject oriented way and all the specifications can be executed without any programming. Very often business people love our approach of describing business processes and they see the advantage of directly executing the process (i.e. create a run-time version). . But because of direct process execution they say the IT department is responsible for such a solution. This means two types of organizations are involved in business process management. The business people consider the aspects strategic alignment, culture and people. Information technology is owned by the IT department. What do we do with methods and governance? The method aspect is divided into two pieces. One method for specifying processes from the business point of view and a separate method for specifying the processes executed by IT. With all the problems related to the transformation of a process specification from one method to the other. With a very complex process governance rule set companies try to bridge the gap between business and IT. This organizational situation does not support a holistic view on BPM in companies.

3   Conclusion

Thomas presented his thesis in a very humorous and light-hearted fashion but the content was very serious and we should think about the remarks he made very thoroughly. I agree that we should consider the soft aspects of BPM and especially the relationship between the social and the technical aspects of BPM e.g. a method for describing a business process that can be accepted or rejected by people who describe processes or should understand a process description, methods should support change management and a process specification should be also sufficient precisely for IT people.

References

[1] Hammer, M.: Hershman w. Lisa; Faster, Cheaper, Better Crown Business (2010)
[2] Dayal, U., et al. (eds.): BPM 2009. LNCS, vol. 5701. Springer, Heidelberg (2009)
[3] Hull, R., et al. (eds.): BPM 2010. LNCS, vol. 6336. Springer, Heidelberg (2010)
[4] Hofstede, A. (ed.): BPM Workshops 2007. LNCS, vol. 4928. Springer, Heidelberg (2008)
[5] ul Haq, I., et al.: Aggregating Hierarchical Service Level Agreements in Business Value Networks. In: Dayal (2009)
[6] vom Brocke, Jan, et al.: (eds.): Handbook on Business Process Management, vol. 1 & 2. Springer, Heidelberg (2010)
[7] Silver, B.: BPMN Method and Style. Cody-Cassidy-Press (2009)
[8] Freund, J., Rücker, B.: Praxishandbuch BPMN 2.0. Hanser Verlag (2010)

Business Process Management – Do We Need a New Research Agenda?

Robert Singer and Erwin Zinser

FH JOANNEUM – University of Applied Sciences,
Alte Poststraße 149, 8020 Graz, Austria
{robert.singer,erwin.zinser}@fh-joanneum.at

Abstract. This article is an answer to the thesis that research in the domain of business process management (BPM) is doing the wrong job, does not deliver results and therefore is responsible for the alleged failure of BPM in the field. We work out that this thesis is not based on any scientific argumentation or proof. Based on the finding that BPM itself does not have a solid scientific foundation we present some thoughts how to come up with a scientific theory of BPM. Additionally we argue that the term BPM has different meanings in different research and application areas. This, logically, leads to different research interests, but all together they give a complex (but fragmented) picture and will emerge towards an unified theory of BPM. The conclusion of this article follows the insight of experts in the domain of BPM research and application, that research in BPM is still not finished and that it is rather at the very beginning. Especially if we understand BPM as one element of sociotechnical systems, which leads us to think about a more holistic approach in the sense of systems theory.

Keywords: Business Process, Business Process Management, Theory, Research, Systems Theory, Enterprise Engineering.

1 Introduction

This article is an answer to the conference presentation of Olbrich [14]. In this section we will summarize the main points from Olbrich. In the following sections we will provide an answer based on "scientific" tradition.

The main proposition of Olbrich can be summarized with the following quotes:

... research has failed the BPM community.

BPM research has ... failed to make any meaningful contributions over the past several years.

... – we made absolutely no progress in learning to handle these capabilities from a personal (e.g. process worker) and organizational point of view. And for this I blame research.

A. Fleischmann et al. (Eds.): S-BPM ONE 2010, CCIS 138, pp. 220–226, 2011.

BPM has until now failed to deliver.

If we accept the fact, that business process management (BPM) does not work in practice as written in many books, learned in company training courses and taught at universities, we clearly can conclude further research need. But the question now is, who is responsible for the failure up to now, or – in our opinion a much more inspiring question – what do we need to do?

At first sight it seems that the statement such as "BPM has until now failed to deliver" has some truth, but in our opinion the situation is much more complex. The first point we have to stress is the fact, that there is no proof for this statement. Nevertheless – and that is a real point for a research agenda – there seems to be no proof at all, that business process management (BPM) is the source for more profit; there are a lot of anecdotal stories and case studies [10][15], but that is not sufficient to count as full scientific proof.

To find out what could be wrong with BPM, we

1. have to clarify what are the scientific foundations of business processes and business process management and
2. only based on this clarification we can derive a research agenda to fill the – assumed – epistemological gap.

If we are going to realize who has been promoting and implementing BPM within organizations during the last two decades, we come up with a clear answer: this was mainly not research driven, but business (consulting and selling of software); companies normally invite consultants and not scientists, e.g. to explain, train and implement BPM. Recently many organizations experience the lack of scientific methodology and are looking now for provable answers on such questions as, "why and how should BPM be adopted for the success of the organization?". The "why" seems to be easier to be answered, than the "how"; a serious calculation of NPV or ROI of the investment in BPM and BPMS (business process management systems) projects still seems to be undiscussed. So let us eat "humble pie" rather than further blame research for non-research responsibilities.

2 Taking a Scientific Approach

To study BPM in scientific tradition, we have to clarify what we mean with taking a scientific approach. A useful discussion of the term "science" can be found for example in Bunge [3][4]. In our discussion we will be satisfied with the following simple definition from Bunge [5]:

> A theory is scientific if, and only if, (i) it is compatible with the bulk of scientific knowledge, and (ii) jointly with subsidiary hypotheses and empirical data, it entails empirically testable consequences.

That means we need a theory, hypotheses, empirical data and testable consequences; a research cycle as discussed by Bunge is shown in Fig. 1. Based on this

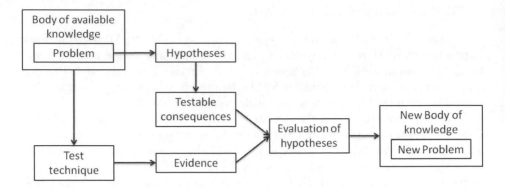

Fig. 1. A research cycle. The importance of a scientific investigation is gauged by the changes it induces in our body of knowledge and/or by the new problems it poses. [3]

we obviously must agree with van der Aalst [1]: "..., a clear scientific foundation is missing". At best we have definitions and some empirical evidence.

The problem is not easy to tackle, because a business process as a research entity cannot be studied isolated from the system it is part of. This is the reason for a long tradition of studying systems as a whole and some serious philosophical questions about mechanistic views of complex systems, which cannot be discussed here.

Some of the ideas of general systems theory (GST) evolved to the holistic concepts of enterprize architecture (EA) and enterprize engineering (EE). All of these findings are concepts and they need research to develop provable methodologies so that we can say: "if we do this, you can expect that".

3   Defining Business Process Management?

Even if we say, that a clear scientific foundation is missing, we have to clarify the entity we want to discuss – so what is business process management? We think one of the reasons for blaming BPM to fail is, that there is no common understanding of the entity "business process", how to implement it and how to measure the economic implications to do – or not to do – business process management.

Depending on a personal point of view, BPM is an idea, a concept or a methodology and even more important there are various stakeholders such as business management and administration, software developers and computer scientists. Each of these parties has their own research agenda. But how is it possible to say, that any research in any of these fields made absolutely no progress as Olbrich states?

From business point of view we follow Hammer [8][9] and others [6] who define a business process as large-scale, truly end-to-end process focusing on high-leverage aspects of the organizations' operations to gain competitive advantage

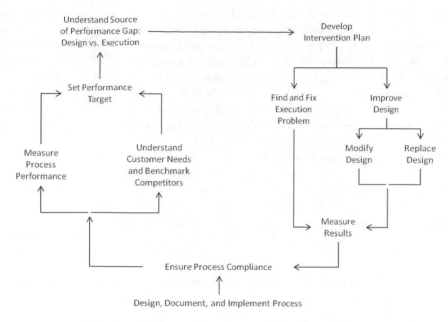

Fig. 2. The essential process management cycle. [7]

and far better results. The essence of BPM typically is shown as a management cycle (see Fig. 2). Many other definitions of the term "business process" and variants of BPM-cycles can be found throughout literature.

But the view of large-scale end-to-end processes is rather contradictory to the view of researchers in the domain of computer science and software development. It is rather clear, that in those domains we are confronted with strictly formal systems. We think, that the core problem is to find a general methodology to transform non-formal systems in a structured way into formal systems to bridge those two views or worlds. But this transformation cannot be automated, it will always be human and knowledge driven. It can be even brought to philosophical questions about modeling of systems and systems theory, as discussed before. Nowadays it is fully clear, that we need a more holistic view on complex systems to gather more insights how to design and manage such systems.

There are many subsystems which are under research, e.g. enterprize architecture (EA), value chains and value networks, business process frameworks, process maturity models, managing (cultural) change, analyzing and modeling service processes, analyzing and modeling complex processes, business process management systems, semantic processes (SBPM) and business rules (BR), business activity monitoring (BAM) and complex event processing (CEP), Petri-nets, discrete event systems (DES), and subject-oriented Business Process Management (S-BPM) etc.

A huge amount of work (useful or not so useful) is done all the time with the aim to develop a better understanding of how to manage complex systems. We cannot blame any of the researchers doing his or her work in their special

area of interest. To use for example physics as an analogue: if somebody does
research e.g. in non-relativistic electrodynamics, maybe this does not lead to
increased knowledge in relativistic quantum mechanics – do we blame him or her?
Nevertheless, all researchers in the domain of physics (and all other domains)
together work to increase their shared knowledge in the whole domain for a better
understanding of nature and systems; it's the same in business management
and the subdomain of business process management. And we further should not
forget, research must be financed; that means there must be good argumentation
why some research is needed to get it funded.

Our conclusion from this is, that Olbrich is not right if he states "BPM research has - for a number of reasons - failed to make any meaningful contributions
over the past several years" and "... - we have made absolutely no progress in
learning to handle these capabilities from a personal (e.g. process worker) and
organizational point of view"; there is no evidence for that.

Contrary, we have to learn to accept, that research in the area of BPM is
ongoing work:

> Despite its widespread adoption and impressive results, BPM is still in
> its infancy. [7]

> ... the BPM community is still short of a publication that provides a
> consolidated understanding of the true scope and contents of a compre-
> hensively defined business process management. [2]

4   Conclusions

Customers care about one thing and one thing only: results. If Olbrich has this
in mind, he is right, that some new BPEL dialects are not important for them;
but it is a – maybe small – part of the whole jigsaw to get a toolbox full of
appropriate tools to solve customer problems.

Put it in a nutshell: we are not at the end of a frustrating journey started
with Nordsieck [12][13], Kosiol [11] and many others, but at the beginning of the
"age of process" [7]. Industry feels the pain when doing BPM; we experience the
fact – and here Olbrich is definitely right – that BPM does not work as intended
and promised. In our opinion – this also proves, the need for research – there
is quite a lack of knowledge in the field. We assume, that there are many new
insights, but they are not well known and internalized in industry. For this we
have no proof, but evidence. To close this knowledge gap intense exchange of
knowledge and experience between industry and research is needed[1]. Research
needs partners from industry and *vice versa*. And we need to include BPM into
academic education of all levels and many domains:

> Universities are now slowly starting to build BPM courses into their cur-
> ricula, while positions such as business process analysts or chief process
> officers are increasingly appearing in organizational charts. [2]

---

[1] See for example http://www.i2pm.net

And we must be aware, that the problem stated is multifunctional. That means many domains must learn to do research across domain borders. Maybe some of the complaints come from the fact, that computer science has incorporated BPM into curricula and has done research over a couple of years. But BPMN, BPEL and Petri-Nets are only useful in certain application scenarios. We need more, much more:

> ..., Strategic Alignment, Governance, Methods, Information Systems, People and Culture. These six factors had been derived as part of a multiyear global research study on the essential factors of BPM maturity. [7]

Olbrich finalizes his paper with the sentence "BPM is an intellectual and not a technological challenge". We would like to adapt this in the following way: "BPM is an intellectual *and* a technological challenge". Both have to come together, however.

There is much more to say, but this cannot be done here. We think a very important conclusion can be drawn from this valuable discussion, as already mentioned before: research, teaching and application in the field is a magic triangle; all three aspects have to work together to bring BPM to the next level. For example, research needs input and funding from industry, industry needs sound new methodologies and well educated workforce to implement BPM to gain sustainable competitive advantage.

References

[1] van der Aalst, W.M.P., ter Hofstede, A.H.M., Weske, M.: Business process management: A survey. In: van der Aalst, W.M.P., ter Hofstede, A.H.M., Weske, M. (eds.) BPM 2003. LNCS, vol. 2678, pp. 1–12. Springer, Heidelberg (2003)
[2] vom Brocke, J., Roesemann, M.: Foreword. In: Handbook on Business Process Management, vol. 1, pp. vii–ix. Springer, Heidelberg (2010)
[3] Bunge, M.: Philosophy of Science: From Explanation to Justification. Transaction Publ. (1998)
[4] Bunge, M.: Philosophy of Science: From Problem to Theory. Transaction Publ. (1998)
[5] Bunge, M.: The GST Challenge to the Classical Philosophies of Science. In: Scientific Realism: Selected Essays of Mario Bunge, Prometheus Books (2001)
[6] Davenport, T.H.: Process innovation: Reengineering work through information technology. Harvard Business School Press, Boston (1993)
[7] Hammer, M.: What is Business Process Management? In: Handbook on Business Process Management, vol. 1, pp. 3–16. Springer, Heidelberg (2010)
[8] Hammer, M., Champy, J.: Reengineering the Corporation: A Manifesto for Business Revolution. Harper Business (1993)
[9] Hammer, M., Hershman, L.W.: Faster, cheaper, better. Crown Business (2010)
[10] Kohlbacher, M.: The effects of process orientation: a literature review. Business Process Management Journal 16(1), 135–152 (2010)

[11] Kosiol, E.: Organisation der Unternehmung. Gabler (1962)
[12] Nordsieck, F.: Die schaubildliche Erfassung und Untersuchung der Betriebsorganisation. Poeschel (1932)
[13] Nordsieck, F.: Grundlagen der Organisationslehre. Poeschel (1934)
[14] Olbrich, T.J.: Why we need to re-think current BPM research issues. Presentation S-BPM 2010 (2010)
[15] Palmberg, K.: Experiences of implementing process management: a multiple-case study. Business Process Management Journal 16(1), 93–113 (2010)

Author Index